Sue Anstiss has driven change in women's spor~~~~~~~~~~ y years. Co-founder of the Women's Sport Collective and a founding trustee of the Women's Sport Trust, in 2018 Sue received an MBE for her services to women's sport. In 2021, she was shortlisted for the *Sunday Times* Sportswomen of the Year Changemaker Award. Sue's award-winning podcast *The Game Changers* amplifies the stories of trailblazing women in sport, and she is now CEO of Fearless Women, a company driving positive change for women's sport. A former GB Age Group triathlete, Sue competed at World and European Championships in her late forties. She is married, with three daughters, and lives in Berkshire, England.

@sueanstiss
www.fearlesswomen.co.uk

Sue Anstiss

Changing The Game

With special thanks to

GAME
ON

Sue
Anstiss

THE UNSTOPPABLE RISE OF
WOMEN'S
SPORT

unbound

First published in 2021
This paperback edition first published in 2022

Unbound
Level 1, Devonshire House,
One Mayfair Place, London W1J 8AJ
www.unbound.com

Text design by Ellipsis, Glasgow

A CIP record for this book is available from the British Library

ISBN 978-1-80018-164-9 (paperback)
ISBN 978-1-80018-062-8 (hardback)
ISBN 978-1-80018-063-5 (ebook)

Printed and bound in Great Britain by Clays Ltd, Elcograf S.p.A

3 5 7 9 8 6 4 2

For
Matt, Molly, Daisy and Tess

In loving memory of
Roy and Pat Anstiss

CONTENTS

FOREWORD

What does the future hold for women's sport and why does it matter? Questions that many of us have been trying to resolve throughout our careers. For those who have seen the impact sport has had on their own lives, and those around them, whether as an athlete, administrator, coach, fan or parent, we know the topic is complex.

I have spent many years being interviewed and questioned on the validity of women's sport. In the past it was always easy to find someone who would simply argue that women's sport was 'less than' men's. The old attitude which questions whether women can play sport and still be feminine (I cannot believe that this is still on the table) is one of the most frustrating things to have to deal with.

This book brings together powerful voices of those who have significant experience at all levels to offer solutions for the future. It offers a compelling history of women in sport, alongside a personal perspective of what the future might hold. It covers some of the biggest issues facing women in sport, from menstruation and misogyny through to lesbianism and race. That it is still not easy to have some of these discussions speaks volumes.

Over the course of history there have been many steps forward and then back, but in recent years the forward motion has accelerated. Barriers are being broken down, change is happening, and it is exciting to see sports and participants embracing opportunities to discuss investment, profile and participation. Understanding the role of sponsors, media and fans will be key to unlocking the future.

The 2012 Olympic and Paralympic Games were a chance to think differently about how our nation views female sport. No single Games is going to change the world, but the success that ensued, with so many British women winning medals, meant that it has since become known as the 'women's games'. As a sports fan this felt like a moment that would be hard to dial back from. But how do we keep things moving in the right direction – especially as we emerge from a pandemic that has once again accentuated the disparity in men's and women's sport?

It is a strength of this book that not everyone featured shares the same view about the way forward. Sue Anstiss challenges us to ask how and when further change is going to happen. What do we need to invest in, not just financially, but also morally and ethically, to ensure we can take women's sport to where it should be?

We can't take anything for granted, but the future looks bright.

Tanni Grey-Thompson, February 2021

INTRODUCTION

We don't want to take over, we just want to take part.

It's been a long time coming, but the landscape for women's sport is finally beginning to shift.

In the past ten years we've seen significant improvements in sponsorship, prize money and professional contracts for sportswomen around the world. There's been increased media coverage for women's sport and recognition of female athletes as role models and activists for social change. The participation gap between men and women is closing, and after decades of sport being led and managed by men, we're finally seeing more women taking influential roles as board directors, editors and producers, coaches and officials.

Yet despite this fantastic and long-overdue progress, female athletes still don't get equal funding or opportunities – even though they train as hard and make the same sacrifices as their male counterparts. In many sports, women receive less prize money, get fewer professional contracts, less sponsorship and a tiny fraction of the media coverage. Girls often don't have the access to the same level of sports, funding and facilities as boys, and across the world women are still less likely to take part in sport than the men around them.

I love sport. Growing up I was a sporty girl, studied sport at university and have been lucky enough to work in the sports sector for over thirty years. But as those years have passed, I've become increasingly concerned about the massive disparity for women in sport. This inequality makes me angry, but I see great hope for the future.

Sport has an extraordinary, unique capacity to challenge and change society. It brings joy and hope to millions. It can positively impact individuals, families, communities and nations – improving physical and mental health, reducing loneliness and building self-esteem and happiness. Sport challenges us to think differently about injustices in society. It's also a multi-billion-pound commercial industry that can transform lives, businesses, nations and regions.

I recognise that sometimes it can be hard for women working in the sports sector to call out the inequalities they experience and to agitate for change. The athletes, coaches, journalists and administrators don't always want to be branded as difficult, or risk being excluded or penalised in the future. We're supposed to be grateful for what we have – happy with small improvements rather than forcefully demanding more. Like many historical fights for gender equality, there is often a backlash from men who feel threatened by change. Does allowing women to have more of something mean they will have to make sacrifices and lose out themselves? Does equal pay or prize money for female athletes and teams result in less income for the men? Will increased media coverage of women's sport result in less coverage of men's sport? Are there fewer opportunities for men to join boards and lead sports because women are now stepping up to take on these roles?

We're living in an age of huge positive change as society recognises injustices that have been experienced by previous generations and attempts to make amends. I am proud and excited to have witnessed the impact of powerful movements in recent years including Black Lives Matter, #MeToo, the Irish referendum on abortion law, HeForShe and the campaign for same-sex marriage. But significant social change doesn't occur without some pain. 'Deeds not words' was the motto of the Suffragettes, and as Frederick Douglass said in campaigning for the end of the slave trade in the US, 'If there is no struggle, there is no progress . . . Power concedes nothing without a demand. Changing the world won't make people like you. It will cause you pain. It will be difficult. It will feel like a struggle.'

While I work in sport, my livelihood is perhaps less dependent than others on toeing the party line. I used to run a sports public relations agency and was sometimes concerned about the negative impact of me publicly calling out the inequalities I saw – criticising media for its poor coverage of women's sport, the governing bodies and teams for their unbalanced funding or the sponsors for not doing enough to 'activate' the female sports properties they might have invested in. I'm less concerned about this now than I might have been a decade ago. Perhaps it's my age, or the fact that I now appreciate action is essential if we're ever going to create the change required in women's sport.

I chose the title *Game On* for this book because it expresses how I feel about women's sport right now. The dictionary says 'game on' is 'used to show that a competition of some kind is about to start, usually when you are excited about it'. The slang dictionary says it's 'an expression used to kick off a contest, issue a challenge, or express general enthusiasm'.

That's it for me. Excited and enthusiastic for the competition but recognising there is still a big challenge ahead.

There's a double narrative for women's sport right now. On one hand there is much to celebrate, with vastly increased media profile, investment and respect for female athletes. Yet in parallel, so much has still not changed, and in some cases we're moving in the wrong direction.

This book follows my journey to understand the history of women's sport, why things are finally changing, what's stopping more rapid progress and how we can ensure this positive revolution in sport continues. How women's sport can transform society for women and girls far beyond the field of play.

I explore the following big questions: Why should we be concerned that half the population have been deprived of access to something so culturally powerful? Why have women been excluded from the world of sport for centuries, their bodies considered too weak to run, jump and throw like men? Why are things changing now and what has made sponsors and the media finally wake up to the potential for women's sport? Who have been the game changers, the trailblazing women knocking down barriers and challenging the status quo for women in the future?

I have focused on the UK – it's where I live and where I've experienced most women's sport – but much of what I share is globally relevant.

I've had the privilege of talking to a range of thought leaders – from high-profile Olympic and Paralympic champions, sports broadcasters and journalists through to sports scientists, CEOs, officials and sponsors. I share some of the stories from the trailblazing women in sport I've spoken to for my podcast, *The Game Changers*, and I also reveal some my own experiences, having worked, volunteered, studied and played sport all my life.

My ambition for *Game On* is that it should offer an enlightened view of women's sport, opening minds to the importance it holds in society, and giving people the rationale, confidence and means to call out inequality when they see it.

The book is a manifesto for women's sport, providing a rallying cry to ensure that the progress we are currently seeing is maintained for the long term and highlighting how women *and* men can play their part in keeping this momentum moving in the right direction.

Let's redress the balance and bring more equality to sport and, through that, more equality to society.

Game on.

I

WHY DOES IT MATTER?

I just think, if you grow up as a girl, it's like there's a room in your house that you're not allowed to go in. That's how I see sport in life. There's a sphere in the world that is hugely powerful and influential, that political leaders fall over themselves to get involved with, and women are obstructed from that space.

I think we cannot live a whole and complete life, we cannot play a full role in society, as long as that's the case.

Anna Kessel, *The Game Changers* podcast, 2019

Sport is something unique in culture. It has enormous potential to be socially disruptive.

Sport plays an important role in reinforcing national identity. In many countries it provides the most popular display of nationalistic behaviour. It's a cultural phenomenon that can unite or divide us like nothing else. Enormous national pride and unity results from success at Olympic Games and World Cups, alongside the tribal division of opposing football fans. Sport makes us healthier and happier as individuals, families and communities. Sport provides a sense of belonging.

Sport's powerful force for good has long been accepted. It was in May 2000 that Nelson Mandela said: 'Sport has the power to change the world. It has the power to inspire, it has the power to unite people in the way that little else does ... Sport can create hope, where once there was only despair. It is more powerful than governments in breaking down racial barriers. It laughs in the face of all types of discrimination.'

Sport is essential for the economy, from the billions of pounds generated by the commercial sports sector through to the huge cost benefits of a healthy population less dependent on the NHS.

For many people sport is their go-to conversation starter.

Business deals are completed over a round of golf or in a hospitality box at a major sporting event. All TV and radio news bulletins end with sport. There are sports pages at the back of every newspaper. Governments and brands invest billions in sport every year.

Yet until now, women have not had equal access to sport and all the benefits it offers. In 2021 that can't be right.

———

There is no doubt in my mind that sport reflects and magnifies key gender issues in society.

The momentous positive shift we've seen in women's sport since the London Olympics in 2012 is in line with the so-called fourth wave of feminism and its focus on empowering women to ensure greater female representation in politics and business. Attitudes around women have changed. From women's bodies to women's rights, powerful campaigns have seen women collaborate and mobilise to call out harassment and misogyny, demanding equal pay and equal opportunities with the likes of #MeToo, No More

Page 3, Time's Up, the Everyday Sexism Project and the Women's Marches.

While historically traditional feminists didn't embrace the potential of sport, in recent years, there's been a powerful interaction between feminism and female athleticism. Generation Z (those born from the mid-1990s to 2010s, such as my three daughters) embracing equality and inclusivity has coincided with huge changes in women's sport. A massive growth in viewing figures for major female sports events saw a global audience of 1.2 billion tune in for the 2019 FIFA Women's World Cup (11.7 million of us watched England's women's team, the Lionesses, in the semi-finals); professional contracts are now in place for UK women in football, rugby, cricket and netball; globally major brands including Barclays, Vitality, Investec, SSE, VISA, Pepsi, Budweiser, Cadbury and Boots are sponsoring women's leagues and events, and increased numbers of women hold senior roles and board positions with sports organisations.

Interest in women's sport has never been higher. Recent key moments have engaged the wider public in discussions around why women's sport matters to society. As athlete activism grows, it's women who are at the forefront.

For many years in the US, Women's National Basketball Association (WNBA) players have led the way in the fight for racial justice and gender equality. Throughout the 2020 basketball season they partnered with the #SayHerName campaign to raise awareness of police brutality against Black women. They stopped playing for two nights in response to the police shooting of Jacob Blake, a twenty-nine-year-old Black American, and were active participants in campaigns to encourage people to vote in elections.

US soccer player Megan Rapinoe using her global profile to

encourage us all to take action for social change; Australian rules football player Tayla Harris taking a stand and igniting a conversation around sexism in sport after an impressive photo of her in full flight attracted a flood of offensive remarks online; WNBA professional player Sue Bird wearing a 'Vote Warnock' shirt in protest at Kelly Loeffler, the senator and team owner opposed to Black Lives Matter; gymnast Katelyn Ohashi performing a perfect-ten floor routine which went viral and generated discussions around body image; Belarus basketball star Yelena Leuchanka being jailed for taking a stand for freedom in her country following the fraudulent election of President Alexander Lukashenko; Naomi Osaka wearing facemasks with the names of victims of police brutality at the US Open; and closer to home, rugby players Florence Williams and Rhona Lloyd calling out Canterbury of New Zealand over their use of airbrushed models rather than female players to launch the new Irish rugby kit.

The list is endless.

Sport's unique positioning means that it has a huge impact on the way in which women are viewed in wider society.

The increased, positive profile of successful female athletes is important for women in all walks of life – not just in sport. It's important that we see women in the sports pages of newspapers, on websites and apps, appearing on TV programmes and talking on radio alongside their male counterparts. This increased, balanced profile will bring confidence for women to achieve anything. It can also counterbalance the negative portrayal and stereotyping of women in the media – showing positive, strong athlete role models.

How does it make young girls feel to never see their sporting heroes in the media? What subliminal messages are we sending our daughters when they grow up in a society that portrays women's sport as less important than men's? What does this say to them about how they are valued in life and work?

As Serena Williams so eloquently explained in 1998, as she questioned the lack of equal pay at Wimbledon: 'Imagine you're a little girl. You're growing up. You practise as hard as you can, with girls, with boys. You have a dream. You fight, you work, you sacrifice to get to this stage. You work as hard as anyone you know. And then you get to this stage, and you're told you're not the same as a boy. Almost as good, but not quite the same. Think how devastating and demoralising that would be.'

Dame Sue Campbell, Head of the Women's Game at the FA, told me why she believes football has the potential to change women's lives more broadly in society: 'If we can change attitudes to women and girls playing football, I wonder if we can change people's attitudes to women in business, I wonder if we can change people's attitudes to the way they are in families, I wonder if we can change attitudes towards what's possible?

'If a little girl wants to be an astronaut why shouldn't she? If a little girl wants to be an engineer why shouldn't she? If a little girl wants to be a great football player why shouldn't she? And if we can open that door in football I wonder if we can open other doors as well.'

I recently heard, and loved, the phrase 'vicarious confidence', the feeling that comes from watching someone like you achieve something magnificent, which in turns give you the belief you can achieve.

Little girls growing up never seeing women's sport miss out on that opportunity to feel pride in female achievements, and they are also less likely to believe they can achieve in sport, too – 'if you can't see it you can't be it.'

Sports have seen a huge uplift in female participation following increased media coverage. Just six months after the England netball team won Commonwealth gold in 2018, regular participation in the sport had increased by 130,000. Such was the impact of the Roses' magnificent win on Australia's Gold Coast that the governing body's session finder had 2,000 per cent more hits in the weeks after it. The FA saw over 850,000 more committed participants after the FIFA Women's World Cup in 2019.

Girls who decide sport is not for them because they've never seen other women playing sport at a high level also potentially miss out on the benefits of sports participation. Aside from all the physical and mental health benefits of playing sport, there are the character-building elements of self-confidence, teamwork, leadership, loyalty, focus, learning how to lose gracefully and so on.

These personal characteristics provide a valuable foundation for future life and they may help in business, too. Research from Ernst & Young in 2013 showed that 94 per cent of women in C-suite roles (the highest ranking executives in the company) had played sports. A large majority of women in the study (70 per cent) said that a background in sport was helpful to their career progression because involvement in sport helped them to work better in teams. Many others (76 per cent) said that the performance of work teams can be improved by applying the techniques and behaviours learned in sport to the corporate world.

In a follow-up study in 2014 that surveyed 400 women from a variety of countries, 74 per cent said they felt sports participation had the potential to accelerate a woman's career and 61 per cent said they felt that their personal involvement in sport had helped their career.

So, if more young girls play sport might this mean we will have more women succeeding in industry in the future?

In addition to giving women more confidence in what they can achieve, and increasing the likelihood that they will play sport, it is important that *men* see women's sport on an equal footing. Ultimately, it's about respect. If men and boys respect sportswomen for their achievements, if they are in awe of their accomplishments, if they celebrate women's victories and the incredible talent on display, surely they are more likely to respect the other women in their lives, too?

Celebrating successful women in sport undoubtedly impacts the way in which a man views his colleagues and female family members.

And recognising that women can be strong and powerful is important for the mental health of men and boys, too. Accepting women's success can reduce the pressure men feel to always be the protector, the breadwinner, the strongest part of any partnership. Allowing women to share these roles enables men to be whoever they want to be in a more balanced, equal society. Less pressure is ultimately better for men's mental health. Men can be themselves.

Sport is also an enormous commercial sector. In 2018, the global sports market was valued at $471 billion according to Statista. When women are excluded from sports throughout their lives it is more likely they will also miss out on the opportunity to work in this incredibly exciting, fulfilling and lucrative sector.

It only takes a quick review of the sporting landscape to see the huge gender imbalance across many roles. From the leadership of major global sports, broadcast and journalism through to sports agents, managers and elite coaches – men (usually white men) still make up the majority of these positions.

Things are changing, often helped by the implementation of governance reviews and quotas, but it's important we recognise that women are still often overlooked with the assumption that they 'don't know sports' like men do. Hard to believe it was forty-five years ago that the Sex Discrimination Act of 1975 stipulated that employers could not discriminate against people on the grounds of their gender.

Finally, what does it all mean to the female athletes themselves? The powerful thoughts of professional female golfer Meghan MacLaren superbly summarise why equality in sport matters. Here's what she shared on Twitter in the summer of 2020:

Please, please bear with me, because I'm more tired than anyone of the supply and demand argument when it comes to gender equality in golf. This isn't a woke millennial take on having every possible demographic equally represented at the highest level. I can't speak for others and how they feel or are valued, I don't have that experience. But I have experience of how it can feel to be a female in this world. That's the point that keeps getting missed. Ultimately, it's just about respect. That's all . . .

Have you ever thought about how opportunity creates opportunity, or how success breeds success, or how talent pushes talent? How many elite female golfers do we miss out on because they can't see their worth? Can't see a role model in the magazine they pick up, because out of almost 200 pictures in a leading publication there isn't one of a woman? Can't see a role model on the first five pages of the golf section on a national news site because it appears women's tours don't exist? . . .

And if we dare to point that out, we are told that the interest just isn't there. That we don't engage, don't entertain, aren't worthy of your time in the way that men are. Why? Because our skills aren't as great? Really? Men's sport dominates primarily because in the beginning and ever since, people with power (. . . men) chose to invest in it . . .

I know times are changing – I'm lucky to be in an era where we can even discuss this. And I f***ing love getting to do what I do for a living . . . but it's 2020 and just look at some of the comments.

I'm not demanding you become a fan of women's golf. Each to their own, genuinely. But everyone needs to recognise that our choice to be a fan is shaped by the way the world works. Not necessarily by us.

2

TWELVE GAME-CHANGING MOMENTS

It's not women's bodies that are the problem, it's their minds. They just don't seem to concentrate as well as men. Which is why they'll never break into the male preserve of championship snooker. Admittedly their shape doesn't help — big breasts can make the game very awkward — but it is that lack of mental control which finally prevents them becoming top class.

Steve Davis, *Sunday Standard*, 1981

We've seen a significant, positive shift for women's sport in the past decade. But this unstoppable rise, with increases in funding, profile and respect for women's sport, hasn't happened in a smooth, linear fashion. Like all social change it's been punctuated with specific events and individual actions that have each shifted the narrative to drive this movement forward to where we sit today.

I'm often asked when I first decided to focus my energy on increasing the impact of women's sport. Had I always been frustrated about the inequalities faced by female athletes, the smaller sponsorship budgets, unequal media coverage, fewer opportunities for girls in sport? For me it's been a gradual realisation. I'm embarrassed to admit that for most of my life it was just something that I accepted. I didn't really question the status quo or feel I had the right to call it out. It was just what had always been for as long as I could remember competing and working in sport.

Women's sport became a real priority and focus for me in 2012 with the London Olympics and the formation of the Women's Sport Trust charity. Looking back over the years since then, there are a number of key moments which have had a significant impact on women's sport in the UK. Here are twelve of those moments, which resonate most with me personally in terms of creating the positive change we see in women's sport today. You may have your own memories of the most important moments. I'd love to hear about them.

I. THE LONDON OLYMPICS – 2012

I'm clearly not alone in citing the 2012 London Olympics as a tipping point for women's sport.

It was, after all, the first Olympics where women competed in all events. There were more women than men on the US team for the first time, with female athletes making up almost half of Team GB. Things have certainly moved on from the first modern Olympics in 1896 when all the competitors were men.

Jacques Rogge, President of the International Olympic Committee (IOC), reflected that the London Games could undoubtedly trigger increased equality for women: 'Opening the Olympic Games to more women is not just a matter of basic fairness. The Games provide a global platform for female Olympians that inspires others to follow their example. More than four billion people, well over half of the world's population, will have access to watch the London Games. About half of that audience will be women and girls, a gender balance few other major sporting events can hope to match. That global reach makes the Games a powerful force for gender equality.'

The fight for equality was on display from the very first night, when Suffragettes, singing their anthem 'March of the Women', entered the stadium as part of Danny Boyle's magnificent Opening Ceremony.

It was also the first time countries such as Saudi Arabia, Qatar and Brunei sent female athletes to any Olympic Games. Some claimed the small numbers of women from these countries (just two from Saudi, four from Qatar and one from Brunei) was token-istic – but for me their appearance sent a significant message that left women hopeful of improvements in the future.

Other female firsts from London 2012 saw Nicola Adams become the first female Olympic boxing champion – the final sport to achieve gender equality – and that extraordinary night for women's football when Team GB beat Brazil at Wembley in front of a crowd of 70,584.

The poster girl for London 2012, Jessica Ennis-Hill, won an extraordinary gold in the heptathlon on Super Saturday, with women changing perceptions in other sports, too. How could you not get emotional watching Jade Jones' enormous passion as she celebrated her Taekwondo gold, or feel the heartbreak of Shanaze Reade, finishing sixth in an action-packed BMX final?

Across the Olympics and Paralympics, British female athletes had incredible success, winning golds in everything from cycling, equestrian, athletics and swimming through to shooting, sailing and archery.

A memorable highlight for me (I know I wasn't the only person in tears) was watching Katherine Grainger finally win a rowing gold with Anna Watkins at Dorney Lake.

The London 2012 Games put our extraordinary female athletes front and centre – and the entire nation loved it.

2. WOMEN'S SPORT TRUST – 2013

For Tammy Parlour and Jo Bostock, the co-founders of the Women's Sport Trust, it was the profile of women athletes during London 2012 that drove them to create their hugely influential charity.

Tammy recalls her frustration when all the wonderful media coverage of female athletes we had enjoyed that summer just dwindled away as the Olympics ended. It was a wakeup call for Tammy (a Hapkido Master), and she persuaded her wife Jo, whose day job was helping companies be inclusive and diverse, to join her in setting up the Women's Sport Trust. I was lucky enough to get involved as one of the founding trustees, when board meetings took place around the kitchen table in Jo and Tammy's home.

What has followed in the past nine years has been quite extraordinary. The impact of this small charity has been transformative for women's sport in the UK and it's little wonder that both Jo and Tammy were awarded MBEs in the Queen's New Year Honours list in 2019 for their services to gender equality in sport.

I asked Jo to tell me more about how it all started: 'Tammy was the trigger. She was the catalyst and she's the pure athlete and the one who really, from a sport standpoint, wanted female athletes and sport to get the profile coverage and investment that it deserved.'

Jo told me the bit that she brought into the mix 'was around inclusion, systemic change, influencing. I think you get a lot of change done by connecting brilliant people to a brilliant idea and then stirring. So much of WST's success has been relational. If you notice that the system's a wee bit broken – so sport wasn't talking to sport, media to media and business to business – they weren't tending to mix much. We stirred them together and made it fun rather than boring.'

One of the most powerful phrases Jo uses (and she really is the queen of superb soundbites) was that the Women's Sport Trust was the 'provocative glue'. We bring people together as a catalyst for conversations behind the scenes. And moving women's sport 'from worthy to irresistible' is a central goal of the WST, whether talking to sponsors, broadcasters, rights holders or sports governing bodies.

The WST's work has included major events such as the powerful #BeAGameChanger Awards, which celebrated the visionaries and game changers driving the future of women's sport at all levels and used their example to inspire action from others.

Partnerships have also played an important role. In 2017 the charity partnered with Getty Images to increase the visibility of female athletes and women's sports, while also challenging the way they are portrayed in imagery. Activities included new creative and editorial collections focusing on women's sport, two paid internships and the establishment of new visual guidelines for the industry.

In 2018 WST launched the #SHOWUP campaign with Sky Sports to encourage everyone to 'show up' and support women's sport by watching, attending or playing. The #Onside campaign also launched that year, in partnership with the Rugby Football Union (RFU), with an ambition to engage men and boys as role models to speak up and take action to support women and girls in sport.

The summer of 2020 saw the launch of the charity's potentially most powerful campaign to date, Unlocked. It paired forty-one elite female athletes, who all wanted to be change makers within and beyond their sports, with forty-one leading figures from business, sport and media. The impact it had on the lives and reach of these athletes exceeded even our most ambitious expectations. I am delighted that Unlocked 2 is now underway.

Finally, during COVID-19, the WST's 'Ambition' project brought together fifty-four leaders from across sport including media, brands, agencies, sports rights holders, national governing bodies and athletes, to consider what needs to change to achieve our ambition for women's sport. The resulting report and recommendations were shared across sport in 2021.

I'm incredibly proud to be a trustee of the Women's Sport Trust.

3. THE WOMEN'S BOAT RACE – 2015

The Women's Boat Race was traditionally held at Henley, the week before the men's Boat Race, which takes place on the Thames in London. This annual rowing race between Oxford and Cambridge Universities' Women's Boat Clubs had first taken place in 1927, when *The Times* reported that 'large and hostile crowds gathered on the towpath' objecting to the women rowing.

As it happens, the women weren't actually allowed to race against each other. This was considered unladylike and some of the male organisers were worried that intense rowing might damage 'women's insides'. The teams therefore rowed one after the other. The early races were not even about the fastest boat; the 'style' of the rowers was judged downstream and the speed on the way back upstream.

The race became an annual competition in 1964 and by 1977, with the boats now racing against each other in a traditional format, the Women's Boat Race was given an annual slot at the Henley Royal Regatta. It might have stayed there for ever but for a woman with a passion to bring some equality to the Boat Race.

Helena Morrissey was the CEO of Newton Asset Management when her investment firm decided to sponsor the women's race in 2011. Until that time the women's event had no funding at all. The female rowers had to buy their own kit and pay for transport, as elite sportswomen have had to do in the past (and many continue to do today).

When Newton's parent company BNY Mellon later took on the entire sponsorship of the Boat Race, Helena Morrissey insisted on a few conditions. The funding must be split equally between the men and women and the women must also receive equal billing to the men. While this clearly upset many traditionalists, it made sense that an event with the massive global profile of the Boat Race should have gender parity. Fortunately, the BBC also supported the new move to enhance what was already one of its highest viewed sporting events.

So, on Saturday 11 April 2015, history was made on the Thames in London, when the Women's Boat Race took place on the same stretch of the river as the men's for the very first time.

The women's event was watched by 4.8 million viewers and I must confess to an emotional tear as I watched the BBC preview compilation video that showed the women in the build-up to the big day, with some fantastic editing and a powerful soundtrack. I'd watched the Boat Race as a child with my parents and never once questioned why women weren't rowing, too. It now seemed so significant to witness them finally receiving equal billing alongside the men.

Clare Balding, who should have been fronting TV coverage of the Grand National that day, made a very public decision to host the BBC's coverage of the Women's Boat Race instead. I asked her why: 'My feeling was, with the women's Boat Race I really wanted to support it. Believe me it was not a financial decision that was sensible, but I felt very strongly that sometimes you've just got to put your money where your mouth is and do it. I don't regret that for a second. My parents didn't understand it. A lot of people in racing didn't understand it, but that's what I wanted to do.'

I appreciate that for many people, the perception of the Boat Race is that it is just a bunch of 'privileged Oxbridge toffs' racing on the water. On some levels it is hard to disagree with this analysis. That said, the Women's Boat Race in 2015 makes my top twelve because it demonstrated the power of corporate sponsorship to drive gender equality in sport on an enormous global stage.

4. GB HOCKEY GOLD – RIO 2016

Hockey has been a part of my life for many years. Not as a player (I'd only played a little at school) but I was welcomed into the 'hockey family' when the sports PR agency I ran began working for the national governing body in 2011.

I had the privilege of working with England and GB Hockey in the build-up to 2012, and then in the years that followed helping to raise the profile of campaigns including Back to Hockey, Hockey-Fest, Rush Hockey and Team Up – all driving grassroots participation in the sport.

At the London Olympics the GB Women had won an emotional medal. Their heroic captain, Kate Walsh (later Richardson-Walsh), was hit in the face by a stick in the opening match against Japan but returned – after surgery to fix her broken jaw – to lead the team to bronze.

Four years on, in 2016, and the team were ranked as one of the best in the world as they headed to compete in the Rio Olympics. The team progressed smoothly through the two weeks of competition to reach the finals without losing a single match, and support for them was building at home in Britain. For many viewers, the sight of these incredible, strong women, sprinting and diving and powerfully striking balls, was in stark contrast to the 'jolly hockey sticks' image many had of the sport.

The final, on Friday 19 August, was against a formidable opposition, the Netherlands, who were hoping to win a third straight Olympic gold.

The hugely competitive match finished 3-3 in normal time, with Maddie Hinch, our extraordinary goalkeeper, having made some remarkable saves.

By the time it came to the penalty shootout, almost 10 million Britons were tuned in. The BBC's ten o'clock news was delayed for the coverage as the nation held its breath (and collectively realised that a penalty in hockey was not just a matter of stepping forward and striking the ball).

After what felt like an eternity, with Maddie Hinch saving all the Dutch penalties and Helen Richardson-Walsh scoring a penalty strike, it was down to Hollie Pearne-Webb to step forward for the final, decisive penalty. The moment at which she scored, and GB Women won their first ever Olympic gold, will stay with me for ever. In writing this I thought it only right to watch that penalty shootout again. Even though I knew the outcome, it is still nail-biting to watch and so emotional to see the GB women and their support staff celebrating afterwards.

Kate Richardson-Walsh, again the GB captain, gave an interesting response when I asked her how she felt as the team gathered for the penalty shootout: 'When the final whistle went, I celebrated maybe a little bit too much, because I genuinely believe in that moment, we had this. And I believed that because we had beaten the Netherlands on penalties at the European Championships the year before, we'd also beaten them on penalties in the European Championships in 2013. So, in the lead-up to Rio, at all major tournaments, we'd had a really good set of results against the Dutch. Coupled with the fact that I know how much statistical analysis, video analysis, practice on the field the goalkeepers and our penalty takers had all done.'

One of my abiding memories of the whole Games is Kate on the podium, lined up with the entire team, holding her gold medal in both hands and gazing at it emotionally. What was she feeling in that moment? 'Just so grateful and proud. It was almost a very quick flashback through everything that I'd been through to get to that point and then not just me, also reflecting on all the women around me, the women that weren't there who hadn't been selected. The women that had gone before us. It was just that whole journey I think in that moment.'

The women's bronze in London and gold in Rio drove thousands of women and girls to start, or restart, playing hockey. I asked Sally Munday what she's most proud of from her time as CEO at England and GB Hockey: 'It's not actually about the gold medal. It's about how our sport used that gold medal and used the bronze medal of 2012 to engage with our clubs and our hockey family to drive more participants. That's what I am most proud about.'

5. MUIRFIELD – 2017

It was March 2017 when Muirfield – one of Scotland's last men-only golf clubs – finally allowed women to join for the first time.

Sadly, the decision wasn't made because members recognised the misogyny of denying women access to their club, nor were they embarrassed following worldwide condemnation of their refusal to allow women in 2016. According to a poll, almost three-quarters of Scots believed Muirfield golf club's ban on women members was 'damaging to Scotland's reputation'. Yet despite groups and individuals campaigning for equal rights, lobbying members and signing petitions, and the Scottish First Minister Nicola Sturgeon saying the club's decision was 'indefensible' and sent 'the wrong signal', the club wouldn't budge.

No. The change of heart occurred only when the club was denied the right to host the prestigious Open championships if it did not comply. The club had hosted the Open sixteen times in the past, but golf's ruling body, the R&A, removed Muirfield as a potential host venue when it failed to allow women to join in 2016.

Funnily enough, only weeks after the R&A announced its decision Muirfield members voted to change the rules to allow women members. When it comes to gender equality, it seems that money talks.

Following the club's change in policy, the R&A immediately announced that Muirfield was once again back in the rotation to stage the world's oldest major.

Henry Fairweather, the club captain at the time, said it was a significant decision for the club, 'which retains many of the values and aspirations of its founding members'. I'm not sure the values and aspirations of those founding members in 1744 included gender equality in any format.

Recognising the significance of the vote, Nicola Sturgeon congratulated the club, tweeting: 'Well done, Muirfield – decision to admit women members emphatic and the right one. Look forward to seeing you host the Open again in future. Scotland is a modern country that wants to see gender equality become the norm across all parts of society and today's decision is another step forward in that journey.'

Tracey Crouch, then UK Sports Minister, added: 'This decision sends out an important message. It is vital that clubs and sports organisations play their part in promoting equality.'

For a sport that is desperate to modernise and bring more women on board this was an important move in the right direction.

Finally, in what could be viewed as a significant turnaround for the club, it has been announced that in 2022 Muirfield will host the Women's British Open for the first time.

6. THE BAN ON 'WALK-ON GIRLS' – 2018

At the end of 2017 some momentous, and in my opinion long overdue, decisions were made by first the Professional Darts Corporation (PDC) and then Formula 1 to stop the use of so-called walk-on girls and grid girls. The discussion around this had been prompted by a phone-in on BBC Radio 5 Live in December 2017, where presenter Jennie Gow had asked whether the use of grid girls was an outdated sexist relic as the gender gap in sport narrows.

The following year, on the back of the #MeToo movement, and the shock of the Presidents Club men-only dinner scandal, sports bodies and broadcasters took the decision that having scantily clad young women accompanying men to the oche or strutting in front of them as they made their way to their cars wasn't quite the right image for sport. We were in the twenty-first century after all.

In response to these decisions, the Women's Sport Trust issued a statement to the media in which we clearly identified why we agreed it was time for sport to change its attitude to using women as accessories in this way:

The Women's Sport Trust believes women in the sporting environment should be judged by their sports appeal and not sex appeal. We've been working with Getty to establish visual standards for the depiction of sportswomen which focus less on what women look like and more on what they achieve.

At a time when so much great work is being done to raise the visibility and increase the impact of women's sporting role models, it's disappointing to see that some of the highest profile international sporting events such as motor racing, cycling and boxing still choose to use women to accessorise their events rather than be a central part of a sport.

What sort of message are we sending women and girls about how they are valued? We're asking them to look at and admire the successful, talented, strong men taking part in the competition, whilst the role of the women is purely based on their physical appearance.

Whilst respecting a woman's right to choose what she does with her own body, we believe there is a clear role for every kind of woman and girl within sport – excelling, competing and winning medals. We want sport to be a place where women of all shapes, sizes and backgrounds feel welcome and able to actively participate.

Sport mirrors and magnifies society. If we depict women in sport in a way that reinforces a narrow stereotype, we add to the pressure young girls in particular feel to look and act a certain way. If we depict women in a central, powerful and sporting role, we create a positive, modern and accurate image to inspire others.

We're confident that the more savvy marketeers and sponsors will recognise that in the 21st century, the presence of grid girls is unacceptable and off-putting for many men and women. By continuing the outdated practice, the likes of boxing, cycling and motor racing are potentially missing out on an opportunity to engage new audiences and excite new fans.

The backlash to this statement was astonishing, as the tabloid media jumped on board and stoked a battle between 'the nasty feminists' and 'the victimized glamour girls'. Such was the vitriol for the Women's Sport Trust on Twitter that I joked about having a T-shirt printed with 'fat, hairy, vegan, lesbian, feminazis' to highlight some of the name-calling our trustees had experienced on social media in the weeks that followed.

It was about this time that I first came across Stacey Copeland, a former England footballer who was now a professional boxer. I heard Stacey talking about the issue on a BBC 5 Live interview call-in and I was in awe. She was so calm and articulate about the whole subject, despite being faced with some very angry walk-on girls in the studio.

Stacey explained to me why she felt the need to talk about the subject: 'I felt strongly about ringside girls from the beginning. The only time I saw women in my sport was when they were dressed in very sexual outfits, walking around a ring with a piece of cardboard with a number on it. And that bothered me. It took so long for women to get the right to box. I know as a female boxer I'm not as accepted as the males, despite doing all the same training as them and dedicating my life to it. Yet somebody who is there just for sexual appeal is? There's something wrong with that picture for me.

'Also, in an age where we are trying to teach boys about respect for women, consent, all of that, to take them to what is a sport event – not a lap dancing club, not a gentleman's club – but sports event, where people are shouting extremely sexualised, crude and, in my opinion, vile things, is totally socially unacceptable. Those boys are watching male role models act like that in a sports environment. To me that is not what sport is at all.'

How do female boxers feel about having ring girls at their events?

'I wasn't a fan of it, so I never had ring card girls from the start of my career. I had kids who were into boxing as my mascots, just like we have at Wimbledon or at football.'

Stacey raised an interesting point that I've found myself making since: 'Imagine if at Wimbledon we suddenly changed and had "court girls" or "net girls" or whatever we would call them. We would be saying "what is going on?!" We would not have them at the Olympics or in football. Just because it has always been that way in my sport it doesn't mean it is right.'

There was huge public backlash against Stacey for taking a stance and publicly speaking out against the use of ring girls, but she feels it was worth it because she is 'on the right side of history with this'.

Stacey wants things to be different for her young niece Ruby, for whom the only women she sees when she watches the Tour de France are the two women giving the winner a peck on the cheek as they pose beside him with a flirtatious leg lifted.

'I want her to grow up not seeing that. And I want her to look back on these things, and say "Auntie Stacey, did there *really* used to be women who walked around a boxing ring in a bikini, with a number on a piece of cardboard?", and I'd say "yes . . . isn't that odd?"'

7. LAUNCH OF TELEGRAPH WOMEN'S SPORT – 2018

In 2018, the *Telegraph* made a big play for women's sport when it appointed Anna Kessel as Women's Sport Editor. To support Anna and her newly appointed team, the paper committed substantial resources and investment to make a space for women's sport online and on its social channels, exploring video and Instagram posts, along with a dedicated monthly supplement and integration into the daily sports sections.

What was particularly exciting about this was that, rather than just appointing one woman to lead coverage of women's sport, Adam Sills, Head of Sport at the *Telegraph*, committed to an entire department. Anna was joined by Vicki Hodges as Deputy Editor, along with three full-time women's writers, Molly McElwee, Fiona Tomas and Katie Whyatt, and a dedicated social media editor, Fadumo Olow, added to the team in 2020. Elsewhere across the paper, in athletics, cycling, swimming, other journalists were covering both men's and women's sport.

In describing the launch of the Telegraph Women's Sport (TWS) Anna proudly declared: 'We are rethinking sports coverage and creating a twenty-first-century approach to sports media. We will showcase diverse women's voices, commit to nurturing new writing across different platforms, and while we want to highlight inequality, we do not want to define women's sport through that lens. Sportswomen are incredible, so let TWS be a space where stories stand on their own merit – not in comparison to men . . . As the United Nations put it, sport has the power to unlock gender equality for women and girls around the world. I am proud that the *Telegraph* is leading this historic step to contribute towards that drive for change.'

I spoke to Anna in 2019 and asked her how things had gone in the early months of establishing the new section: 'Of course there's challenges and we're talking about changing a structure. I don't just want us to work in a silo. We have women sport specialist journalists, but it's really important that we work right across the range of writers that we have. And so that means having conversations around: "OK, what's our content going to be? I know you've written for thirty years and you've won every award under the sun but . . ." and it's been wonderful that those male writers have been really open to that and interested and keen to do something new and fresh.'

I'm a huge fan of all the *Telegraph* has done and there's no doubt that its investment in women's sport sent ripples across the media, encouraging other national newspapers to invest more in reporting and featuring women's sport on their pages. One of the most refreshing elements has been the way in which TWS has not been afraid to tackle controversial issues. From menstruation, motherhood and sexual abuse through to concussion, racism and fat-shaming, the team at the paper have covered topics that impact women and girls far beyond the world of sport.

Anna and her team have created an environment where high-profile sportswomen feel comfortable to share unapologetically their stories with moments of joy and glory, alongside emotional vulnerability. The voices of sportswomen have been amplified with regular columnists including sprinter Dina Asher-Smith, former Paralympic cyclist and swimmer Sarah Storey and footballer Jordan Nobbs, along with thought-provoking features from the likes of former England rugby player Maggie Alphonsi and former England cricketer Ebony Rainford-Brent. In January 2021 it was wonderful to see Naomi Osaka as guest editor of a monthly supplement dedicated to athlete activism. Anna has also explored new voices, giving a platform to a broad range of women beyond those typically reporting on sport, with guest writers including authors Poorna Bell and Caroline Criado-Perez.

TWS has helped to address the under-representation of women's sport, giving 29 per cent more coverage to women's sport in its first year than any other newspaper. In fact, according to research from the Women's Sport Trust, the paper had 'near parity' of key sports coverage over the summer of 2019, with 45 per cent of lead sports articles featuring women's sport. It's no wonder TWS has already won multiple awards.

'We predicted that Telegraph Women's Sport would bring about a revolution in sports coverage – and it has,' reflected Anna on the section's anniversary in 2020. 'We are thrilled to see women's sport elevated onto front pages and making national headlines, but there is still much to be done in working towards parity for women and girls at all levels, from closing the school sport gender gap to equality for elite sportswomen. At TWS we are committed to telling these stories, highlighting injustice and championing sporting excellence along the way.'

8. NETBALL GOLD COMMONWEALTH GAMES – 2018

'It's pretty addictive watching international netball, isn't it,' was my husband's comment as he, like many others, found himself drawn to the games taking place during the Gold Coast Commonwealth Games in 2018. As a dad of three keen netballers, Matt's watched a lot of the sport courtside over the years, but I loved how he was now utterly drawn to watch these incredible female athletes at the very top of the international game.

For England, the Commonwealth Games on the Gold Coast marked a significant moment in the team's history. In the past decade, the England Roses had consistently lost out to the Australia Diamonds or the New Zealand Silver Ferns in most major championships.

By way of background to the huge success of these southern hemisphere teams, the game was originally introduced as 'women's basketball' in around 1900, and rapidly spread across schools in both countries. Jumping forward to 2008, the ANZ Championship launched with five teams from Australia and five from New Zealand, and regular TV coverage, becoming the first semi-professional netball league in the world.

The league ran until 2016, when a new ANZ Premiership launched in New Zealand, and in Australia Suncorp Super Netball launched, a new, nationally exclusive league with increased funding and media coverage.

By 2019, the salary cap for each team in the Suncorp League was around £300,000, with an additional £85,000 for clubs to provide players with employment, education and to pay for ambassador roles. With accommodation and private health insurance also provided, and average pay for players around £40,000, Super Netball was the place to be if you were a woman wanting to earn a living in sport in Australia.

I was lucky enough to visit Netball New South Wales in 2019, home to the Giants and Swifts, two of the top teams playing in the league. It was astounding to see the professional setup in Sydney and the enormous publicity generated, with players appearing on billboards and buses, to promote the league.

Many English players were understandably drawn to play down under, including Roses stars Helen Housby, Jo Harten, Serena Guthrie, Geva Mentor and Nat Haythornthwaite. It's this experience, of training and competing with the best professional netballers in the world, that may have made all the difference to the result at the Commonwealth Games on 15 April 2018.

Pamela Cookey, former captain of the Roses who had also played for a time in New Zealand but retired before the Commonwealth Games, told me about a defining moment for the England team in 2013 when they won a Test series 3-0 against Australia. 'That was where the belief started and where we saw it was now possible. It wasn't just a one-off game where we beat Australia or New Zealand which we'd done in the past. It was three solid games. We saw they weren't unbeatable. They were just a group of players – two arms, two legs – just like the rest of us who played netball.'

The Commonwealth Games final followed a nail-biting semi-final against Jamaica, where, having been six goals down at one point, Jo Harten's dramatic goal in the last second clinched a 56-55 win. That in itself had been pretty emotional for the Roses, as they'd lost in the semi-finals of the past four Commonwealth competitions. History was already being made, as it was the first time since netball was introduced at the 1998 Games that Australia and New Zealand were not playing each other in the final.

My sleepy daughters and I set our alarms for the middle of the night to be sure we didn't miss the historic final of England versus Australia. An incredible 1.8 million people in the UK did the same, and what a final it turned out to be.

I was beginning to lose hope a little in the final quarter when England fell four goals behind, but they made an impressive come-back and with just twenty seconds on the clock it was 51-51 and England was taking the final centre pass.

With just five seconds to play, Jo Harten missed a shot and then so did Helen Housby. In terms of what then followed, you couldn't have written a better bit of sporting drama. The buzzer sounded, but a penalty shot was given for a contact on Housby. She calmly shot the goal that won Commonwealth gold: 'As a shooter you dream of that moment. Commonwealth Games final, last-second goal, but you never believe it's really going to happen. It's the best day of my life,' she later told the media.

What followed in the coming months, and why that moment makes my top twelve, was the profile that netball received in the UK and the enormous increase in women and girls playing the sport.

The year closed with a final netball highlight, with the Vitality Roses winning two awards at the BBC Sports Personality of the Year Awards. Having been awarded Team of the Year, the Roses went on to beat the England men's football team, Alastair Cook, Tiger Woods and Tyson Fury, with the most public votes to win 'Greatest Sporting Moment of the Year'.

What a wonderful inspiration for any young (and old) netballers watching that night, to hear the words of England captain Ama Agbeze: 'It's been a very long journey. Billie Jean King said that you stand on the shoulders of those who went before you, and we're very tall girls – we've been standing on a lot of shoulders.'

9. BARCLAYS SPONSORSHIP OF THE FA WOMEN'S SUPER LEAGUE – 2019

In what I feel was a watershed moment in 2019, Barclays announced the biggest ever investment a brand had made in women's sport in the UK. The multi-million-pound partnership with the Football Association, worth over £10 million, saw the top tier of women's football renamed as the Barclays FA Women's Super League (WSL) from the 2019–20 season through to July 2022.

It wasn't just elite sport that benefited from the investment, as the relationship saw the FA, Barclays and the Youth Sport Trust working together to drive the growth of the women's game at grassroots level, too. Barclays became the lead partner of the FA Girls' Football School

Partnerships, a nationwide scheme to increase girls' access to football at school with the ambitious goal of all girls having equal access to football in schools by 2024.

Commenting on the deal at the time of the launch, Jes Staley, Group CEO of Barclays, said: 'Barclays' multi-year investment is also our salute to the professionalism of the FA Women's Super League players, and we hope it will help take the game to new heights, making England's domestic league a world leader. Our commitment to women's and girls' football, at a crucial time in its development, goes beyond pure sponsorship – we believe it can be a key to increasing participation, development and the wider visibility of the female game.'

In addition to this huge public deal, Barclays also supported other organisations working behind the scenes to drive equality in the world of football. The progressive brand increased its funding for Women in Football, the charity which lobbies against sexism in the game and also sponsored my own podcast, *The Game Changers*, enabling me to create a number of new series dedicated to 'Fearless Women in Football'.

Aside from the transformative impact Barclays' funding will have on women's football in the UK, for me this deal had even broader impact. The fact that a brand as big and powerful as Barclays, with a long-standing tradition of sponsoring men's sport in Britain, was backing *women's* sport on this substantial level sent a powerful message to other brands considering entering this space.

Here's hoping many other major brands will follow Barclays' lead.

10. THE FIFA WOMEN'S WORLD CUP – 2019

The FIFA Women's World Cup was a game-changing event for women's sport on many levels.

Globally, a reported 1.2 billion people watched it on television, the most in the history of the tournament. Half that vast audience were European, with viewing figures in South America up 500 per cent from the Women's World Cup in 2015. An incredible 82 million people watched the final.

In the UK, the profile of women's football reached new heights, with 28.1 million tuning in to watch the BBC coverage across the event, more than double the numbers from Canada 2015, which attracted 12.2 million. The BBC also reported 13.1 million match requests (live and on-demand) on BBC iPlayer and BBC Sport.

Millions watched Scotland in their first ever World Cup; 1.7 million watched England versus the USA in the semi-finals. If only we had made the final – just think what the numbers might have been then.

With a gender split of 62 per cent male and 38 per cent female for the total tournament audience, it was clearly not just women watching women's sport as critics sometimes claim is the case.

As players like Steph Houghton, Ellen White, Karen Bardsley and Lucy Bronze became household names in England, this was the moment that propelled Megan Rapinoe to global stardom. Already established as a much-admired athlete activist for bravely being the first soccer player to take the knee in support of US football quarterback and civil rights activist Colin Kaepernick, it was her Twitter spat with US President Donald Trump that made us love her even more.

Rapinoe had openly told reporters that she would not visit the White House if the US women's team won the World Cup. Her comments later went viral on social media, when a video was released ahead of the quarter-final against France where she said to camera that she was 'not going to the f★★★ing White House'.

Trump couldn't resist taking to his beloved Twitter to respond: 'I am a big fan of the American Team, and Women's Soccer, but Megan should WIN first before she TALKS! Finish the job!'

And she did just that, scoring a penalty in the final and winning the Golden Boot and Golden Ball, in addition to the team trophy.

And she didn't go to the White House.

II. FALLON SHERROCK AT THE PDC WORLD CHAMPIONSHIPS – 2019

After all the furore around the Professional Darts Corporation (PDC) deciding to stop using walk-on girls in darts in 2018, only to see they were still employing plenty of young women in skimpy shorts waving pom-poms as the 'Official PDC Darts Dancers', I have to say watching the darts wasn't a priority for me around Christmas 2019.

That all changed with the arrival of Fallon Sherrock.

There are few 'firsts' left for women in sport, but one that made global headlines was when, on 17 December 2019, Fallon Sherrock became the first woman to beat a man at the PDC World Championships, held at Alexandra Palace in London.

What a pleasure to see the hundreds of noisy men in the crowd finally celebrating a woman for her talent and skill, rather than the tightness of her top or the length of her legs.

Fallon beat Ted Evetts 3-2 in the first round of the 2020 World Championship and spectacularly followed this up with a 3-1 win over eleventh seed Mensur Suljović in the second round. She finally lost 2-4 to Chris Dobey.

Becoming a poster girl for the sport literally overnight, the affectionately named 'Queen of the Palace' received supportive messages from the likes of Billie Jean King, with media from all over the world wanting to talk to her. Her Twitter following shot from 15,000 to 100,000.

She even appeared on *Good Morning Britain* the day after her first victory, winning more of the nation's hearts by beating Piers Morgan live on the show (did he really think he stood a chance?).

I asked sports reporter Jacqui Oatley, who's covered darts for many years, if she thought that Fallon's success would open the door for other women in the future. 'Well, this has been an absolute revelation because there aren't too many sports firsts left, are there? She was so cool and so calm, and with darts being such a meritocracy, it's not like football where you can't have men playing against women, you can absolutely have women playing against men in darts. There is that psychological barrier for the men, whatever people say, they really don't want to be on that big stage being booed and being beaten by a woman, even though Ted Evetts was incredibly magnanimous.

'It was phenomenal. The PDC is trying to grow the game into different territories, and that first victory almost overnight changed darts for ever.'

Jacqui was keen to remind me that, while it was Fallon who made the headlines, there are lots of other fantastic female darts players breaking new ground, including Lisa Ashton, who won a tour card as a professional, and Mikuru Suzuki, the back-to-back women's champion.

Who knows, maybe I'll be watching the darts again in the future after all.

12.   CLARE CONNOR APPOINTED PRESIDENT OF MCC — 2020

Clare Connor being named as the next President of Marylebone Cricket Club (MCC) was symbolic of the enormous change in women's cricket when it was announced in the summer of 2020.

The former England captain, who was named Head of Women's Cricket at the England and Wales Cricket Board (ECB) in 2007, and is now Managing Director of Women's Cricket, will become President of MCC in 2021. She will be the first woman in this prestigious role in the club's 233-year history, leading one of the oldest institutions in any sport and heading a club that did not even allow female members until 1998.

Even now MCC members are mostly male. According to the *Telegraph*, in 2019 MCC had 217 women as full members of the club. With the total membership of 18,000, that's just 1.2 per cent.

Considered by many the most exclusively male of sports, 'the gentlemen's game' has changed significantly for women in the past decade, under the guidance of the much-admired Clare Connor. Such has been her impact that she has been awarded an MBE, an OBE and a CBE for her services to the game.

Reflecting on her appointment, Clare told the BBC:

I am deeply honoured to be named the next President of MCC. Cricket has enriched my life so deeply already, and now it hands me this wonderful privilege. We often need to look back to see how far we've come. I made my first visit to Lord's as a starry-eyed, cricket-obsessed nine-year-old girl at a time when women were not welcome in the Long Room. Times have changed. Now I find myself entrusted with this remarkable opportunity – the opportunity to play a part in helping MCC, cricket's most influential club, to thrive and grow in an even more modern and inclusive future.

My belief is that the game is for everybody and we haven't always behaved that way as a game. That's not a criticism of anybody. The game has, for a long time, been set up in this country and overseas to cater for men and boys. And we're at an exciting crossroads in society more widely and in sport and in cricket where there is a huge commitment to making the game more inclusive and more diverse. And that's not just about gender. That's all areas of inclusion and diversity.

Clare's appointment is symbolic of a wider shift for women's cricket as its popularity and growth continues across the world. I was lucky enough to be at Lord's on 23 July 2017 to witness England Women winning a thrilling World Cup final against India in front of packed (and wonderfully noisy) stands. March the 8th 2020 saw another record-breaking attendance, when 86,174 fans packed the Melbourne Cricket Club for the ICC Women's T20 World Cup final.

Women's cricket needs more investment if it's ever to reach the levels of the men's game, so it was hugely welcomed in 2020 when the ECB announced a funding boost for women's cricket of £20 million over the next two years to increase grassroots participation and make cricket a gender-balanced sport. The ultimate goal of the ECB is to invest £50 million over the following five years, which will ensure funding for forty full-time professional, domestic contracts, along with the existing professional contracts for England Women's elite players, creating a pathway for Under-11 to Under-17 levels and raising the profile of the women's game through The Hundred – a new domestic tournament which now begins in the summer of 2021.

It's an exciting time for women's cricket and with a woman like Clare Connor at the helm it will get even better in the future.

As I write this book, we have seen COVID's disproportionate

impact on women's sport – as the pandemic exposed the inequalities already at play in the wider sporting landscape.

Across many sports, women's leagues and championships were cut before men's, and less investment available for testing and equipment has seen elite women's teams prevented from training and playing like their male counterparts. This has made employment more precarious for many professional and semi-professional female athletes.

As sport returns, there's the added risk that the hugely reduced income across the entire ecosystem may see clubs fall back to prioritising their 'traditionally more profitable' investment in men's sports.

Despite concerns that the progress we have seen during the past decade could be lost completely, looking back at these incredibly positive twelve moments I feel confident that will not be the case. There have been too many significant changes that have caused us to shift our view on women's sport for that to happen. I look forward to witnessing many more in the next decade as we make our progress towards equality.

As stated by UN Women in their report *COVID-19 Women, Girls and Sport: Build Back Better*: 'Women and girls must be equally participants and leaders in the process of building back better, so their gains are not lost, and a better future for all becomes a reality, where women and girls can participate in, work with, govern and enjoy sport on an equal playing field.'

3

THE FEMALE FRAILTY MYTH

Girls are sometimes pretty and wear nice clothes and can sit on coaches to watch us play cricket . . . but girls cannot run, jump or climb trees.

Eton schoolboy, *Physical Culture*, 1895

I am fascinated by the story of women's sport. How beliefs about women's bodies and the impact of physical activity, held so long ago, still have a massive influence on women's sport today.

The more I've read, the more I can see that much stems from the Victorian ideal of femininity: the perception of the passive, gentle, delicate woman who would have neither the strength nor the desire to take part in strenuous activity or sports.

These attitudes were reinforced by the 'female frailty myth', a long-held, unproven medical belief that strenuous sport would damage women's bodies and make them infertile. Girls were taught from an early age that they would become masculine and sterile (and their uteruses could fall out) if they participated in a vigorous activity like sport.

Because of these views, 'the weaker sex' was prevented from

taking part in sports for decades – women banned from distance running and hockey through to ski jumping and boxing. Hard to believe that London 2012 was the first Olympic Games where women were allowed to compete in every sport.

Throughout history women have suffered discrimination in sport, with men's sporting dominance going far beyond their physical ability to be faster and stronger in most head-to-head competitions. Men have held power in most sports, excluding women from any control over the very sports they might have played. Sports promoters and agents were predominantly male, and, with fewer women in corporate roles, sponsorship decisions were made by men. Since the early days when sports sections became a regular part of national newspapers the sports media has been male-dominated. This not only resulted in men's sport always being the priority, but in many cases, if women's sport was reported at all, it was depicted as 'unfeminine and unnatural'.

What fascinates me now is how these archaic attitudes towards women's involvement in sport still have such a significant impact on attitudes to women's sport today. It perhaps helps to explain why women's sport still trails men's in terms of funding, sponsorship and media coverage.

Sport and recreation have been a part of British society since the Middle Ages, with sports and games often part of celebrations and festivals for working people while the wealthier classes enjoyed golf, archery and riding. But organised sport, as we know it today, with its clubs and rules and leagues, was not created until the late eighteenth century.

Masculine sporting pursuits grew in popularity in Britain partly to counter men's fear that the 'foppish' behaviour of the French court might influence them. Just think back to those images of aristocratic French men with wigs, powdered faces, elaborate clothes and stockinged legs.

In the US after the Civil War, male sport was seen as the path to virile, athletic manhood. It was also a way to provide discipline for the 'unruly masses', and to achieve 'muscular Christianity'. According to Susan Cahn in her book *Coming on Strong*, sport and physical activity were thought to contain men's sexual energy, instil self-discipline and 'strengthen a man's moral fibre through muscular development'.

In England, formal, organised sports, with new rules and regulations, were being developed for boys attending public schools including Eton, Harrow, Rugby and Winchester. For the schools to play against each other competitively 'compromise laws' for football were drawn up by Cambridge University. Across the world, away from schools and universities, independent sports clubs were also developing for men and boys.

At a similar time in the US, the expansion of higher education had driven the growth of sport on college campuses. Collegiate athletic programmes were established, with paid administrators and professional coaches for the young men attending. Organised sport was seen as something to focus the minds of underprivileged young men, too, and was therefore adopted as a tool by YMCAs, churches and welfare workers.

So where were the women at this time? As sporting prowess and athleticism became associated with masculinity and manhood, it was little wonder that women struggled to find their place in the world of competitive sport.

Some women had been competing, however, even in the eighteenth century. The first recorded women's cricket match in England took place in 1745 'between eleven maids of Bramley and eleven maids of Hambledon all dressed in white', which paved the way for more women to take part in regular village cricket matches by the end of the century.

Sadly, though, nineteenth-century science characterised women as the inferior, weaker sex who were ruled by their reproductive systems, which resulted in pain and illness, mood swings and regular bleeding. Another belief at the time was that women were born with a finite amount of energy and if they used it on too much physical activity in sports, they would not have enough energy to give birth.

Self-professed medical experts did recommend some level of physical activity to help women strengthen their bodies, but this was more likely to be in the form of vigorous walking, dumbbell exercises or dancing than any involvement in competitive sport.

Even as the bicycle was becoming popular across the world in the 1880s and 1890s, with an estimated 30,000 women taking up cycling in the USA alone, critics were warning of dangers for women which included uterine displacement, spinal shock and pelvic damage. I particularly liked their warning that avid cycling could harden the face muscles into a hideous 'bicycle face' with a protruding jaw, wild, staring eyes and strained expression.

Working life was transformed by industrialisation in the nineteenth century and, despite many working-class women taking physical jobs in factories, the medical community become fascinated by women's fragile bodies and minds, often prescribing complete rest as cure for many ailments including 'female hysteria'.

With no real scientific evidence, doctors began to attribute traits of passivity or hysteria to female biology. The womb was seen as the basis for all female behaviour and any damage to it through exertion would result in deranged behaviour and breakdown, jeopardising women's ability to conceive or potentially producing damaged offspring.

These unfounded beliefs resulted in the control of women's bodies by the (male) medical profession. It was generally accepted that women were weak, delicate and prone to nervous exhaustion. Women's perceived lack of natural sporting ability was assumed to be because of their physical incapacity rather than anything to do with the excessive restrictions in their everyday lives.

The way in which these attitudes still impact women's sport today can very clearly be seen in the world of Grand Slam tennis. The argument I so often hear about why women should be paid less than men is that they only play three sets versus men's five sets. It turns out the reason for this dates back to 1902 and, perhaps unsurprisingly, it was men who made the original decision.

Despite the US Women's Singles Championships being played to five sets from 1891 to 1901, in 1902 the all-male team at the US Lawn Tennis Association decided in their wisdom that five sets was 'too strenuous' for women. Though many leading female players challenged this decision at the time, all Grand Slams chose to follow their advice, and have done so ever since, despite repeated protestations from the Women's Tennis Association (WTA).

To counter this concern about women's weak health, the 1880s saw the development of women's physical educators. In 1879, the London School Board appointed its first Lady Superintendent of Physical Education (PE), who drove the development of colleges where middle-class women would train to become PE teachers. At the same time in the USA, women were training women as PE instructors who went to work in newly established PE departments in colleges and universities across the country.

While this might have been a positive move for women's involvement in sport and recreation, it only reinforced the idea that the sole purpose of physical activity for women was to improve their 'weak' health.

Along with this perception of the weak female body, social conventions about femininity also impacted the development of women's sport. It's been suggested that the negative obsession with the way sporting women looked was because men felt threatened. If muscular activities like sport and exercise were what distinguished British men from the foppish Frenchman, then their masculinity came under threat when the same activities were undertaken by women. One way of dealing with the threat was to belittle the women who tried to play.

The very idea of 'female athletes' made people anxious that men might lose their physical supremacy and, because of that, society might lose distinctly male and female characteristics. Women's sport therefore became associated with weakness, lack of aggression and looking good.

It is perhaps unsurprising, then, that no women took part in the first modern Olympic Games in 1896. By 1900 there were 'officially' just two sports organised for women – tennis and golf. I was shocked to learn that even then, early forms of golf restricted women to 'half swings' because anything else would be unladylike. 'Not because we doubt a lady's power to make a longer drive,' explained Lord Wellwood in a contribution to *Golf* by Horace G. Hutchinson in 1890, 'but because that cannot well be done without raising the club above the shoulder. Now, we do not presume to dictate, but we must observe that the posture and gestures requisite for a full swing are not particularly graceful when the player is clad in female dress.'

It was also around this time that the medical profession was developing the field of sexology, with its notion that heterosexuality was the norm and homosexuality was abnormal. So-called experts claimed that homosexuality in women could always be suspected in females who had short hair, dressed in men's fashions or 'enjoyed sport like their male acquaintances'. The public took to this view which implied that any woman who ignored the requirement to look 'feminine' while exercising must therefore be homosexual.

A positive shift for women's sport in the US arrived in 1901, in the form of Constance Applebee, a graduate from the British College of Physical Education. Constance was unimpressed with the range of physical activities for women on offer at Harvard College, where she was then studying, which at the time included musical chairs and 'drop the handkerchief'. She explained to her cohort that they were party games, but for real exercise women in England played hockey. Constance went on to tour US colleges, spreading the word for hockey wherever she went.

I love her attitude in justifying women's sport to prominent leaders. She said to one university President: 'You want all these students to go out and do something in the world. To get the vote. What's the good of their having the vote if they're too ill to use it?'

In the early 1900s publications in Britain emerged that were focused on women's sport including *The Hockey Field* (1901), *Ladies Golf* (1912) and *Golfing Gentlewomen* (1914). By 1914 *The Badminton Magazine of Sports and Pastimes* even had its own women's section, but the coverage remained incredibly chauvinistic: 'Let young girls ride, skate, dance and play lawn tennis and other games in moderation but let them leave field sports and rough outdoor pastimes to those for whom they were naturally intended – men.'

While these publications did help to build a community for women interested in various sports, the national press were still patronising about female participation. Women's cricket matches drew big crowds, but even W. G. Grace, who had a very talented cricketing daughter, said it was 'only a game for schoolgirls that ought to be abandoned when they grow up'.

Women's place in society was changing dramatically, however, thanks to the huge impetus of the Women's Suffrage Movement. Despite several positive changes for women at the end of the previous century, women still did not have the right to vote. Emmeline Pankhurst's Women's Social and Political Union adopted a more militant approach to gaining suffrage and, because of sport's links to masculine identity, chose to target male sporting events for their demonstrations.

It is estimated that a sixth of the attacks organised by Suffragettes were on sports venues. Traditional male sports were their main targets, including golf clubs, where women had been excluded or viewed as second-class citizens. Acid was used to burn 'Votes for Women' into the greens. Cricket pavilions were burned down, racecourse grandstands, boating pavilions and billiard halls attacked, and attempts made to disrupt the Boat Race. The terrible climax of the campaign was Emily Davison's death, when she tried to stop the horse of King George V in the 1913 Epsom Derby.

While these shocking events may have helped women to eventually get the vote, they probably did not help the cause of allowing women more access to sport. As a *Times* journalist pointed out at the time, 'attempts to spoil sport are not likely to win favour for any cause from a sporting nation'.

And then came the First World War and the Suffragettes' militant action ended to help with the war effort. With men away at the front, women took up roles in factories and businesses and in many cases had more time and opportunity to play sport. Before this, family life and men's financial power had often limited women's opportunities.

As women moved into munitions work, they got better pay and had more leisure time. They began to play football in large stadiums in front of big crowds and in the process raised hundreds of thousands of pounds for charity.

By Boxing Day in 1920, when Dick, Kerr Ladies played St Helens Ladies, they drew a record-breaking crowd of 53,000 at Everton's Goodison Park, with an additional 14,000 waiting outside without tickets. By 1921 there were 150 women's football teams in the UK.

———

The commercialisation of sports began to take off in the US in the 1920s. Enterprising businesses saw the opportunity for leisure to be sold to consumers in the form of equipment, clothing and entertainment. Professional sports developed including baseball, boxing, horse racing, swimming, golf, tennis and American football, with huge audiences paying to watch sport as entertainment.

Alongside this, cultural changes for women saw the advent of the flapper era. Slim, short-haired, confident women who celebrated their independence reflected the break with tradition and female athletes shared many of their characteristics.

Teenager Gertrude Ederle symbolised all this when the Olympic swimming medallist from New York became only the sixth person to swim the English Channel, two hours faster than the five men who had gone before her. I love how much that must have annoyed many men at time.

Alongside teams like Dick, Kerr Ladies playing in front of packed stadiums in the UK (bigger than the crowds that had been watching men's football), national events were developing in the US for women's college sports such as swimming, basketball and athletics – attracting advertisers, media and huge crowds. In 1920 the US sent its first women's team to the Olympics.

The media at the time particularly liked the idea of women in tennis, golf and swimming, as they were sports that men felt emphasised the grace and femininity of the female body. A new ideal of womanhood was evolving – 'a mix of athletic femininity coupled with an undertone of sexuality'.

Male sports promoters looked to maximise the link between sporting success and sexuality to attract crowds, just as the media were beginning to focus on sexual attractiveness to explain the value of women's sport. In describing a 1925 athletics event with over 5,000 young women competing, the *Baltimore Evening Sun* stated: 'It was a girly show if ever there was one. It was a great gathering of budding and full-blooming beauty.' Good Lord.

As if that wasn't bad enough, I was shocked to discover that beauty contests were added to the sports arena, and from the late 1920s national basketball tournaments also crowned tournament 'beauty queens' from among the players.

I spoke to Gail Newsham, author of *In a League of Their Own!* and an expert on the Dick, Kerr Ladies, about what was happening in the UK around this time. She told me: 'In 1921, 5th of December 1921, the FA banned women's football. They said women couldn't play on league grounds anymore. That it was dangerous sport for women. It could affect their fertility – all of those kinds of things. And for fifty years women's football was in the wilderness.

'I think the Goodison match was the turning point, really. We can't have that – 53,000 – because it was the second biggest crowd recorded at the time, since records began in 1888.'

As Gail says, the FA claimed the decision was made on two grounds: first, because football was 'unsuitable for women' and secondly because women were getting too much of the expense money – in other words they were being paid as semi-professionals. 'Complaints having been made as to football being played by women, the Council feel impelled to express their strong opinion that the game of football is quite unsuitable for women and ought not to be encouraged.'

To disprove the medical claims the team invited twenty doctors to watch a game. The doctors declared it to be 'no more taxing than a day's heavy washing', agreeing there was no medical reason why women's football could not continue. Sadly, though, despite this, the ban in England remained in place and then travelled across the world to countries including Germany and South America.

In Brazil – birthplace of Marta, generally accepted as the greatest female player of all time – a law from 1941 to 1979 completely banned women and girls from playing football. Females were not allowed to play competitively, to play in schools or even for fun in the park. The draconian law stated that women could not practise any kinds of sports that were 'incompatible with the female nature', based on a belief that it was dangerous for women to play football as it could damage their ability to have children and to work.

It seemed that men felt threatened, particularly in their traditional areas of influence. The world of traditional men's work was changing, and women were beginning to enter the workplace and make demands around equality in relationships. Some believe that as changes like this occurred in society, men were desperately seeking areas they could protect and hold on to as their own – and sport was one of those areas.

Bans on women's football across the world remained in place for around fifty years, until 1970, when they were gradually lifted in a piecemeal way. FIFA began to take charge of women's football, with the unofficial Women's World Cup in Mexico in 1971; the final between Mexico and Denmark, which Denmark won, was played in the Azteca Stadium in front of a crowd of 110,000.

———————

The 1960s and 1970s proved to be an important time in the progress of all women's sport across the world, as leaders in the feminist movement recognised that the high-profile nature of sport could help support the women's liberation movement.

In 1972, Billie Jean King won the US Open, receiving $15,000 less than the men's champion, Ilie Năstase. She very publicly stated that she would not play the next year if the prize money was not equal. In 1973, the US Open became the first major tournament to offer equal prize money for men and women. Disappointingly, it took another thirty-four years for Wimbledon to do the same in 2007.

An important event that undoubtedly helped improve opportunities for women in sport across the world was the 'Battle of the Sexes' in 1973, where Billie Jean King, at just twenty-nine, took on and beat Bobby Riggs, a fifty-five-year-old former professional player. Viewed by around 48 million people worldwide (and many more since the story was told again in the superb film of the same name in 2017), it was a real watershed moment for the profile of women's sport. Not only did it show that a woman could compete on a level with men, but it highlighted the commercial viability of women's sport for entertainment.

Around this time, in response to the smaller prize money and lack of women's events put on by the USLTA (US Lawn Tennis

Association), which made it hard for women to earn a living from playing tennis, Billie Jean led a group of female players to form their own tour. They found a sponsor in cigarette brand Virginia Slims (providing a more elegant route to lung cancer for women) and, as other sponsors came on board, by the end of the year nearly forty players had registered for the tour, with an impressive prize pool totalling nearly $310,000.

On the back of the success of the Virginia Slims Tour, King negotiated with the USLTA to create a women's division in 1973. Known as the Women's Tennis Association (WTA), it remains the most profitable US professional women's sport organisation. 'We were at the height of the women's movement and it was an exciting time to be campaigning,' said Billie Jean King years later in an interview with the *Telegraph*.

The year 1972 was also the one in which Title IX was passed into law in the US, in the words of historian Mary Jo Festle, 'the biggest thing to happen to sport since the whistle'. Title IX provides all US citizens with equal access to any programmes or activities that received federal financial assistance, and, importantly, this includes sport. It means US public schools (the equivalent to state schools in the UK) are legally required to provide girls and boys with equitable sports opportunities. American universities that had offered thousands of sports scholarships to male athletes had to offer the same opportunities to female students.

In the five decades since Title IX was enacted, sports opportunities for girls at US high schools have increased by more than 1,000 per cent and by over 600 per cent for women in universities and colleges. Before Title IX, one in twenty-seven girls played sports in the USA. Today it is two in five.

Women's involvement in the Olympics also made progress

around this time, and in 1964 women were finally allowed to compete in a team sport for the first time when volleyball was added to the line-up. This was followed in 1976 with basketball and handball, in 1980 by hockey, in 1996 by football and in 2016 by rugby sevens.

It was not until 1984 that endurance sports for women were included in the Olympics, with the inclusion of cycling and the marathon. It will be 2024 before we see 50 per cent male and female participation.

———————

The final decades of the twentieth century proved to be an important time for equality in sport. Special action groups for women were created with Women's Sports Foundation, founded by Billie Jean King in the US in 1974, the Canadian Association for the Advancement of Women and Sport, established in 1981, and the Women's Sport Foundation (now Women in Sport), founded in the UK in 1984.

Sport and physical activity were recognised as a human right in the International Charter of Physical Education and Sport, adopted in 1978 by UNESCO: 'One of the essential conditions for the effective exercise of human rights is that everyone should be free to develop and preserve his or her physical, intellectual, and moral powers, and that access to physical education and sport should consequently be assured and guaranteed for all human beings.'

The Brighton Declaration was established by an International Working Group on Women and Sport in 1994, organised by the British Sports Council and supported by the International Olympic Committee (IOC). This independent coordinating body of government organisations aimed to be a catalyst for the advancement and empowerment of women and sport globally. The international treaty has become a road map to support the ongoing development of a more fair and equitable system of sport and physical activity, fully inclusive of women and girls.

In September 1995, more than 17,000 participants and 30,000 activists headed to Beijing for the opening of the Fourth World Conference on Women, with a single purpose in mind: 'gender equality and the empowerment of all women, everywhere'.

Sport was directly referenced in the Beijing Platform for Action, which resulted in the sports ecosystem and stakeholders having a key role to play in ensuring gender equality on and off the pitch.

Also in 1995, the IOC established a Women and Sport Working Group to advise the Executive Board on policies to ensure gender equality. This was elevated to the status of a Commission in 2004, and the Women and Sport Commission now meets once a year to monitor the participation of women in the Olympics as well as their representation in decision-making.

———

Along with tennis and its three sets for women, the female frailty myth impacts other sports today. In badminton women play to 11 points, but men play to 15. Women's basketball quarters in the WNBA (Women's National Basketball Association) are ten minutes long, but the NBA quarters are twelve minutes. In athletics, women's shot, javelin and discus typically weigh less than men's and hurdles are lower. In golf, 'ladies' tees' are closer to the green. In artistic gymnastics men compete in six events compared to just four for the women. Both complete a floor routine, but the men tumble silently for seventy seconds, while the women perform to music for ninety seconds and must also incorporate dance movements 'to express their personalities' – something not required for the men.

After much debate in recent years and a campaign called #RunEqual, one very outdated gender imbalance in English sport that could finally be settled in 2021 is the distance of cross-country races. While women and men race over the same distances on the roads and the track, and the IAAF (International Association of Athletics Federations) have equalised the distances run in the World Cross-Country Championships, in England women's cross-country races are often much shorter.

In regional championships senior men run 15km with senior women running 8km – just over half the longer distance. In the English National Championships, the difference is 12km to 8km, not such a big difference, but the men are still running 50 per cent further. I love the example that campaigners share to illustrate how ridiculous this is – it would be like the London Marathon being 26.2 miles for men and only 14 miles for women.

———

While Victorian attitudes have much to answer for with regard to where women's sport is today, Moya Dodd, former FIFA Council member, and now one of the most influential women in global sport, is clear about how more recent history has impacted the progress of women's sport.

She told me:

One of the great travesties of sport in the twentieth century, actually I think the greatest injustice with world sport, ever, has been the exclusion of women from football. We would be living in a different world if the national bodies like the FA, and the international bodies like FIFA, had taken it upon themselves to allow, to just permit, women to go ahead and play, and then to create competitions in which they could participate.

We all know how popular football was in the First World War for women, this was a window of time where the men weren't playing, so in a sense there was plenty of bandwidth for women to show what they could do, and not withstanding they probably had no history in playing the game, they got out there and they did a good enough job that 53,000 people showed up to watch them by 1920.

Then there were deliberate measures to exclude women, and then our grandparents, and parents, and we grew up in this world where women didn't really play sport and nobody was interested in watching it, so there was no professional career path.

That was the world we lived in for pretty much all of the twentieth century, and it has taken a hundred years for us to get back to the point where you are seeing, once again, tens of thousands of people in stadiums watching women's sport.

4

FULL COVERAGE

Sport is home to one of the most intense and most historically enduring gender divisions in journalism, in terms of who is permitted to cover which sports as journalists, how athletes are covered, as well as in terms of which genders are served as audiences.

Deborah Chambers, *Women and Journalism*, 2004

Throughout the day, as we have already noted, every TV and radio news bulletin ends with a sporting round-up. The back pages of every newspaper feature sport. Conversations at work revolve around the weekend's games. Mass events unite us as families, communities and nations as we gather around TV screens. Sport provides a unique platform to reach and influence people of all ages on a global scale.

Yet women feature so rarely in the media coverage.

Professor Toni Bruce, an expert in the field of gender and sport, explains that within society we are literally enveloped in 'mediasport' – 'any sport not experienced in the space where it happens, but represented through the media'. In our global, corporate sporting world this makes mediasport almost inescapable, reaching millions, if not billions, of people. And because this coverage of sport sits within the *news* media, audiences naturally associate it with objectivity and balance. They believe the way in which sport is shown is a truthful reflection of society.

'Mediasport is not an innocent player in society – the ideologies, attitudes and values that are present in mediasport production powerfully shape our understanding of ourselves and others,' explains Professor Bruce.

It seems remarkable that it was just a decade ago, in 2011, that the BBC Sports Personality of the Year panel selected an all-male shortlist of ten contenders – and no one on the panel thought that might be an issue? Even more shocking was the fact that lads' mags *Nuts* and *Zoo* were included on the judging panel that year. Neither of them put forward a single female to be in contention for the shortlist. Even in 2020, only one woman, record-breaking jockey Hollie Doyle, made the shortlist of six.

Much referenced research from Women in Sport back in 2010 showed that less than 5 per cent of sports coverage in the media included women.

Not a lot has changed since then, and it is the same the world over. Professor Mary Jo Kane, the founder of the US Tucker Center for Research on Girls and Women in Sport, says that in the course of forty to fifty years of research and hundreds of studies about the representation of women's sport, the results have been amazingly consistent: only 4–6 per cent of the whole landscape, be that print, broadcast, online or social media, is given over to women's sport. She points out that this gives a false representation of women taking part in sport at all levels.

Despite dramatic increases in women participating in sport at all levels globally, averages are 10 per cent in print media coverage and 5 per cent in broadcast media. 'A damning indictment of the institutionalized sexism of sports reporting' is how Graeme Turner described the situation in 1997. Not much has changed since then.

An ongoing study in the US that tracks the amount of TV coverage for women's sport since 1989 shows that it has continued to hover around 2 per cent for the past decade. In 2013 it fell to an all-time low of 1.6 per cent. In 2015 it reached the grand heights of 3.2 per cent.

I try to make it a habit to count the number of female sports stories on the major sports channels including BBC, Sky and BT Sport. On a particularly bad day, perhaps just two or three stories of the seventy featured on either homepage or app will include women's sport.

The BBC recognised its previous poor performance in terms of the coverage of women's sport and in 2019 launched its #ChangeTheGame campaign, with the goal of providing unprecedented levels of women's sports coverage across the summer. At many points in the following months the balance of coverage on the BBC's homepage took a huge shift to approach a 50 per cent share for women's sport stories. I commented on Twitter at the time that it felt as if we had moved into a wonderful, parallel universe, where parity of women's sports coverage was the norm for a few weeks.

This increase in coverage was certainly helped by a summer of major women's events including the FIFA Women's World Cup, the golfing Solheim Cup, the Netball World Cup and the Women's Ashes, which provided the BBC, and other sports channels, with great content and an engaged audience.

Sadly, it would appear that #ChangeTheGame did not transform the coverage long term, and those fantastic levels of coverage on

BBC channels were not maintained in the six months that followed the busy summer. Women's sport stories returned to levels of 10–15 per cent in the autumn of 2019. Some positive news at least, as this was higher than they had been before the summer, and still more than the 4 per cent average of Sky Sports and even less for BT Sport.

It was the same in print media, as Clare Balding pointed out to me:

> 2019 was always going to be a massive year because it's not an Olympic year, there wasn't a men's football World Cup to compete with. The combination of the Women's Football World Cup and the Netball World Cup happening so close together and virtually overlapping and Wimbledon being right there as well. That meant women's sport was going to be at a level of exposure it had never been at before, but do you know what? As soon as the Premier League season started again, you would open a newspaper and go, well the women clearly aren't doing anything today, and again not on the Monday, Tuesday, Wednesday or Thursday.
>
> Oh, there's a tiny little two lines there about Charlotte Dujardin being eliminated at the European Championships. And I just think, 'come on, guys'. There's so much written that's not really news but just creates a noise around male sport.

The BBC is certainly much better in its coverage of women's sport than, say, ten years ago, largely driven by Barbara Slater who became the BBC's first female Director of Sport in April 2009. A former gymnast who represented Great Britain at the 1976 Olympic Games in Montreal (she carried our flag at the Opening Ceremony), Barbara has been outspoken about the BBC's need to do better. On the decision to show more archives of sporting events when there was no live sport in the spring of 2020, during the COVID-19 pandemic, she reflected:

I think amongst that archive there probably is an element of truth that our output [in the past] was dominated [by men], but we will be making sure we celebrate women's achievements just as much.

The broadcaster has an enormous role to play in making sport visible, but it needs the buy-in of multiple stakeholders. It needs sponsors, governing bodies, the written press and the competitors themselves. We could not have delivered the audiences last summer [2019] had it not had that collective will from across the industry. I don't think any one element can do it on its own. It requires invest-ment from the governing bodies. It requires much wider cultural changes of attitude. If you look at the quality of the coverage of the Women's World Cup, it was multi-camera, it was covered like a main event, it was broadcast like a main event.

A concern of mine has always been that, although you might have fantastic leadership from the top of the BBC Sports department from Barbara Slater and the women's sport leads Anna Thompson and Vicks Cotton, does this fully filter through the entire organisation? What's the attitude of the digital team as they upload the latest stories that they judge will appeal to sports fans? Sadly, I think many in these roles naturally revert to what they know, not viewing the potential stories through the lens of equality.

A simple example of this that I remember vividly came during the Rio Olympics in 2016, when Britain won its first Olympic medal in the women's 4x100m relay for thirty-two years. You would have understandably expected this to be the lead story on the

BBC website that afternoon. But frustratingly (until some prompting ensured it was rightly updated) it wasn't the extraordinary Asha Philip, Dina Asher-Smith, Daryll Neita and Desiree Henry who topped the BBC Sport news page that day, but the fact that Adam Gemili had placed fourth in the men's 100m.

Don't get me wrong, I'm a huge fan of Adam Gemili, but at the time it really struck me that someone in the BBC team clearly decided that his fourth place was a more significant achievement than the women's record-breaking medal-winning performance.

I'd encourage others to call out this bias and inequality when they see it. We all need to make more noise to remind media that coverage like that is simply unacceptable.

When it is high-profile individuals making the point, that's even better.

In 2015, Andy Murray was shocked to see the placement of the story about Katarina Johnson-Thompson's gold medal in the pentathlon at the European World Indoor Championships on the BBC homepage. 'Why is Johnson-Thompson gold medal story headline number 22 on the BBC sport homepage right now? Complete joke,' he tweeted.

Go Andy.

The UK's print media is no different. In the last decade you could often read the sports pages of a broadsheet or tabloid newspaper and not find a single article or mention of women's sport. Not one. A sports quiz in this weekend's Saturday *Times*, for instance, had only two questions out of twenty-five that even mentioned women's sport. I don't understand how, in 2021, when someone had created the quiz and it had then been edited, laid out and proofed, no one thought the quiz looked a little imbalanced.

Reasons for the lack of female coverage vary, but the main excuse has been that there is just not the audience for women's sport. Websites and newspapers research what their customers want, and funnily enough it turns out they think they all want Premiership football, along with men's rugby, cricket and boxing.

But is this really the case, or is it more a matter that sports media is predominantly run by men who naturally revert to writing about what they know – men's sport?

Researchers refer to the 'gatekeeping theory' which helps us to understand who makes up the media and how those decision makers shape what gets covered. According to data on Associated Press Sports Editors in 2016, less than 10 per cent of sports editors or assistant sports editors were women and women also make up a minority of reporters (12.6 per cent) and columnists (12.4 per cent).

A report from the Women's Media Center in 2017 found that 89 per cent of sports coverage in the US was written by men.

Obviously, a huge majority of the gatekeepers are men, and, of those men, almost all are white.

The gatekeeping occurs at many different stages, from selecting what gets covered, to producing and editing content and then deciding what is published or transmitted. When an editor claims 'no one is interested in women's sport' and fewer resources are dedicated to covering women's sport, this is gatekeeping. Professor Mary Jo Kane, who has done vast amounts of research in this space, is clear in her opinion that when a sports editor claims 'no one' is interested, it really means *he* is not interested.

Along with gatekeeping another key consideration is the way in which women's sport is 'framed' for the audience. Sports coverage often minimises the competence of female athletes and highlights their feminine traits, their sexuality or traditional gender stereotypes. They are also often 'infantilised' by commentators, with references to 'the girls' or 'ladies'.

If we look back at the history of the sporting media, you could understandably feel that things have not changed significantly since the first sports pages emerged in the nineteenth century.

Sports journalism effectively began with specialised magazines for sports such as horse racing and boxing in the 1820s before newspapers became affordable and accessible to all along with rising literacy rates. In the US, 'yellow journalism' saw publishers looking for the most sensational stories that would appeal to the masses and sell copies. A very similar approach was taken by our own tabloid press and 'red tops'. Sport was ideal for this.

In the UK Saturday sports papers were hugely popular in reporting men's sport. The local newspaper, published on a Saturday evening soon after that afternoon's games finished, contained information about the sports played that day. A different paper, the 'sports pink' or 'green 'un', was produced in each area covering local teams in depth.

As newspapers grew, they saw that they needed a distinct sports section and in the US by 1920 every major paper had a sports section, often taking up nearly 20 per cent of the space. The journalists were men and they primarily wrote about men's sport for male readers. Sports journalists were hugely powerful at this time, as newspapers provided sports fans with the only real opportunity to find out about their team's performance.

———

Despite many attempts to create print media outlets dedicated to women's sport over the years, the majority haven't survived. In the US these have included *Sportswoman*; Billie Jean King's *womenSports* which became the Women's Sport Foundation's *Women's Sport*s and then Condé Nast's *Women's Sport + Fitness*; *Real Sports*, which was published for five years; and *Sports Illustrated for Women (SI Women)* which ran for just 20 issues. Closer to home in the UK there was the magnificent *SportsSister*, created by Danielle Sellwood and Louise Hudson, which I still believe was very much ahead of its time.

With coverage of women's sport growing in the past decade, it appears that new media is succeeding where traditional print did not. Well-respected websites, podcasts and collectives dedicated to women's sport are generating large followings, often created in direct response to the lack of coverage in traditional print and broadcast media.

Newswires and digital channels for women's sport have emerged, including the likes of espnW and GiveMeSport Women. Siren, in Australia, is a collective of women's sports advocates, content creators and fans who wanted more from mainstream coverage of women in sport. Its website and newsletters deliver 'feminist content that challenges the status quo of sport media'.

If you're a fan of women's rugby in the UK the Scrumqueens website has long been a much-admired voice for women's rugby union, with podcasts such as *Women's Rugby Pod* and *Try Hards* growing in popularity and reach. If you want to know more about the Women's Super League, or have a passion for women's football, download the FA Player app, watch Sky's *Women's Football Show* or listen to TalkSPORT's *Women's Football Weekly* podcast or *The Offside Rule: WSL Edition*. For something more informal, there's *Two Girls Talk Balls* or *The Players* podcast. If your passion is cricket, there's *No Balls*, the cricket podcast, or *Women's Cricket Chat* and if women's basketball is more your thing, you could follow the WNBA via *Swish Appeal*, *High Post Hoops* or *WNBA Nation*.

For more general women's sport coverage, there's now plenty of podcast choice including *Women Who Sport*, *Just Women's Sports*, *Fired*

Up Sport, Her Spirit, In Her Corner, Burn It All Down and, if it's not too self-indulgent to mention here, my own podcast *The Game Changers*, which features interviews with trailblazing women in sport.

The new channel espnW had a clear ambition to change the conversation around women's sport when it launched in 2010. The global multi-platform brand sits across digital, television, radio, films, events, educational platforms and social media and is dedicated to 'engaging and inspiring women through sports'. It continues to see massive growth as sports fans of both genders use new media to watch games, gain insights about their favourite players and teams and join communities and forums.

It is not solely new media though; as mentioned in my Twelve Game-Changing Moments, in 2018 the *Telegraph* launched Telegraph Women's Sport. In describing the launch, editor Anna Kessel said: 'As the United Nations put it, sport has the power to unlock gender equality for women and girls around the world. I am proud that the Telegraph is leading this historic step to contribute towards that drive for change.'

When I asked Anna more about the section's manifesto, she said the aim was to have 'unprecedented coverage of women's sport, which, to be fair, was starting from a very low baseline of two per cent newspaper sports coverage dedicated to women. I don't know what the stats are now, but it's rocketed.'

Anna explained that they now have an entire department: 'There's me and Vicki Hodges the Deputy, we've got three full-time women's writers: football then across sports. We've also got a rugby writer who splits her time between men's rugby and women's rugby. We've got a cricket writer who splits her time between men's cricket and women's cricket and then right across the paper, athletics, cycling, everybody is doing both men and women's sport, which is really, really exciting.'

In a further boost for their women's sports coverage, the *Telegraph* make it freely available to all, unlike the rest of the newspaper which now sits behind a paywall.

While I applaud both espnW and Telegraph Women's Sport, and also *The Times* for appointing Rebecca Myers to specialise in women's sport, there's a danger if women's sport becomes 'siloed' away from the main sports section and therefore doesn't receive exposure to general sports fans. Editors may feel they have 'done their bit' for women's sport with dedicated sections or writers and therefore do not need to ensure there's gender balance across the mainstream coverage.

Sky Sports also announced some bold plans to increase its commitment to women's sport in 2020 by expanding its existing coverage and strengthening its digital output, building on the fantastic work it has done in recent years across women's cricket, rugby, football and netball.

The station announced that live women's sport would be showcased to brand-new audiences via Sky Sports' YouTube channel with events such as the Women's Six Nations, WNBA, Vitality Netball Superleague and women's cricket among those to be made freely available for any viewers.

It was also predicted in the British media that Sky Sports would be the new broadcast partner for the FA Women's Super League from 2021, as they swooped in with a landmark offer to take all coverage of the top tier from BT Sport. Rumours of this deal came a few weeks after the WSL agreed a US rights deal with NBC, the American broadcaster which is also owned by Sky's parent company Comcast.

Sky have also been a very supportive partner to leading women's sport organisations such as the Women's Sport Trust and the

Women's Sport Collective, the network for women working in sport which I co-founded with Kate Hannon in 2020.

As we've seen with the BBC, though, the positive message at the top doesn't always seem to filter across the entire organisation. For all the magnificent work Sky are doing in some areas, they have then let themselves down in the past by broadcasting promotional videos with a compilation of sports or events that don't include any women (beyond those cheering in the crowd of a men's game). Or in another example, an enormous Sky Sports advertising hoarding on the side of a building on the A4 (heading into London) that only featured male sports stars. Hopefully, this is becoming a thing of the past as attitudes change throughout the organisation and they work to maximise their formidable female sports rights.

The demand to watch women's sport is growing, especially around big, global events. In 2019, a combined audience of 1.2 billion tuned in to watch coverage of the FIFA Women's World Cup across all platforms – a record for the event. The final attracted an average audience of 82.2 million TV viewers – a significant 56 per cent increase over the 52.5 million that watched the US women beat Japan in 2015.

The semi-final, which saw the Lionesses lose 2-1 to the US team, attracted a UK TV audience of 11.7 million, making it one of the most watched TV programmes of the entire year (beaten by the nation's favourite, *Gavin and Stacey*, on Christmas Day). A total audience of 28.1 million (47 per cent of the UK population) watched some of the BBC's coverage of the tournament.

FIFA President Gianni Infantino commented on the 'cultural phenomenon' of the FIFA World Cup that has the power to attract media attention and provide a platform for women's football to flourish: 'The fact that we broke the one billion target just shows the pulling power of the women's game and the fact that, if we promote and broadcast world-class football widely, whether it's played by men or women, the fans will always want to watch.'

It's such a key point. If women's sport is promoted and broadcast, then people will watch it.

Ahead of the 2019 Women's World Cup the national bodies worked hard to ensure we got to know the English and Scottish players – giving us a reason to care about them and want to follow their success. With dedicated TV documentaries, newspaper and magazine features and social media takeovers, the players' profiles were promoted, and the public bought into their stories.

Other major women's sports events that have attracted great viewing figures when promoted well include the final of the Women's Rugby World Cup in 2017. A thrilling but heart-breaking game for Red Roses fans saw the Black Ferns beat reigning champions England in front of a TV audience of 2.6 million.

One of my most powerful memories of watching women's sport happened along with over 9 million other viewers, when the GB Women's Hockey team won gold at the Rio Olympics in 2016.

And where women's sport has always had equal billing to the men's there is little disparity in the viewing figures. An incredible 16.3 million of us tuned in to watch Jess Ennis-Hill win Heptathlon gold at London 2012, with 17.1 million watching Mo Farah win the 10,000m later that same night.

In recent years both the US Open and Wimbledon have, on occasion, seen the women's finals attracting more viewers than the men's, and data from leading data analysis firm Nielsen showed that approximately 14.3 million US viewers tuned in to watch the 2019 Women's World Cup final on TV, compared to 11.4 million for the 2018 men's World Cup final – a 22 per cent increase in viewers.

Other women's sports showing massive growth in viewership include basketball, with the WNBA reporting record increases in 2019. Its 2020 Draft, where teams select new players for the next season, was held virtually because of COVID-19 and broadcast on ESPN and became the most watched WNBA Draft in sixteen years, up 123 per cent over the 2019 Draft.

More good news from the National Women's Soccer League (NWSL), where viewership was up 493 per cent in 2020 following a new partnership with CBS and Twitch. The league also recorded its seven most-watched games ever, including a record 653,000 viewers of the NWSL Challenge Cup championship.

Commenting on the dramatic improvements, Commissioner Lisa Baird told *Insider* that in the past, the NWSL has only been available on cable networks, limiting fans' ability to access games. She believes the switch to network television contributed significantly to the league's huge ratings spikes in 2020. 'The numbers you're seeing are truly the increase, but last year, most of our games were on cable,' Baird said. 'The comparison is broadcast to cable, so let's just be very upfront about that. That is one of the major reasons we had such tremendous growth.'

The article goes on to point out that for years in the US there has been an assumption that 'the audience just isn't there' for women's sports. This creates a self-fulfilling prophecy, leaving leagues like the NWSL and WNBA with no real platform to share their product.

It looks like things might have changed at last in 2020, as, along with the NWSL deal with CBS, the WNBA agreed an extensive schedule of games which were broadcast on ESPN, ESPN2 and ABC in the summer. It was ESPN's largest WNBA schedule ever and included thirty-seven live regular-season games, playoffs and the whole 2020 finals.

'We and the WNBA deserve to be proud of women's sports and what we've done,' Baird said. 'It's just having that platform to tell the stories. We worked really closely with CBS. They were pretty bullish on women's soccer and said, "Yeah, we're going to give you an enormous platform." And we were able to carry that audience that we developed and bring it in to show people great games.'

Similar bold moves are taking place for women's sport across Europe. In November 2020, the Dutch public-service broadcaster NOS agreed to a deal for the TV and radio rights to all matches played by the national women's team, the reigning European Champions. The broadcaster's extensive female football portfolio already includes the delayed Tokyo Olympics, the UEFA Women's Championship and shared coverage of the top-level domestic league. Why the increased investment? In 2017 the Women's Euros were a massive draw for NOS, with 4.1 million people tuning in to watch the Dutch national team win the final. It took 83 per cent of the TV market share.

In Australia, coverage of women's cricket has grown from a one-hour highlights package fifteen years ago to 130 hours of live free-to-air coverage in 2019–20. This included thirty-six of the Women's Big Bash League games and all Australian international games. The league has grown to be the fourth-highest viewed league in Australia (male or female), recording over 300,000 viewers several times in the 2020 season, 30 per cent up on the previous year.

—————

So, we will watch women's sport when it is available, but, sadly, so much fantastic content is just not available for audiences to see. When it is hard to find on obscure channels or streamed on websites it's only the really dedicated fans who are going to gather round a laptop or iPad to watch some poor-quality broadcast of the sport they love.

This was highlighted in my own home this weekend. We'd watched some fantastic men's Premiership Rugby coverage on Friday night. Despite the lack of any crowds because of COVID, the broadcast included superb, multiple camera angles and editing, knowledgeable commentators, witty former players as pundits, plentiful game stats and fascinating interviews with players and staff.

The next day saw me attempting to watch the only women's Premier 15s game being broadcast this week. It was a superb, exciting battle that saw Susie Appleby's newly formed Exeter Chiefs beating two times Premier 15s champions Saracens Women 22-14, and in the process halting their thirty-three-match unbeaten run. Both teams played exceptionally well in a hugely entertaining game.

What a disappointment then, to have to watch the game on a dodgy live stream from England Rugby. Limited cameras meant there were few close-ups of the action, commentary could have been better and technical issues resulted in there being no sound at all in places. Hardly the way to convince new viewers to the Premier 15s that women's rugby is worth watching. It's the same the world over. Talking to Jessica Luther for the book *Loving Sports When They Don't Love You Back*, written with Kavitha Davidson, WNBA player Imani McGee Stafford says: 'The truth of the matter is that today, right now, fans have to do a lot of homework just to be fans. I always say we just have the best fans in the world because they literally have to go on a scavenger hunt to be our fans.'

The accessibility of coverage is also a consideration. While there might be hundreds of hours of women's sport being broadcast via the red button, YouTube channels and sites like The FA Player, getting the women's product on free-to-air, mainstream TV and radio is surely essential if women's sport is ever going to be accepted as equal to men's by the mass market. Free-to-air media like the BBC, ITV and Channel 4 is where women's sport will pick up new sports fans who are interested in all sport, along with those who only tune in for the major events.

Fortunately, most of the major women's sports events are now better covered than ever before. We saw this in the summer of 2019 when the FIFA Women's World Cup and the Netball World Cup were broadcast in their entirety on the BBC including qualifying rounds and all nations.

And when women's live sport resumed at the end of the summer during the 2020 pandemic, it was great to see the BBC, Sky and BT Sport collaborating to ensure coverage of women's football and cricket was freely available for everyone to see.

Similarly, it was such a positive move when the BBC broadcast two England women's rugby matches against France in November 2020. This was the first time women's rugby had been shown live on the BBC, but it had taken much work at the RFU to make it happen, investing in the production at a very challenging time for the sport. Hopefully, the success of this content will demonstrate the potential audience for women's rugby and more games to be broadcast in the future.

Outside of the major events, where women's sport has fallen down in the past is the lack of week-to-week coverage. Kelly Simmons, Director of the Women's Professional Game at the Football Association, explains: 'I think we've cracked pinnacle events in women's sport: Olympics, World Cups. Whatever the sport, big moments, big audiences, big profile. But what we haven't cracked, what we are starting to crack with the Barclays FA WSL, is that regular coverage. So, the sport doesn't disappear until the next two-year or four-year big major event. That real breakthrough into mainstream – and I think with the WSL we can really do that. And if we can be the breakthrough sport for women, that is hugely powerful for women and girls in wider society. It's bigger than football.'

In Women in Sport's 'Where did all the Women Go' report in 2018, the charity also highlighted that the success of national female teams has been an important driver of media coverage, often filling a void when our men's national teams have performed less well. The authors then raised the question of how women's sport can remain visible in the media, regardless of success in the future. Despite recent high-profile wins at major championships in hockey, cricket and netball, will we keep seeing more highs and lows in coverage in the future?

The report went on to recognise that, along with a team's success, the decision to give women's sport significant coverage was often due to the persistence of individual journalists and media outlets. Coverage often relies on having strong allies within media organisations, so how can sports support these individual journalists in the future with great content and access to players?

Finally, the report recognised that better scheduling of events can also create more opportunities. This is something that the FA has been particularly good at, working with the men's game and actively targeting the gaps in the football calendar

The quality of the coverage itself can also be a huge issue. A sports broadcast that includes a wide variety of camera angles and great editing can be a joy to watch versus a match covered with a couple of static cameras.

I'll confess that I've never been a massive cricket fan. It wasn't a sport I watched much growing up and I've never seen the attraction of following an event that could last for days, played at what I felt was an incredibly slow pace. But watching the coverage of the Women's T20 World Championships from Australia in 2019 was a revelation. With multiple angles, close-up coverage, views of every player, clever visual analysis, witty, knowledgeable commentary – it was fascinating. I found myself completely drawn into the exciting games and began regularly tuning in so I didn't miss a match as England progressed through the rounds (until sadly missing out on a place in the finals because of rain).

As I watched, it dawned on me that a big part of the attraction for me on this occasion was the superb visual and audio coverage. For much of women's team sports there just isn't the budget required to provide that quality of coverage with amazing close-ups and replays.

Critics of women's sport will always suggest that the imbalance of media coverage is just the result of what's popular and what's not. If people were interested in women's cricket or rugby or football in the way they are men's, it would be allocated comparable coverage.

It brings us back to the chicken and egg scenario, where eminent gender studies scholar Professor Cheryl Cooky suggests that most of our perceptions about women's sport are attributable to the media coverage we see. Men's sport will always be seen as more enthralling than women's when it has higher production values with more cameras, replays and close-ups, professional commentary and half-time analysis, on-screen graphics and pre-game build-up with engaging back stories of players and teams.

How can women's sport ever compete? With limited camera angles, less professional commentary and few players' back stories, the coverage will never be as engaging to watch, which in turn means it won't attract the same size audience.

Investment in high-quality production will make an enormous difference to the perception of women's sport and the viewing figures. Congratulations to the broadcasters, sponsors and rights holders who are committed to investing in this area to ensure women's sport is seen in all its glory.

———

Another issue that appears to result in less printed media coverage for female sport is that, along with the lack of women working as sports journalists, there's an assumption that female journalists will be the only ones reporting on women's sport.

This belief that 'women write only for women' is something that dates right back to the early years of newspapers when editors saw the need to recruit female writers but confined their reporting to fashion and society news. A new kind of 'women's journalism' evolved, with female journalists only writing stories which would appeal to women readers. Other topics (including sport, of course) remained covered by men for men to read.

Many researchers over the years have exposed the fact that sports media is mainly 'written by men, for men, about men'. But having male allies call out the sexism in sports coverage can also drive significant change. David Stern, the Commissioner of the NBA, was renowned for supporting the WNBA against what he thought were media attacks or an indefensible lack of interest, attending events like the Associated Press Sports Editors convention where he would 'invariably get into arguments'.

'We felt the WNBA didn't get the respect that we thought it deserved,' Stern said. 'The way the editors decided on what to cover was, they said, part art and part science. I used to always tweak them. I'd say that sounded like excuses, and I reminded them that's the way the old boy network always cut down on minorities and women getting jobs.'

———

Another fascinating dilemma when it comes to building an audience for women's sport is, who should the media be targeting? Writing about espnW, the world's leading portal for women's sport, Anya Alvarez, a former golf professional and contributing writer, says:

> Only twenty-eight per cent of espnW's audience is female according to a 2017 comScore report. While it was created with the intention of serving a female readership, it continues to struggle to connect with them. Why? Because they're targeting the wrong audience. Trying to reach women who don't play sports and who weren't given equal opportunity to play sports growing up is a misguided strategy.
>
> Before Title IX, one in twenty-seven girls played sports. Now, two of five girls play sports. That means close to twenty million girls in the United States under the age of eighteen are active athletes. That is your market: not the women who didn't play sports growing up. Get those twenty million girls to women's sports events and you'll have an audience who will become lifelong fans, because loyalty to a sports team is about engendering a connection early on.

Stats from Nielsen show that there is latent demand for more women's sports coverage from both men and women. Their 2018 research across eight key markets around the world (US, UK, France, Italy, Germany, Spain, Australia and New Zealand) found that 84 per cent of sports fans are interested in women's sport. Of those, 51 per cent are male, which confirms it's not just women who are interested in watching women's sport. There's a gender-balanced audience for it with a major opportunity to engage male fans, too.

Perhaps surprisingly, it's men who make up the majority of fans for the Women's Tennis Association, the Ladies Professional Golf Association and the WNBA. A third of all US major league sports fans (for the likes of the NFL, major league basketball and the NBA) are women, with 47 per cent of Australian sports fans now female according to the Australian Bureau of Statistics.

It's clearly not a binary matter of men supporting men's sports and women supporting women's sports, as many people assume.

———

Digital presents a fantastic opportunity for women's sport as we witness a shift away from linear TV coverage and print media as the main route to consumption.

While the survival of men's sport often depends on broadcast revenue, that's not been the case for the women, which might now be an advantage. Women's sport has the opportunity to pivot its offering, to be more creative in the ways it serves its growing audience, as, unlike traditional media, digital time and space are unlimited and in effect 'free'.

The growth of social media also provides the potential to move away from traditionally male-biased mainstream media, growing fan communities and raising the profile of women's sport. Individuals can become journalists themselves with blogs, websites, podcasts and YouTube channels, joining forces to promote their favourite athletes and teams.

The entry of platforms like Facebook, Instagram, Netflix, Twitch and Prime could also be great news for women's sport as they help drive ticket sales and merchandise, building new audiences and marketing athletes to current and new fans.

In 2020, Amazon's live streaming platform Twitch announced a three-year deal to show US National Women's Soccer League (NWSL) games. As part of the deal, Twitch has the exclusive rights to live stream NWSL games outside the US, showing all 108 regular-season games, the playoffs and championship to viewers worldwide. Twitch is also collaborating with the NWSL to create additional content from the league and its players.

For those who might not know, Twitch pioneered the idea of live streaming people playing video games and understandably has a very young, male audience. Sports programming enables the platform to diversify and appeal to a broader audience and presents a fantastic opportunity for women's sport.

Watch this space.

While many sports undoubtedly need to do more to understand how they can use digital to drive the commercial value of women's sports, some organisations are already embracing this change. For the 2019–20 season, the Football Association launched The FA Player, its live streaming platform dedicated to women's football.

Free to use and available online and via an app, The FA Player provides live access to all Barclays FA WSL matches, a live match from each round of the Women's Championship, archive Lionesses footage and interactive engaging content from the players. It quickly reached over 100,000 subscribers.

Commenting at the time of the launch, the FA's Kelly Simmons said: 'This announcement is a pivotal and significant step in the FA's journey to grow the women's game and attract new audiences. We know people want to watch football in different ways, with content that's quickly and easily accessible.'

Anecdotal reporting indicates that it is often stories about women's sport that get the biggest pick-up on social media. The most viewed clip on the England and Wales Cricket Board's Facebook page in 2019 was a catch by Fran Wilson and, at the time of writing, Rugby Football League's most watched video in 2020 was an incredible tackle by Kelsey Gentles.

Audiences *are* interested in female athletes and these numbers will grow further if they are given access to high-quality content.

There's a young engaged fanbase on digital and it's now down to the rights holders and sports bodies to package the women's product and deliver it in a way that appeals, investing in top-quality production and distribution.

As Chris Hurst, a fellow Trustee on the Women's Sport Trust board and leading digital sports consultant, told me:

Digital platforms present an excellent way for sport's stakeholders – be they governing bodies, media or brands – to use their platforms to tell the stories that may not have gained mainstream media exposure previously. They also allow stories to be told in a very targeted and personalised way to different audiences. UEFA's #WePlayStrong campaign is a great example of this, making sport more accessible to a female audience and driving greater interest in women's sport overall.

I would expect that during the next decade gender parity of coverage on a governing body's own social media accounts will become a greater area of focus. The rise of branded digital content, delivered in partnership with sponsors who want their brands to be associated with both the men's and women's teams, will be a major driver of this change.

I also think that the rise of sport OTT platforms [Over-The-Top, where content is streamed directly to consumers], allowing governing bodies and leagues to go direct to the consumer, as part of a well-structured broadcast rights package, with a mix of free-to-air, pay TV and short-form digital clip rights that can be syndicated to third-party platforms, will be a real area of evolution. It will help industry leaders better understand the audience consuming women's sport and what content they want to see more of.

I wouldn't want success in the digital space to mean that women's sport gets overlooked in more traditional sports broadcasting – there's no doubt that linear, free-to-watch TV is essential if women's sport is to reach a new audience – but it's certainly an area where women's sport has an opportunity to thrive especially, as Chris suggests, when it's part of a well-structured integrated package.

5

IT'S A SELL-OUT

The whole idea that there is no demand to watch women play sport is the biggest fallacy that has been sold to us. It is not something that occurred naturally. It is something that occurred because of the active suppression and eradication of women from the sporting landscape.

Moya Dodd, first woman on the FIFA Council,
The Game Changers podcast, 2020

Looking back to those extraordinary crowds in the 1920s, where over 50,000 people paid to watch women's football in England, it's little wonder that people like Moya Dodd call out the naysayers who comment that there will never be an audience for women's sport. Similar sized crowds would gather across Italy and France to watch women's professional football in the 1980s, but it's taken decades for the numbers of spectators flocking to watch women's sport in the UK to get back to those levels. And then only sporadically at major events.

Some women's sports, including tennis, track and field, cycling and triathlon, have always attracted similar crowds and spectators to the men's – especially when events are combined. But team sports, traditionally the preserve of men, have been slower into this space.

Women's football has certainly been the trailblazer in this area in recent years, perhaps no surprise for the world's biggest sport. And being the most popular global game means the success in football has rippled out to bring commercial opportunities for all women's sports.

Attracting spectators and fans is essential if women's sport is to grow and develop. Not only are spectators an income source through ticket and merchandise sales, but packed crowds make for a good visual spectacle which in turn attracts TV channels and broadcasters.

In terms of attracting spectators, 2019 was a real turning point for women's football. The continuing growth in the popularity of women's football in Spain saw records broken for a women's club game when 60,000 fans watched Barcelona beat Atlético Madrid at the Wanda Metropolitano in March 2019. Earlier that year, a crowd of over 48,000 had gathered for Athletic Bilbao's cup game against Atlético Madrid at the San Mamés Stadium in Bilbao.

In Mexico, Liga MX Femenil had set the previous crowd record for a professional women's football match in May 2018, when 51,000 came to watch rivals Rayadas and Tigres Femenil.

In the USA, the Women's Soccer League was also breaking records, with one of the largest stadiums, Portland Thorns' Providence Park, hosting nine of the top ten highest attended games in the league's history. Four of those games took place after the FIFA 2019 World Cup and in August 2019 Portland Thorns hosted North Carolina Courage in front of a record crowd of 25,000. Two months later they attracted the second biggest crowd in NWSL history, when they played Washington Spirit in front of 24,500 fans.

And then in the summer, despite some issues around ticket sales, 57,900 fans watched the USA beat the Netherlands 2-0 in the final of the FIFA 2019 World Cup at the Stade de Lyon. Great numbers, but still a long way from the biggest attendance at any women's game, set at the 1999 World Cup Final, when 90,000 fans watched the USA beat China at the Rose Bowl Stadium in LA. The game ended with a nail-biting penalty shootout that the USA won 5-4.

Here at home, the Barclays FA Women's Super League opened in September 2019 with a record-breaking crowd of 31,000 at the Etihad Stadium to see Manchester City take on Manchester United. The following day I was lucky enough to be in the crowd at Stamford Bridge to see Chelsea beat Spurs 1-0 in front of 24,500 fans; the atmosphere was incredible. Later that same month 77,768 packed Wembley Stadium to watch England's women play Germany in a friendly, close to the crowd of 80,203 who had flocked to the same stadium during London 2012 to see the USA beat Japan.

It isn't just football that saw growth in crowds in 2019. In Australia women's leagues such as the Rebel Women's Big Bash and the Women's Australian Rules Football league (AFLW) began to attract large audiences along with more sponsorship deals and broadcast revenue. Having watched my first AFLW game in Sydney in 2019, I can fully appreciate why the sport draws such big crowds. What a spectacle it is. Fast, powerful and incredibly physical.

The ICC Women's World Cup final in July 2017 was a sell-out, when a crowd of 24,000 filled Lord's to watch England beat India by just nine runs, a thrilling game and one of the closest finals in the tournament's history. Again, there was an extraordinary atmosphere at Lord's that day.

Then, in March 2020, the T20 World Cup final smashed the women's cricket attendance record at the Melbourne Cricket

Ground with an attendance of over 86,000 watching Australia beat India.

The 2019 Netball World Cup in Liverpool sold a record-breaking 112,000 tickets for the event, and rugby, too, has seen growing numbers of spectators for the women's game. In the first game of the Six Nations in 2020, 14,000 watched France versus England in Pau and then 11,000 came to the Twickenham Stoop for England versus Wales. Just two years before there had only been 4,000 at the corresponding fixture at the same venue. Red Roses games at Sandy Park in Exeter have shown there is a huge appetite for the women's game. There was an extraordinary atmosphere in the crowd when England played Italy in March 2019 with 10,545 tickets sold, a record attendance outside a World Cup.

Clubs like Harlequins, playing in the Premier 15s, have been regularly attracting crowds of over 4,000 for their big games. Smaller numbers than the men's games but showing considerable growth. Here's hoping that if England Rugby successfully bid to host the 2025 World Cup, we might see a sell-out at Twickenham in the way we have for the Lionesses at Wembley.

Driving the size of crowds is high on the agenda for those working in women's sport, although in the era of COVID this has clearly been a challenge for everyone. Understanding who makes up the crowd for women's sport is interesting. Anecdotal evidence says the crowds for women's sport include more families and females, but more research is needed in this area if we are to build further to impact the numbers.

Understandably there has been a pushback from those working in women's sport to the assumption that it is just women who are the potential audience for women's sport. Ultimately their goal is to have men *and* women watching women's sport, especially as men are currently the biggest audience for sport.

Clubs like Manchester United, Chelsea, Harlequins and Saracens have worked hard to encourage their existing male fans to also embrace the women's teams. In 2018 Manchester City launched Same City, Same Passion, a club-wide campaign that focused on promoting the women's game by demonstrating that the same skills, excitement and passion exist wherever a ball is kicked.

'Misconceptions about the professionalism and quality of women's football still exist and that needs to change. Same City, Same Passion aims to highlight that the similarities between men's and women's football are far greater than the differences and, regardless of who's playing, it's just football,' said Omar Berrada, the club's Chief Operating Officer.

Although around 15 per cent of Premier League football fans are female, historically women have been less likely to watch sport, primarily because they have less leisure time than men. In many homes, women pick up the majority of unpaid work including the household chores, childcare and caring for elderly relatives. Because of this, in the UK men enjoy nearly five hours' more leisure time every week than women and the difference is particularly pronounced at weekends – a time when men might be attending live sports events or watching their favourite teams on TV.

So, men have been the default target audience, but, as society shifts, and we see more balance in the sharing of support in the home, it could be that attracting women to watch will be key to the growth of women's sport. I've been lucky enough to attend a number of netball internationals and netball Superleague events over the past decade, and the passion and noise emanating from a crowd of women and girls is something quite exceptional to behold.

Other attempts to attract new fans for women's sport have come in the form of showcasing the women's game alongside the men's. The RFU has tried this with varying degrees of success by hosting double-headers and having the Red Roses play either before or after men's internationals at Twickenham. I've attended a few, and while I appreciate the best intentions of having the women run out after the men's and potentially getting the game seen by 70,000 spectators, it must be soul-destroying for the female players to watch the crowd rapidly dwindle until only a few thousand are left in the stands by the end of their game.

Putting the women first as a curtain raiser has to be the better option, but I've been told there are issues around the women 'spoiling the pitch' (seriously) ahead of the men's game and their presence restricting the big game build-up and interviews for TV. Having the women on after the men also means that the RFU can offer free or very cheap tickets for fans of the women's game to attend after the men's game, which they would not be able to do if they were playing first. With either option, it is a pretty long afternoon of sport (and drinking) for anyone who wants to watch both games.

Having the women's games stand alone is something that has worked for other sports, and as women's rugby has grown in popularity it does seem that this approach is working. If it goes ahead at all in 2021, the women's Six Nations will be separated from the men's. It will be interesting to see how successful this format is and whether having its own time in the sporting calendar and not being tagged onto the men's games will be better for the profile of the women's championship. It's something that's occurred because of COVID but might turn out to be much better for the women's game in the long term. Another issue in the 2020 season was that all the women's games started at the same time, so aside from the fact that you'd struggle to find many of them on TV, even if you could, you couldn't watch them all without multiple screens on the go.

The ambition around attendance at major women's sport events and fixtures is also something that's up for debate. 'Shocking' is how one industry expert described the England women's cricket venue selection post-World Cup, with the team not returning to play at Lord's or the Oval. The original Women's Euro venues showed a distinct lack of ambition to fill the biggest grounds in the country for crowds wanting to watch the Lionesses or other top European teams play. Similarly, it was hugely disappointing to see England's fixture against Ireland in the 2019 Six Nations taking place at Castle Park in Derby, a ground with a capacity of just 5,000, when previous England women's internationals had enjoyed attendances of over 10,000.

For the WSL the challenge has been translating the fantastic numbers for opening games, often played at the big-name stadiums, to ongoing numbers throughout the season. I was shocked to learn the average attendance for FA WSL games in 2018 had been around 1,000, although when the season was terminated early in 2020 the average had reached nearer 3,500.

Kelly Simmons at the FA was thrilled with the way 2020 started though:

Opening games of the season smashed all records with average attendances around ten thousand versus nine hundred or so in 2018. So, we're two hundred and fifty per cent up and we are absolutely thrilled. How have we done this? We've worked really hard to make sure we pull through some of that interest and engagement in the Women's World Cup. We really focus on the calendar, which is obviously challenging because there is so much men's football and sometimes we can't avoid it, but we focus on putting our biggest games in the best slots. We focus on the FIFA men's windows when there is no Premier League and work with the clubs to put big games in men's stadiums.

We have seen some phenomenal attendances. I'll never forget going to Tottenham versus Arsenal – it was about 28,000 – and you could hear the atmosphere. You've got the Arsenal fans chanting down one end and the Spurs fans singing at the other end and it looked incredible. That's what we can deliver. We've done it at Stamford Bridge and the Etihad. We have really amplified those big games and invested in what we call 'big games bigger', trying to keep up profile and build attendances. We had a big women's football weekend where we smashed all records again that was deliberately put when there was no men's football on.

I think one of the really pleasing things is some of the big games in the women's stadiums sell out. Arsenal and Chelsea particularly have started to sell out some of their bigger games, which gives us new and interesting challenges. A great problem to have.

I asked Lionesses and Manchester City captain Steph Houghton what she felt could be done to increase the numbers of spectators for the women's games in the WSL:

We need to try and find a regular slot when all the games are played. I appreciate that sometimes for television purposes the games' timings are changed, but when these games get changed late on it's hard for fans to adjust when they are going to watch the games. Obviously, it is hard with the men as well, in terms of the clashes with their games.

But we can promote them so much better and we can get them out there – really push them hard as much as we possibly can. It's more an issue of people knowing when the game is than if they want to actually come. The tickets are cheap enough. Manchester City fans have got a lot of opportunity to come and watch the women play. We play exactly the same as the men in an unbelievable stadium with great pre-match entertainment. It's more a matter of trying to get people *to* the game. Once they are there, they enjoy it.

Former England player Eniola Aluko agrees. Now director of women's football at Aston Villa, Eni was playing at Juventus for a record-breaking game in 2019 which attracted almost 40,000 fans. I asked her how we could increase the crowd sizes for women's football, and she said it's about people 'sampling' the women's game.

A marketing strategy is needed. It's a risk, but it's needed because you've got to be able to give people exposure, a taster. I use the analogy of sometimes when you go to a market and somebody gives you a taster of food and you taste it and that's what makes you want to buy it. Not because you were thinking of buying it before. That's the way I kind of see women's football. That you need to get the masses to taste it first, and then they'll come.

How you get them to taste it is up to you. Free tickets or very cheap tickets – it doesn't really matter. In Juventus' case it was a top-of-the-table clash and a title decider. Juventus versus Fiorentina. Juventus is very much a club where people turn up to go on tour in the masses, so people see it as a stadium experience.

That said, Eni is wary of putting too much pressure on the women's game in the early years of its development in the UK: 'I think we need to remove this pressure of selling out stadiums – sometimes men's stadiums don't sell out. We are putting so much pressure on the women's game – it's like we've got to get there. No, let's see the progress. Let's celebrate twenty-five thousand people coming today, because five years ago twenty-five thousand people wouldn't have come.'

Smaller crowds for the women's games do mean that spectators are able to enjoy a far more fulfilling fan experience, getting close to their heroes. As previously mentioned, in rugby, football, cricket and netball, it's not unusual to see elite players on the sidelines for over an hour after the game has finished, signing autographs, taking selfies and chatting to fans. This is something you rarely see in men's sport.

Fans can attend a whole season of WSL games for the price of one Premier League game so there's plenty of opportunity to target those who love live football but perhaps can't afford to watch men's matches live.

Women's football is also far more family-friendly, with less anti-social crowd behaviour – in fact, the clubs often don't even specify home and away seating because separation isn't needed. As football pundit Ian Wright told me: 'What I do love about the women's game is the ambience of the fans. It's a whole different vibe to the way the fans behave in the men's game. It's much better, more friendly – it feels lovely. And it's the kind of atmosphere where you can bring your daughters too.'

One of the key rationales for increasing crowd sizes for women's sport is that spectators generate funds that can then be used to pay players and staff and build the sport. This includes the income from spectator ticket sales and spending on merchandise or food and drink sold on match days, along with increased sponsorship in match programmes and hoardings to reach fans in the stadium.

Offering a different fan experience from men's sport is something that is being explored by various teams and leagues. Head down to the South Coast to watch Lewes FC Women (the first club in the world to invest equally in their male and female sides) and you'll enjoy a very special day with bubbly on tap in the bars, locally made vegan pies and live music.

Opinions vary on the best approach to fill stadiums for women's sport. Some believe you should never give away free tickets as it devalues the product and then becomes harder to charge for attendance in the future, the theory also being that if people have paid even a small amount for their ticket, they will be more likely to attend on the day. This was certainly the case for the opening games of the 2019 FA WSL season, when more people paid for tickets to watch Manchester City versus Manchester United at the Etihad than watched Chelsea play newly promoted London rivals Spurs at Stamford Bridge for free. The free Chelsea tickets were rapidly snapped up, but 15,000 who obtained tickets did not show up for the game.

Another important reason for charging something for tickets is to generate income to help fund the women's game. As the AFLW has grown in popularity in Australia, officials have been criticised in the first two seasons for giving away free entry since the players' wages remained low as a result.

Even before COVID-19, the world was changing, and it was getting harder to get younger fans to sit and watch live sports events in their entirety. Changes in technology and the way in which sport is consumed may provide a huge opportunity for women's sport in terms of the development of live streaming and innovative methods of sharing engaging content and telling stories.

This is one place where women's sport might have an advantage. Without the history and tradition of men's sport and the dependence on enormous crowds to sustain it, women's sport can potentially be nimbler and pivot its offering for fans.

6

SHOW ME THE MONEY

Sponsors and brands are looking at women's sport with new eyes.
They are looking at what they can get from women's sport from
the story and the purpose. Ultimately, it's about what it says
about them as a brand.

Lisa Parfitt, co-founder, The Space Between

I started my career in sports sponsorship, working for Gatorade, the
US sports drink. Our goal at the time was to build the authenticity
and credibility of the brand in sport ahead of a planned UK launch
in 1992. We seeded the product into a range of sports and high-
profile teams, establishing partnerships and increasing the visibility
of elite athletes drinking the product. Looking back, it shocks me
to see that, despite the fact that almost all the work we did was in
men's sport, I never saw this as an issue. I do not remember ever
really thinking about it or questioning it.

Apart from some work across Europe in more gender-balanced
sports like athletics, triathlon and tennis, the majority of the deals
we negotiated were for male team sports including the England
football team, England and Scotland rugby, England cricket,

England basketball, the British Basketball League and Premier League teams including Arsenal, Leeds and (at the time) Nottingham Forest.

Promotion for the brand included one of my all-time favourite TV adverts, 'Be Like Mike', but watching the fantastic Gatorade athlete Michael Jordan in the Netflix documentary series *The Last Dance* in 2020, I was struck by the absence of females in the world of the Chicago Bulls. No female players, no coaches, administrators and very few female journalists.

My highlighting this is not to call out Gatorade, who were clearly focused on building presence with the biggest sports at the time (and have gone on to back many female athletes, teams and campaigns since the 1990s), but more to highlight how much things have altered in my own awareness and perception. As the years have passed my filter for equality has significantly changed through the work I have done in women's sport. I look back and think: how could I not have seen or questioned that at the time? I imagine that is still the case for many people working in sports marketing today. It's been easy to stick with the high-profile sports and names and that's meant that men's sport continues to receive the most investment.

Throughout the history of sports sponsorship in the past fifty years, deals have mainly been negotiated by senior managers in sports and corporate organisations, and, in both cases, these were predominantly men. Both tended to be influenced by male beliefs and networks, which has meant that sponsorship deals are often skewed that way, too. According to research in this area, there are three interlinking reasons for the historical lack of sponsorship in women's sport.

First, decisions have been made based on the potential financial outcomes of a deal which often include networking opportunities.

In many cases, those making the decisions (usually men) see *men's* sport as the best place to socialise and entertain their usually male customers in hospitality boxes.

Second, media coverage and the metrics of 'exposure' are often cited as a major reason for sports sponsorship. Because men's sport has always received substantially more media coverage, those making sponsorship deals believe men's sport will always give greater exposure (albeit at a higher cost than the women's equivalent in many cases).

Finally, previous trends often influence sponsorship decisions. Sports sponsorship can be an expensive investment with no guarantees of success, and so those making the decisions want to justify their decisions based on what competitors have done before them. If brands A, B and C have signed sponsorship deals with Premiership Rugby teams and seem to be getting good exposure and hospitality, it's much easier for a marketing manager to follow suit and sign a deal with another men's team, rather than invest in a women's team or league which might be as yet unproven.

———

All that said, it is fantastic to see that investment in women's sport sponsorship is on the rise. From 2013 to 2017 there was a 47 per cent increase in the number of deals being done and a 38 per cent increase in the average deal size. That was before the huge deals that followed in 2018–2020.

In 2018 UEFA announced a $28 million partnership with credit card firm Visa, the first stand-alone sponsor for the women's game in a deal that runs until 2025. The FIFA Women's World Cup in France in 2019 saw six unique event partners (compared to three from the previous tournament in Canada) generating an estimated $12.76 million.

In 2019, it was announced that the prize money offered in the inaugural Shiseido Women's Tennis Association Finals in Shenzhen would be $14 million, doubling the previous $7 million. This means the WTA tour's prize money has increased 90 per cent in the last decade.

Winner Ashleigh Barty earned $4.42 million in prize money, significantly more than the winner of the male equivalent ATP tour final, Stefanos Tsitsipas, who won $2.87 million in 2019.

Women's sport in the UK currently generates approximately £350 million per year in revenue. Over half of this is from two sports – football and tennis. According to research from Two Circles and the Women's Sport Trust, by increasing and driving fan interest in women's sport this annual revenue could increase to £1 billion in the next decade, an increase of over 200 per cent.

Despite much of women's sport being invisible during 2020, at the end of that year, Izzy Wray, a consultant in Deloitte's Sports Business Group told the *Telegraph* that her company predicted 2021–2 could be the breakaway season for women's sports. They anticipated revenues could top $1 billion as audiences reach record highs and significant increases in brand sponsorship agreements and TV rights deals lead to an increased demand for women's sport. 'Prior to Covid-19, matchday audiences, TV viewing figures and fan bases for women's sports had been building at a phenomenal pace. As social distancing measures lift, pent-up demand for live sporting events will collide with the growing fan base for women's sports. Brands have a significant opportunity to seize the moment to explore new opportunities in the market, which have the potential to bring immense value, not only in monetary terms, but also as a signal for their support of gender parity.'

Brands are now choosing to sponsor women's sport not because it is the right thing to do, but because they are seeing the power of women's sport to engage the public and drive sales. Research from Nielsen in 2018 showed that women's sports are seen as more progressive, less money-driven, more family-oriented and cleaner than men's sports. Women also see women's sports as a lot more inspiring than men's.

The Nielsen research also showed that 84 per cent of general sports fans have an interest in women's sport, and, of those, 51 per cent are male. It is clear that women are interested in watching women's sport, but women's sports also represent a major opportunity to engage male fans.

Heather Rabbatts founded the Women's Sports Group which renegotiated the Women's Super League broadcast deal on behalf of the FA. She told me: 'Some of the values around women's football, that sense of collaboration, that sense of professionalism and passion but not tribalism, are very attractive to brands and broadcasters. It's exciting for any sponsor or broadcaster supporting women's sport as they're getting involved in a sport that's growing and moving forward. That offers some real opportunities in terms of their own return on investment.'

Commenting on the change in attitude towards sponsorship of women's sport, the FA's Kelly Simmons says: 'We are seeing two things when we talk to brands. One, that they don't want to be in a men-only space, and secondly, they want community activation and engagement as opposed to traditional badging and eyeballs. Things have very much changed.'

In the UK women's team sport has attracted big brands in recent years, with Barclays announcing the biggest ever sponsorship of women's football in this country in 2019 when they became title sponsor of the WSL. The deal, worth £10 million over three years, also sees Barclays supporting the FA Girls' Football School Partnerships. This support enables the Youth Sport Trust and the FA to create strategic partnerships with families of schools that are committed to the growth and development of girls' football with the ambition that all girls will be able to play football in schools by 2024.

I asked Kelly Simmons why she thought we were seeing this growth in sponsorship deals for women's football: 'A range of reasons – changes in society, changes in sports sponsorship and changes in what brands want. If you look at society there is a greater challenge on everybody, including brands, to be inclusive and diverse and support women. That whole movement has helped change the environment. You have also seen a change in sponsorship, and sports sponsorship, with brands wanting to demonstrate a better purpose, a wider purpose, and wanting to put back into society.'

How companies are viewed by their staff and customers is always important, as Kelly explains: 'Barclays were really keen to be seen internally as an inclusive and diverse employer and, therefore, reviewing their sponsorship portfolio and having been a big investor and supporter in the men's Premier League, it made absolute sense that as part of that portfolio they would support the top of the women's game too.'

One of the first big brands to sponsor women's sport in the UK was Kia in 2014, when the car manufacturer announced the first stand-alone sponsorship deal for women's cricket. The announcement was a huge boost for the newly professional England Women's squad and demonstrated that women's cricket, and women's sport more generally, was a viable commercial option for big brands.

Talking to Sue Mott in 2017, President and CEO of Kia Motors (UK) Paul Philpott explained why the decision made absolute business sense:

> Women are pretty influential in the car-buying process. Around fifty-five per cent of our drivers are women and I've seen studies that estimate eighty-eight per cent of car purchases are influenced by women.
>
> That was the spur, the catalyst for us. It made sense. Women are a powerfully influential consumer base. Women are brilliant sporting heroes. We looked at the England Women's cricket team, then led by Charlotte Edwards and subsequently by Heather Knight: they had talent, capability, skill and the commitment to take themselves to number one in the world. There weren't many teams in the country – men or women – who could say that. The opportunity to be associated with such success and with a challenger brand themselves was a great opportunity for Kia.

In fact, it's estimated that women drive 70–80 per cent of all consumer purchasing through a combination of their own buying power and influence. Even when a woman is not paying for something directly herself, she's often the influence or veto vote behind someone else's purchase, be that a partner, child or elderly parent. With this in mind, it's extraordinary really that more brands haven't thrown themselves behind women's sport.

Paul Philpott goes on to identify another key advantage of women's sport: 'Kia were a challenger brand back in 2014 . . . still looking for something different to give us a disproportionate return on our investment.'

Ultimately brands are looking at what they invest and the return they will get for that financial investment. Women's sport is at a point where it offers incredible value to brands: the opportunity to associate with a sporting property that would be multiple times more expensive for the male equivalent.

Brands also find that access to athletes is so much better with women's sport. 'At a human level, working with the athletes is such a pleasure,' says Philpott. 'If we were to sponsor a major Premiership football team – we wouldn't have access to the players, we wouldn't have access to the management, we'd just be an asset. Whereas the beauty of our association with England Women's cricket is that they are known to us, they're individuals, they're people. We feel how passionate they are and how much they appreciate our sponsorship. It's a two-way relationship.'

Other brands that have been real trailblazers for women's sport include Ricoh, who sponsored the Women's British Golf Open for twelve years before title sponsorship was taken up by AIG in a new five-year deal launched in 2019, and SSE, whose landmark moment in the history of women's football saw the energy brand in the first ever major sponsorship of the Women's FA Cup competition. Reflecting on that deal, Lisa Parfitt, co-founder of sports marketing agency The Space Between, says: 'It really was ahead of its time. You had a client and a brand who were willing to overlook media value and broadcast minutes for the story and the purpose behind what they wanted to achieve as a brand. We are continuing to see that in the approach of brands.'

While it is usually the men's side of a sport that gets the biggest investment from sponsors, in hockey's case it was the women's game that took precedence when Investec came on board in 2011. The huge success of this partnership lay in the enthusiasm of the financial services company to fully activate the sponsorship with the female athletes, as Sally Munday, the then CEO of England Hockey, explains: 'Yes, they gave us a pot of money, and that was very welcome, but also we went on a journey with them around London 2012 to really try and raise the profile of the women's squad. They put the women's pictures all over London on taxis and billboards. They really helped us in terms of trying to change the perception of the game and change the image of how the women were seen. Our players love working with Investec because Investec look after them.'

Sadly, making the most of the sponsored properties, known as activation, is a place where some sponsors of women's sport have fallen short. From my own days in sports sponsorship back in the nineties, the rule of thumb was that a sponsor should commit twice the actual price of a sponsorship to activation. If you spent £50,000 on a shirt sponsorship, you should commit a further £100,000 to maximise what you've bought. A case in point would be Tyrrells, the premium potato crisp manufacturer, who were much celebrated as the first title sponsor of the Premier 15s, the top tier of the women's English rugby union domestic league in 2017. Unfortunately, many in the sport felt they failed to maximise this relationship in terms of building the profile for the sport and the league. The relationship ended in 2020 when the contract with the RFU was not renewed for another term. Here's hoping that Allianz, announced in the autumn of 2020 as the new sponsor for the Premier 15s, will do a better job.

A sponsor that has always been great at aligning themselves with women's sport and activating its properties well, is Vitality, working with netball, hockey, cricket, rugby and football. Clearly the profile and branding from the events they support is a key consideration, but Vitality's approach has been different from many brands in that it's far from a 'badging' exercise and much more about how they can help a sport to achieve its bigger goals.

Lisa Parfitt explains: 'Vitality started very early in netball and they've grown with them and supported them. Fundamentally they've been able to change the sport by funding professional contracts. The reason that the Vitality Roses play and are being paid is because of Vitality.'

One of the main reasons Vitality, a health and life insurance firm, has invested so much in women's sport is that it reinforces the brand's drive for gender parity, which is enhanced by the fact that it's possible to have a much larger presence in a sport or at a major event. 'A key part of our strategy is around ownership,' says Nick Read, Commercial Director at Vitality. 'Where we can "own" a sport, or an event, that is a core constituent part of our strategy. Take the Women's Hockey World Cup in 2018: it was very ownable.'

This clearly wouldn't have been possible for the brand in the world of men's football, which is another sport where Vitality has a large presence, but where there are myriad other brands. This is a significant advantage for brands coming into women's sport right now.

Businesses are also keen to understand if the audience for women's sport matches the audience they are trying to reach. It's wrong to say that 'women's sport is just for women' – for instance, more men watch women's football than women – but there are definitely sports that do appeal to women, and for the brands that want to target women this can be incredibly powerful.

Similarly, it is often via the sponsors that change at a structural level can be made in sport. If decisions are being made within a sport that will damage the progression of women, then letting the sponsors feel the wrath of consumer opinion can be hugely powerful. After all, women make up over 50 per cent of the population and control the majority of buying decisions in the home, so some well-directed activity on social media, especially when amplified by high-profile influencers, undoubtedly makes brands sit up and take notice. This in turn impacts the teams and organisations. Ultimately, money talks.

———

In the early days of sports sponsorship 'the Chairman's whim' was the phrase used to describe many decisions made about which sports an organisation supported. The Chairman loves golf so the company sponsors tournaments where he'll get to present the trophy to his heroes; he's a big rugby fan so they sponsor the RFU and he can entertain clients at Twickenham, meet some stars and watch every game live; his wife loves tennis, so he sponsors Wimbledon and they have Centre Court seats for the family each year.

Times have changed and sponsorship decisions are more often based on more sophisticated metrics of reaching potential customers via broadcast and branding.

That said, it's been interesting to see an element of 'the Chairman's whim' emerging in the past decade which might benefit women's sport. For many of the big brands backing women's sport you'll often find the senior decision-makers talk about their wives and daughters, and the recognition that now is the time to invest in women's sport to ensure more equality for the next generation. It's not that these – mainly male – decision-makers hadn't had wives and daughters in the past, but that we're now living in a time when they are more conscious of being called out by females in their family for the decisions they are making, which is hugely positive.

'It's possible I was also very receptive to the idea because of my previous experience of women's sport. Not only do I have a daughter but my first real exposure to big-time professional women's sport was when I worked in Germany. I went to the Women's World Cup final in 2011 in Frankfurt with my eight-year-old son. It was a real spectacle. It was end-to-end, went to penalties, we didn't leave the stadium until quarter to midnight. The atmosphere was fantastic. The game was dynamic, passionate but fun, too. My son still talks about it to this day,' says Kia CEO Paul Philpott.

In an era of #MeToo and #TimesUp businesses are also recognising the need to display better gender balance across their organisations. Where they spend their sponsorship money can have a significant impact on their staff and customers. A major corporation can no longer claim to offer gender-equal business practices only to then solely sponsor men's sport. If it wants to have a truly inclusive culture, then redressing the balance of its public-facing sponsorship activities will be key. And, of course, we are also seeing increasing numbers of women on corporate boards, which in turn brings more balance to investment decision-making.

Sally Horrox, co-founder of sports marketing agency Y Sport, explains how the conversations she is having with brands have changed: 'A few years ago it might have been unusual to have included the women's game or women's sport, or the reach to females, in those conversations,' she tells Richard Gillis on the *Unofficial Partner* podcast. 'Now it's just absolutely par for the course and it's expected. Because the boards of those brands, against their own governance structures, and their own commitments to shareholders, need to demonstrate that they are fair and even in the way they distribute their marketing funds.'

The importance of reaching communities is also highlighted by

Sally Hancock, Sally Horrox's co-founder, who worked with SSE when they became the sponsor of the Women's FA Cup. 'I think it's taken one or two savvy brands to be brave and really step up to the plate. SSE definitely led the way with that, and it's often cited. And the results of that and the impact and reach – not just at the BBC broadcast Wembley FA Cup level – but right down to community grassroots. Other brands looked at that and started to think actually there is a right seam of opportunity here. This is our audience. This is the community we sit in. These are our customers. It's about time we took a closer look at what we are doing, and try to make sure we are applying a more diverse approach about what we're doing now.'

The way in which sponsorship properties are sold is also changing and this needs to continue for women's sport to evolve. If brands only consider historical audience figures and media coverage, then often women's events can't compete because they haven't had this exposure. Brands that are more forward-thinking, willing to be open-minded in their desire to help shape this emerging market, will see great returns on their investment as they also help create a more equal future for society.

Talking to me about new opportunities for brands ahead of the FIFA Women's World Cup in 2019, former Lioness Eni Aluko said: 'Since the #MeToo movement women are now seen around the world as deserving of more. More equality, bigger voice, more powerful. So, from a brand perspective harnessing the powerful women in sport to enhance their brand makes sense for where we are in the world in terms of women.'

Sponsoring women's sport isn't just about doing it because it's the right thing to do, though. Even before the Women's Boat Race joined the men's on the Thames in 2015, Helen Morrissey, who had led Newton Asset Finance to sponsor the women's event, said: 'Newton's sponsorship also made fantastic business sense – and my hope is that other companies will see this and follow suit. Even before taking account of the likely global attention around this year's historic race, the metrics used to gauge "payback" of Newton's sponsorship monies suggest we have already achieved at least a threefold return on our investment.'

As consumers, we can all play our part in this area, by showing support for the brands that back women's sport. From the products we buy in supermarkets to where we bank, from the insurance policies we buy to the cars we choose – we can all make buying decisions that reward the brands who have thrown their collective weight behind women's sport.

———

Another route to income for some sports is the sale of broadcasting rights.

In the UK, the commercialisation of TV rights has been the foundation for the growth of the Premier League – its income has rocketed alongside the desire of fans worldwide to follow their favourite clubs and players. Broadcasters compete to become official rights holder of the competition and the enormous fees paid are then distributed across the Premier League clubs. Back in 1997 the rights were sold to Sky for £670 million. The rights to show Premier League games from 2019 to 2022 were sold for £4.4 billion amid speculation that new organisations might begin to enter the bidding, including the likes of Amazon, Facebook, Netflix and Twitter.

The way in which the rights to women's sport are being sold has changed in recent years. In the past it was very common to sell the rights to the men's team or league to a sponsor and then 'tag on' the women's, too, ensuring they received a small proportion of the funding. At a time when there was little demand for women's sport, this felt like a fair way to ensure women got some of the pie and it also enabled the commercial team to enhance a sponsor's package.

What we are now seeing is the 'unbundling' of these rights – selling the women's sport as a stand-alone entity. Many would say the huge success the FA have had in attracting sponsorship for the women's game is because they unbundled it from the men's. As Heather Rabbatts, Chair of the Women's Sport Group, explains: 'What's important for women's football is that it has its own appointment to view. It's not just seen as an intro act for male football. It actually stands by itself and has proven its value.'

Selling women's sport in this way not only means more access to funding but gives brands the opportunities to shape the relationship with women's sport and the messaging around it. 'When we talk about unbundling it is about selling women's football, selling women's cricket, selling women's rugby. They are different sporting experiences. Of course, if you love rugby you may well love women's rugby and men's rugby or you might be somebody who just loves women's rugby, or somebody who just loves women's football. This is an opportunity to put women's sport properly and squarely in the front window where it belongs,' says Heather.

The FA has had much success in selling the rights to the WSL from 2021, and although the numbers are a tiny fraction of the income generated for the Premier League it will make a significant difference to the women's game.

Other sports like rugby are also unbundling the rights to the women's element, with the Women's Six Nations looking for a new broadcaster and sponsors when the England Women's relationship with Sky comes to an end. In 2020 the agency CSM was appointed to source new commercial partners for the competition.

World Rugby, too, have been inspired by the success of federations such as UEFA and the FA, and in 2020 unbundled the women's rights. As Katie Sadleir, General Manager of Women's Rugby at World Rugby, explained to me, it's not enough to be growing the percentage of investment into women's rugby from the World Rugby pie; it was important to grow 'the whole pie':

> If all we were doing was robbing Peter to pay Paul, then we weren't actually getting significant gains in terms of standing on our feet saying women's sport is important.
>
> We developed a separate commercial strategy. We did an analysis of what was going on in the unions around the world to see where they were at with their own commercial strategies and we decided to unbundle the commercial rights for women and men.
>
> Most international federations did as we did in the past. When they sell the rights for their men's World Cup, they also throw in the rights for the women's World Cup, and some of the other events as well. It's not saying in any way that the sponsors who had been given the women's rights weren't passionate about women's rugby, but the internal cashflow didn't materialise and we weren't seeing the activation to the same extent.

World Rugby are now in the market seeking six global partners for women's rugby over the next six years to include the next two World Cups. I wish them well.

For many women's sports it's not a matter of selling your rights but hoping that a TV channel will cover your sport at all. Despite not having a male equivalent sport 'to hang on to the coat tails of', in the words of former CEO Jo Coates (née Adams), England Netball did a great job in this area.

In 2005 they teamed up with Sky and invested their own money in the production costs for Superleague games to show there was an audience. The national governing body effectively paid to get itself on TV, a brave move for any sport. When they renegotiated in 2013 Sky agreed to pay for production but took some of the commercial rights in exchange. By 2016 England Netball had its commercial rights back and the shows were fully produced by Sky with high-quality production, graphics and analysis.

As the audience for women's rugby increases this is certainly an approach that rugby could take. Last year I watched the most amazing game as Harlequins Women played their long-time rivals Saracens at home at the Twickenham Stoop. The game entered its final thrilling moments. Saracens had staged a remarkable comeback from being 24-7 down at half-time to now being ahead 27-33, and Harlequins were desperately close to scoring in the 80th minute with a huge push around their goal line.

I sat on the edge of my seat, my hand covering my mouth in a mix of excitement and dread (Harlequins were a client at the time). I remember my overriding thought at the end of the afternoon was that I had been lucky enough to be present at one of the most astonishing and gripping games of rugby I'd ever seen, yet it was witnessed by a crowd of only a few thousand and those able to watch on England Rugby's live stream.

If only that wonderful match had been broadcast more widely – reaching a mass audience on mainstream TV; what a superb advert it would have been for the women's game.

Here's hoping that, with a new sponsor for the Premier 15s, we might see a shrewd broadcaster step forward, too.

––––––––––

A final observation is the presence of investors in men's professional sport. Look at the ownership of the biggest football and rugby clubs and, along with a few investment groups, you'll primarily see male millionaires and billionaires with vast sums to spend on a sport they love. It's the same across the world.

Women's sport hasn't historically appealed to these wealthy men and, if we were hoping that female billionaires might redress the balance, unfortunately that's less likely when for every female billionaire there are 8.4 male billionaires.

Of course, there are male owners who appreciate the value in women's sport. I asked Emma Hayes, the Chelsea manager, about this and she told me: 'In my opinion the women's game has a debt of gratitude to Roman Abramovich. Because from the off he has always been really interested in it. He loves the team. He's such a big Chelsea fan as well as an owner and that is hugely influential.'

For some women's clubs where they find investment is a matter of principle. Lewes FC has a funding model that sees over 1,600 small owners investing in the club – I'm a proud Lewes FC owner myself.

I asked Maggie Murphy, General Manager at Lewes FC Women, if the club's hugely ethical stance on all things would make it difficult to take investment from a billionaire businessman waltzing in with a huge cheque to transform the club. She was pretty forthright in her response: 'If there are some shady billionaires out there that want to give us money, you're not welcome. Of, course I need more money, we have so much more ambition, so much potential and we know that we need money to take us to that next level, but we are only going to take good people's money, and we are not going to compromise our values, because then we have not achieved anything. The hypocrisy would be terrible.'

In 2020 it was wonderful to witness the arrival of Angel City, the majority-female-founded Los Angeles NWSL club which is backed by A-list celebrities such as Eva Longoria, Jennifer Garner, Natalie Portman, Serena Williams and her two-year-old daughter Alexis Ohanian Jr along with former US Women's National Team players Julie Foudy, Mia Hamm and Abby Wambach. The new franchise, which launches in spring 2022, says it wants to write a new playbook and 'reshape exceptions and think differently about ownership, ticketing, partnerships, and community collaboration'.

It was also announced in January 2021 that twenty-three-year-old Naomi Osaka, Forbes highest paid female athlete in 2020, had invested in another NWSL franchise, North Carolina Courage. Osaka commented that she admired everything that Courage does for diversity and equality in the community.

Here's hoping these moves might mark the beginning of more women investing in female sport.

7

EQUAL PAY FOR EQUAL PLAY

Everyone thinks women should be thrilled when we get crumbs and I want women to have the cake, the icing and the cherry on top too.

Billie Jean King, 2016

A challenge often made to women's sport is whether the quality of play is as good as men's. Never mind the fact that women are physically different from men – so the very best women may not be able to run as fast, or kick or throw as far as the best men – but the widely held belief by many male sports fans that women footballers, cricketers and rugby players do not play with the same level of skill as men.

It is an interesting argument and I've often found myself defending women's sport, citing that it's a different game and it's not fair to compare men's with women's.

That said, the reality is that, until recently, women in these sports may not have had the equivalent levels of skill demonstrated by the men because they've been amateurs, deprived of the chance to play full time like their male counterparts. With insufficient coaching throughout their careers, and inadequate opportunities at a youth level, until very recently many have only trained a few nights a week, often juggling full-time jobs with playing their sports. How can anyone expect women to play with the skill and experience of men – who have been fully professional for decades – when this is the case?

This is where the development of professional contracts in women's sport is already having a massive impact.

In sports where men and women have always had equal opportunity to train and perform, equal access to sports science support and funding, you do not see any difference in the intrinsic skill levels. From triathletes, gymnasts and swimmers through to rowers, golfers or cyclists, the skills of the men and women are equal, with just power and strength the differentiators in performance.

It's been a strange history for professional women's sport, as Ali Bowes and Alex Culvin explain in the introduction to their book *Issues and Debates in the Professionalisation of Women's Sport*:

> It was the individual games of golf and tennis that really broke new ground for western women in sport, specifically in the United States. Initiated in the wake of the second wave feminist movement in the 1950s and 1960s, most notably with the formation of the Ladies Professional Golf Association (LPGA) and the Women's Tennis Association (WTA), the sports are now considered the most successful, popular and, significantly, lucrative forms of professional women's sport. The move for other sports, and specifically team sports, to follow this shift towards a professional era has been slow, sporadic and marred with difficulties.

As Ali and Alex point out, in terms of individual sponsorship, the sports that have led the way are tennis and golf with professional athletes such as the Williams sisters, Naomi Osaka and Sharapova earning eye-watering amounts in comparison to many other female athletes.

In fact, nine of the world's ten highest-paid female athletes in 2020 make their living playing tennis. The only exception is Alex Morgan, co-captain of the US women's football team, who is in tenth place, earning $4.6 million from income and sponsorship.

In 2019 Osaka earned $37.4 million from prize money and endorsements, setting an all-time earnings record for a female athlete in a single year. Maria Sharapova previously held the record with $29.7 million in 2015. Serena Williams was the world's highest-paid female athlete in each of the previous four years, with annual income ranging from $18 to $29 million. During her incredible career Serena has also collected over $300 million from endorsers.

Despite the success of a few female athletes, it is disappointing that in 2020 only two women – Serena and Naomi – appear on the *Forbes* ranking of the 100 best paid athletes in the world. Perhaps this will change in future decades. We live in hope, but across most sports, female athletes get substantially less media coverage and this in turn makes them less appealing to sponsors.

Attempts to establish professional women's sports leagues, so that female athletes could be paid to play in the way men are, have met with mixed results across the world.

Basketball is one of the earliest examples with the inaugural Women's Basketball League established in 1978. Unfortunately, it only lasted three seasons. The 1990s saw the unsuccessful Women's Basketball Association (1993–5), which evolved into the more sustainable and successful Women's National Basketball Association established in 1997. Even during the sporting hiatus caused by COVID-19, the WNBA has continued to break new ground, with its 2020 Draft ratings broadcast on ESPN up 123 per cent on the previous year, with 387,000 viewers and 6.5 million social media video views.

On 14 January 2020, the WNBA announced new league-wide

contracts that will change women's basketball for ever. Talking to the *Telegraph*, Chiney Ogwumike, Vice-President of the Women's National Basketball Players Association, commented: 'People were calling this agreement ground-breaking, and as I heard it more and more I realised it wasn't ground-breaking, but ground-establishing.'

Along with much-improved salaries, the new terms include employees' rights, better travel conditions and full maternity pay, plus financial compensation for veteran players involved in adoption, surrogacy and fertility treatment. A salary cap increase of 30 per cent means players can now earn from $130,000 to $500,000. Still nowhere near in the region of the top men playing in the NBA, where average salaries were $7.7 million in 2020, but a substantial increase which should enable women to stay and play in the US rather than being drawn to Europe.

Some of the overseas teams had been tempting players with up to ten times their WNBA salaries. With a short season for the WNBA, the result was many women competing all year round, risking exhaustion and injuries in the process. In addition to this, there was the emotional distress of being away from loved ones for half the year and the inability to market yourself to sponsors in the US when you're not living there for the majority of the year.

Several attempts have been made to professionalise women's football in the US, starting in 2001 when the Women's United Soccer Association was established as the world's first women's football league. All players in the eight teams were to be paid as professionals and former England captain Kelly Smith was one of the overseas players included. After just three seasons, however, with losses of around $100 million, in September 2003 the league suspended its operations.

In 2009 the Women's Professional Soccer League launched with seven teams and big plans for future expansion. The chance to play professionally attracted many great English players, including Eniola Aluko, Anita Asante, Karen Carney, Katie Chapman, Gemma Davison, Lianne Sanderson, Alex Scott, Kelly Smith and Karen Bardsley. Once again, the league failed to survive and in 2012, after a number of legal and financial issues, it was suspended.

The current professional league in the US is the National Women's Soccer League, which was established in 2013. Learning from the previous failures of professional women's leagues, the NWSL put systems in place to protect its future, including subsidies from governing bodies, lower operating costs, salary caps and an even distribution of players. With the ability to now play professionally in the Barclays FA Women's Super League, few British players remained in the NWSL in 2020.

While the NWSL has so far lasted longer than its predecessors, and the popularity of women's football in the US remains incredibly high after another World Cup win in 2019, driving attendance and sponsorship for the league is still a challenge.

To help address this, Budweiser, an NWSL sponsor, launched the #WontStopWatching campaign when the US team returned from the World Cup to encourage fans to attend league games. In October 2019, Megan Rapinoe fronted the brand's Future Official campaign to attract new brand sponsors to the league.

'When the US Women's National Team returned from France, the next step was making sure fans continued to support women's soccer on a year-round basis. And they answered our rally cry by supporting the NWSL with both record attendance and viewership this year,' said Monica Rustgi, Vice-President of Marketing for Budweiser. 'Now, with the "Future Official Sponsor" campaign, we turn to other brands and encourage them to support the league like passionate fans.'

The NWSL was the first US women's sport to return after the

COVID-19 lockdown and it looked like that momentum from 2019 was going to be maintained. The opening game of the NWSL Challenge Cup broke the previous ratings record (190,000) with 572,000 viewers on CBS. Houston Dash won the final over the Chicago Red Stars, breaking NWSL domestic television viewing ratings records, with a 653,000 average on CBS.

Interesting developments in the autumn of 2020 saw a flurry of the very top US players heading to play in the FA WSL, when the US season was dramatically shortened because of COVID-19. World Cup winners Rose Lavelle and Sam Mewis signed year-long contracts with Manchester City. Tobin Heath and Christen Press signed with Manchester United, with their shirts outselling any of the Manchester United men's players for the first weeks after they arrived. Alex Morgan, famous for miming 'sipping tea' after scoring against England in the World Cup semi-final (it made some England fans angry, but I thought it was very funny), arrived to play for Spurs. Jess Fishlock, Wales' most capped player who's had enormous success in the NWSL at OL Reign alongside Megan Rapinoe, also returned on loan to play at Reading FC. What these players do for the profile of women's football in the UK will be interesting to see, especially when you consider Alex Morgan had more Instagram followers – 9.2 million – than the official Spurs men's account at 8.8 million.

Professional soccer also had a stuttering start in Australia, where the Women's National Soccer League initially lasted just eight years, from 1996 to 2004. In 2007 the W-League was established, with all clubs but one aligned to the existing men's A-League teams' business model. In 2017 Westfield came on board as the title sponsor of the league, and a collective bargaining agreement that year enabled the W-League to remain competitive with player salaries in comparison to other leagues around the world.

Since 2015, though, Australia has seen a huge growth in professional women's sport. Along with netball and basketball, the change has primarily occurred in what were traditionally male sports – namely football (soccer), AFL, rugby league and rugby union.

In 2018 the Men's and Women's Cricket Big Bash League finalists received equal prize money and, according to Sporting Intelligence, three of Australia's competitions are among the ten best-paid women's sport leagues in the world including Super Netball League at number two, Women's Big Bash League (cricket) at number eight and W-League (soccer) at number nine.

———

So, what's the state of play for women's professional sport in the UK?

In May 2014, the England and Wales Cricket Board celebrated 'the dawning of a fully professional era' for women's cricket in England as they announced that eighteen players had been awarded fully professional contracts. The Sports Minister at the time, Helen Grant, said it was 'a significant step not just for women's cricket, but for women's sport . . . it demonstrates to girls and women throughout the country that a career in sport is a realistic aspiration for them'.

Building further on this – and perhaps in response to the success of Australia, who have over 100 women playing professionally or semi-professionally – in 2019 the ECB announced an initial £20 million of funding over the next two years to allow forty full-time professional contracts to be awarded in addition to the existing twenty-one England centrally contracted female players. Clare Connor, England's Managing Director of Women's Cricket, said: 'Over the last five years, Australia have made similar investments which we are about to make. There's no getting away from the fact we do need to close the gap, certainly around the number of female players who can make a living playing the game.'

In December 2020, the ECB confirmed the allocation of professional players to the eight teams within the new women's regional set-up, adding a further sixteen players to the list of contracted professionals. This means that forty-one female cricketers have now signed full-time domestic contracts.

The Rugby Football Union have had a mixed record when it comes to their efforts to professionalise the women's game. In 2014, amid much noise and celebration, twenty contracts were awarded to women playing sevens in the build-up to the Rio Olympics. This was then expanded to forty-eight contracts, including sixteen full-time deals for those playing fifteen-a-side.

Uproar then followed in 2017, when the RFU announced it would not be renewing the contracts of the England Women's fifteen-a-side team. The Shadow Sports Minister, Dr Rosena Allin-Khan, along with 124 MPs from across the political spectrum, wrote to the RFU to complain about the policy of 'cycling' between contracts for sevens and fifteen-a-side rugby as it was unfair to expect the athletes to pause and resume their careers every two years. 'Surely the RFU should be focused on investing in both aspects of the women's game and should be prepared to back this up with secure contracts for both teams – sevens and fifteens. After all, this is the commitment the RFU has made to the men's game,' she added.

It was therefore a cause for much celebration in January 2019 when the RFU finally awarded full-time professional contracts to twenty-eight fifteen-a-side players ahead of the World Cup in 2021. Some of the best players can also earn income from the clubs they play for, though this is limited, with little income for the Premier 15s from rights, sponsorship or central funding.

Sadly, this situation changed again during the summer of 2020 as a result of COVID-19. Unlike the ECB, who ring-fenced the money for women's contracts, the RFU cut all professional contracts for sevens players – both male and female – and reduced funding for the Premier 15s by 25 per cent.

Being paid to play netball is the reason why many British players moved across to play in Australia and New Zealand in the past decade. Leagues there benefit from sponsorship and revenues that see average player earnings of around £40,000 a year. The popularity of the sport there also means athletes are more likely to receive personal endorsements. I was lucky enough to visit Netball New South Wales in 2018, and it was fantastic to see massive billboards adorned with images of English players Jo Harten and Helen Housby, who also appeared on the sides of buses advertising their games.

With team salaries in the UK's Vitality Netball Superleague capped at £75,000 between ten players, the semi-professional players would struggle to survive without additional jobs and income. Although Sport England funding had enabled the England Roses to play full-time netball ahead of the Commonwealth Games, in October 2018 it was announced that Vitality would extend its support of England Netball, and that as part of that agreement the Vitality Roses were created, ensuring the women could remain on full-time contracts.

When it comes to football, for decades the women's game has been an amateur, voluntary-led sport in the UK. Even those playing at national level did so for free, sometimes paying for their kit and contributing to their travel costs for away games.

Things changed in 2009 when England put eighteen of its top players on central contracts, and there are now twenty-six England players earning an annual salary, with the WSL teams paying top players, too.

A slight caveat to this positive news of 'professional contracts' for women in sports including cricket, rugby and football is how much these contracts are actually worth. It's upsetting to learn that in some cases these contracts may only just be above the minimum wage.

As Hannah Thompson, a doctoral researcher at Loughborough University working with elite female athletes, points out:

> It's great news that this is happening and certainly something to celebrate, but we mustn't lose track of how far female athletes still have to go towards true equality with their male counterparts. There's a difficult tension to navigate here. The gratitude our sportswomen are expected to show for finally being paid, versus the fact that it's about time, as they've waited so long for any change. We need to celebrate the small wins, and it's hard not to be grateful for the fact that things are finally shifting, but we can't become complacent when the amounts being paid are relatively low and incomparable to the men.
>
> Being paid is just the start and it's long overdue. The problem we have now is female athletes having the option to be paid in the sport they've dedicated their lives to, but still on relatively low pay. It's choosing this versus leaving sport to progress in an alternative career where salaries may be more attractive with better employment rights.

When the central contracts were first introduced in football, England players received £16,000, an amount that has now been increased to £20,000. Some might call this laughable as male Premiership League footballers earn more than that in a single day, but Kelly Simmons at the FA says that's not a fair comparison: 'Men's football is a hundred and fifty years old and a multi-billion-pound industry, so I don't really compare the women's game to that. It's about turning what was amateur into a professional sport.'

The women's game developed further in 2011, when the FA launched the WSL and most teams were predominantly semi-professional. Following the 2017–18 season, the WSL became a fully professional league for the first time, with eleven teams for the 2018–19 season.

So there, within the space of a decade, women in this country are now able to play professional sport. Not only does this mean the quality of the sport on display is rapidly increasing, it also gives immense hope and inspiration to young women who can now aspire to earn a living playing the sport they love, just like the boys.

————

Aside from players' salaries in the NWSL, in the US the national women's football team's battle for equal pay became very high profile in 2019, especially after they'd won their fourth FIFA World Cup (they've also won five Olympic gold medals).

In a lawsuit filed by twenty-eight women's national team players against US Soccer in March 2019, the players sought $66 million (£52.8 million) in back pay and damages under the Equal Pay Act and Title VII of the 1964 Civil Rights Act. They claimed they had not been paid equally under their collective bargaining agreement in comparison to what the male players received through their deal.

The women wanted the same bonus structure as the male players, but US Soccer argued that the women actually made more than the men, both overall and by game average. During the court case, the women's position was strengthened by the vocal support of male players, with the US men's team issuing a statement that criticised US Soccer, saying: 'the federation continues to discriminate against the women in their wages and working conditions.'

There was huge public support for the women's claim, which became amplified further when it was revealed that the lawyers for US football's governing body had made submissions claiming the job of a male footballer on the national team 'requires a higher level of skill based on speed and strength' than their female counterparts. Seriously. In 2020. Unsurprisingly this statement attracted global criticism, and even sponsors like Coca-Cola, Budweiser and Volkswagen got involved and called out US Soccer. This comment was later removed from the legal submission and the US Soccer President, Carlos Cordeiro, resigned as a result.

Despite this, the backing of many high-profile people across the world, and the fact that the national women's team were ranked first in the world compared to the men ranked at twenty-two, in early 2020 a judge rejected the claim that the women were underpaid compared to the men. He ruled that the pay case did not warrant a trial.

The women's team were shocked by the outcome and have said they will appeal the decision and never give up the fight for equality. Molly Levinson, the players' spokeswoman, said: 'We are confident in our case and steadfast in our commitment to ensuring that girls and women who play this sport will not be valued as lesser just because of their gender.'

In May 2020 Joe Biden, then the Democratic candidate for the presidency of the United States, declared his backing for the US women's team, tweeting that the players should not 'give up this fight' for equal pay and threatening to withdraw funding from the governing body should he win the White House. 'To US Soccer: equal pay, now, or else when I'm president, you can go elsewhere for World Cup funding.'

Now that Joe Biden is President, we will watch those developments with interest.

At the end of 2020 the two sides finally settled on the working conditions and it was announced that the United States Soccer Federation will now 'implement revised policies on four working conditions: charter flights, venue selection, professional support and hotel accommodations' to equalise the treatment of the men's and women's teams.

Women's footballers are clearly finding their voices when it comes to unequal pay across the world. National teams raising issues about the unfairness of pay and conditions in recent years have included Scotland, Denmark, Nigeria, Puerto Rico, Brazil, Argentina, Ireland, Spain, Trinidad and Tobago, Colombia, Chile and Jamaica.

Some positive news elsewhere in the world comes from Norway, where, since 2017, its male and female footballers have received the same pay for representing their country. In 2019 the Dutch Football Association announced that their national women's team would receive increased compensation for the next four years until they reach an equal pay-out with the men in 2023.

Following the FIFA World Cup in 2019, Australia followed suit. In November that year it was announced that the Westfield Matildas would now earn the same as their male counterparts, share an equal split of all commercial revenue and that their travel, coaching and operational support would be brought up to the same standard as the men's. This followed years of lobbying by the women, who had even cancelled a sell-out tour of the US in 2015 amid a row about their pay, which the players said was so low it was illegal.

In September 2020, Brazil made sporting headlines, announcing that its women's national players would now be paid the same as male players for representing the country. Rogerio Caboclo, President of Brazil's football association, the CBF, said: 'There is no more gender difference, as the CBF is treating men and women equally. What they will gain by conquering or by staging the Olympics next year will be the same as the men will have.'

This prompted the FA to announce that the England women and men were *already* receiving equal pay, something that had, in fact, been in place since January 2020.

———

Along with contracts to play professionally, prize money can also make a massive difference to women's sport, rewarding players for the time invested and covering the costs of backroom staff. In 2020 we witnessed both the good and the bad in this area in cricket and football.

The Hundred is a new format of cricket from the ECB, which was due to launch in the summer of 2020, but because of COVID was postponed to 2021. The new 100-ball competition, which features eight city-based teams, includes men's and women's events running simultaneously. There was much celebration in the cricketing world, and more widely across women's sport, when in March 2020 it was announced that both the men's and women's Hundred competitions would offer equal prize money with the prize budget of £600,000 being split equally between the competitions. Heather Knight, the England captain who will lead London Spirit in The Hundred, commented: 'It is brilliant news. To have equal prize money is a statement by the ECB to put women's cricket alongside men's cricket.'

Of course, it is wonderful news, and hats off to the ECB for making this commitment, but if we look a little deeper into The Hundred, in terms of true equality for the female players there's still quite a way to go. For while the prize money is equal, and the female players will also be treated equally to the men during the tournament in terms of travel, accommodation and access to sports science support, the contracts for the women playing are substantially smaller than in the men's competition. The players are paid in various salary brackets and the highest for the women is £15,000, compared with £125,000 for the men.

Having spoken at length to the ECB about why this is, I 'sort of' understand the reasoning. In 2019 the ECB launched their ambitious action plan to make cricket a gender-balanced sport. A commitment of £20 million was made for women and girls' cricket over the following two years, with a potential £50 million over the next five years. It is a huge investment that will positively impact everything from grassroots and schools, through the pathway regionally into the national game.

I say that I 'sort of' understand, because I do appreciate that to attract the male players to The Hundred the contracts had to be significant, whereas the current salaries of the female players are only a fraction of the men's. But what an incredible global statement of equality and respect for female athletes that would have been if the ECB, within this radical new format of The Hundred, had also chosen to be radical in their treatment of their female players. It could have gone a long way towards shifting the historical patriarchal stereotype of cricket. After all, it took 200 years for women even to be allowed to enter the Long Room at Lord's, with the world's most famous cricket club, Marylebone Cricket Club, finally allowing female members in 1999.

When it comes to equal pay in football, there is one club that's had a significant global impact, and that's Lewes FC, the first club in the world to pay its male and female players equally. I asked Maggie

Murphy, General Manager at Lewes FC Women, to tell me more: 'A lot of people talk about pay parity; it is actually a lot more than that. Yes, our playing budgets are the same, but actually it is about splitting the revenue equally. We have the same marketing budgets, we both play on the same pitch, we have the same training facilities. When decisions are made, it is not a case of what do the men want, and then what do the women want, it is a case of having everyone round the table and deciding what happens.'

Maggie's enthusiasm for all that Lewes is doing to help drive equality in women's sport is infectious. In 2019, the club led a high-profile campaign calling for equal prize money in the FA Cup, where the women's prize pool is currently less than 1 per cent of the men's. Let me repeat that. *Less than 1 per cent of the men's.*

Maggie explains why their initiative gathered so much traction and why it matters to the future of women's football:

> People weren't aware of just how big the gap was until we started talking about it. When we went into our fourth round FA game, we won £2,000, but if we were men we would have won £180,000. I can win the league with £180,000. I can improve our facilities and our infrastructure. I can provide even better coaching to one hundred girls in our pathway if you give me £180,000 for a single game. But we got £2,000.
>
> Then the next game against Arsenal, we could have won £3,000, but the men were set to win £360,000. It is not just the number, it's also the fact that for the men's side they keep doubling the prize money, but for the women we are going up in smaller increments.

Other arguments made against making this change for equality include suggestions that it might 'kill grassroots men's football' if you took away the money. In fact, Maggie explains, 80 per cent of the men's FA Cup money is paid in the final few rounds, where it's generally the Premiership teams playing. So, no impact on men's grassroots football at all.

Maggie makes a final powerful point about investment.

We are not blind to the fact that women's football doesn't yet generate as much money from revenue and broadcasting, but then there hasn't been any *investment*. How can I generate bigger crowds, or how can I go on a marketing drive, if I have just won £2,000 in my FA Cup? Imagine what I could do with £180,000.

We have this idea that men's football got to the size it is all by itself, and that is not the case. They have had huge amounts of investment, public money – taxpayers' money, your money, my money – for decades in the use of public facilities, in the use of public grants. Even Wembley Stadium hosts so many more men's sports fixtures than women's, but it got £120 million of taxpayers' funds just a couple of years ago. So, our money is constantly being skewed towards investing in the men's football, and we are just getting pennies and we have got so much potential.

We just need to shift somehow. If we agree that the current divide, which is less than one per cent of what the men earn, isn't good, but we aren't ready for equal prize money, when should the prize pot be equalled? I'd be willing to have those conversations. OK, let's all agree it's going to be equal by 2040, so what do we do in order to get up there in 2040? At the moment there is nothing. No one can think that the current status quo is OK – let's try to figure out how do we get to the equal prize money.

I have no doubt that more and more women's teams, along with sponsors, media and influencers, will get behind this campaign for more equal prize money in the future. There are so many inequalities in women's football and more battles to be fought, but it really does feel like the prize money issue is important because the disparity is so tangible and clear for all to see.

In 2020 it was announced that Vitality would be the new sponsor of the FA Cup. Perhaps they will join the call for more equality in funding, too?

———

To finish on a more positive note, despite the gaping inequality with the FA Cup, and issues highlighted by the US women's football team, prize money in women's football has increased significantly in the past decade. Industry sources say the total pot in 2019 was $30 million, compared to just $6 million in 2007. That said, it's still nowhere near the amounts to be won in the men's game, and prize money for the last men's World Cup was about ten times that on offer to the women in 2019.

Research from the BBC that was published in March 2019 suggests that 83 per cent of sports now offer men and women equal prize money – much improved from the 70 per cent back in 2014. This is obviously fantastic news, and a move in the right direction, although some sports like football still have some enormous salary discrepancies.

To illustrate this point, a global sports salary survey in 2017 revealed that if you combined the salaries of *all the women* playing in the top-tier football leagues in England, France, Germany, USA, Mexico, Sweden and Australia, they'd still be *less than* the £32.9 million earned by Neymar in his contract with Paris Saint-Germain in 2018 . . .

We have some way to go, then.

8

WOMEN TALK SPORT

From Motty to totty as girl power conquers Match of the Day.
Daily Mail, 2007

In early 2020, during the COVID-19 lockdown, cricket writer at the *Telegraph* Isabelle Westbury took to Twitter to share her thoughts on the lack of female representation in today's sports coverage and why she thought it was such a problem: 'More men named John wrote in the sports pages of today's national newspapers than women full stop. Across the sports pages of last Sunday's nationals, 8 Johns wrote articles, as did 4 Neils (!) and a total of 7 women. Of 166 sports articles just 3 were on women's sport (<2%). Normally, female coverage & representation in print sports media is bad. This is worse.'

Isabelle went on to explain that the low numbers of female sports writers are often disguised by the larger proportion of women in broadcast sports media. Why are there more women in broadcasting? Isabelle feels the more visible roles make it easier to hold broadcasters accountable and create change:

Also, there is probably a pretty-woman-fronting-the-sports-coverage element to it (unfortunate but true), which you don't get with a print by-line.

It's also easier to enter the broadcast media because it's almost entirely freelance and self-employed, even at the top. Contrast this to senior sports writers as decent salaried employees. This is an almost exclusively male domain. Change is happening here, but slowly, and we're not at a stage where it's manifested in senior sports writing roles.

Many junior writing roles, however, where there are (some) more women, are part-time (contractors, without employee benefits, either) and poorly paid. So, the end game is: most women in sports media are in broadcast/or are freelance and on insecure contracts. So, when a pandemic hits, and sport vanishes, so do the women covering it. No sport is broadcast and newspapers, who are suffering a big financial hit, scale back, dispensing of anyone who is not an employee.

Well boohoo, you might think, some women have lost their jobs. So have many others. The problem is, this impacts not just the women covering sport, but the women playing it too.

All of the three articles on women's sport last Sunday were written by women. Frustratingly, we remain at a stage where it is still almost exclusively women writing about women's sport. Some notable exceptions but broadly, this is the case. Why? Meh. It's not as though men are incapable of watching women play sport or learning about it. It just isn't done enough. Nor is it encouraged by editors. Stereo-typing, lazy assumptions, cheap commissioning all at play.

So, with no sport, the (almost exclusively male) writers still with a job are writing about what they know. It's human, to revert to default. I would. But it means articles on historical stories from an age when almost all coverage was of male sport. Articles on off-field luxury lifestyles (so, male athletes), generous donations (again, only male sports stars with means to do so), big money takeovers and transfers.

So, here we are. Few women covering sport, fewer women being covered.

It's a difficult challenge with an ambitious end goal of male and female sports journalists able to report equally on male and female sport. While some male journalists consider women's sport to be 'second class' to the male equivalent and prefer to stick with covering the sports they know, other men have been hugely supportive of women's sport. I can understand, however, that some of these male journalists worry about the approach they should take. Do they fully embrace covering women's sport but risk being accused of stepping in to take opportunities from female colleagues when they perhaps aren't as familiar with the sports and players?

I remember there being much criticism of some of the very famous male rugby broadcasters brought in to commentate on the Women's Sevens at the Rio Olympics. While they were well-meaning and professional, they clearly did not have the background knowledge of the women's game, or the GB players, in the way they would have for the men's games. From a quality of coverage perspective, it would have been far better to have had pundits and commentators who were familiar with the women's game – the likes of Maggie Alphonsi or Sue Day – who had both done a great job of commentating on men's and women's rugby in the past.

It is possible for this older generation of established male sports journalists to find the right balance, though, as Rebecca Myers from *The Times* saw at the FIFA Women's World Cup in 2019. Rebecca was full of praise for the 'country's heavyweight sportswriters, mainly male and middle-aged' who descended on France to report, 'sensing a raw public appetite and dawning of a momentous new age'.

'These men have been the embodiment of the feminist phrase "male ally", highly conscious of being sent by their sports desks to "parachute in" and steal by-lines from their more junior female colleagues. Instead, they have set out to champion us, tweeting out our pieces and praising our work. They have taught us not only how to match their impressive red wine consumption, but to be prouder, more confident, and to blow our own trumpets.'

And while I absolutely believe that more women throughout sports journalism will eventually result in increased coverage for women's sport, it doesn't necessarily follow that, just because a woman is at the top, the content at the paper or station will naturally become more balanced.

A case in point is the *Mail on Sunday*. Despite having a female Sports Editor, Alison Kervin, for over a decade, no one would claim the paper is in any way a champion for the coverage of women's sport. I do wonder if this might be because, as the first female sports editor at a national newspaper, Alison was keen to establish herself as a 'traditional sports editor' and actively chose not to cover more women's sport?

This point is reinforced in the US, as Toni Bruce says in *Communication & Sport:* 'One myth that needs addressing is the claim that more women in sports journalism would create change. Evidence to date suggests that women journalists make little difference; a combination of their low numbers and the overwhelmingly "macho" habitus of sports journalism makes for complex negotiations for female journalists.'

Historically we have had great female sport reporters, but, as Toni says, there have not been enough to cause change. Resistance to them has included men assuming women wouldn't understand the game or know the rules, something Jacqui Oatley tells me was as issue she experienced:

> The biggest barrier was the mistrust of 'what on earth would she know?', 'I bet she doesn't know about our team', 'bet she couldn't have that passion'. I've actually heard these things, which are hilarious.
>
> There was a manager I interviewed after a Premier League game. I could tell he was a bit of a dinosaur even though he wasn't that old, but I could just tell he was looking through me. I was asking very fair questions. I just knew he thought what was the point and then I thought, well I'm just going to remark on a couple of his tactical changes, and he looked at me suddenly – looked me in the eye – and he said, 'You know your football, don't you,' and I just thought oh – this is pathetic. Really it was quite pathetic.

Another issue was that women were not allowed access to the male changing rooms, where male reporters would get post-match interviews with the stars of the sport.

'This is not a fight about nudity, it's a fight about power and access,' said one of the contributors to the ESPN documentary *Let Them Wear Towels* which highlights the challenges female journalists faced at this time.

In the US, it was not until 1978 that female sports journalists were allowed to enter locker rooms for interviews. Melissa Ludtke, a *Sports Illustrated* reporter, sued the New York Yankees for not letting her interview players in the locker room during the 1977 World Series and a judge ruled in her favour, saying it was in violation of the Equal Protection Clause in the 14th Amendment.

Talking about this new, post-match access to the locker room, the hugely respected award-winning British sports journalist Sue Mott, who was working in the US at the time, says: 'If the men were allowed in the locker room, so were we. It was excellent access, but I often had to keep my eyes on the ceiling.' Sue would go on to become Sports Feature Writer of the Year in 1995.

Though it was a positive outcome for female sports reporters, sadly many women were punished as a result. 'After I "broke the locker room barrier" in 1975 . . . the hate mail started. I was "a whore", a "prostitute" and women's libber!' said Robin Herman, the first female sportswriter for the *New York Times*.

Female journalists were also harassed by players and coaches who did not want them in the locker rooms with their male equivalents. Lisa Olson, a journalist who complained about being harassed in an NFL locker room in 1990, then faced such public hostility – obscene phone calls, hate mail and death threats – that she left the US for six years to work in Australia to get away from the abuse. And this was before the days of trolling on social media.

In terms of women coming into sports journalism, regrettably it does not look as if much will change anytime soon. A quick straw poll of current sports journalism courses in the UK shows that, while more women than men graduate each year with journalism degrees, when it comes to sports journalism women make up less than 5 per cent of the intake each year.

Things can also be tough after graduation when you enter the world of work, as former sports reporter Jo Tongue remembers: 'I found it really difficult going out to football clubs. Part of my job was to go to press conferences or go to football grounds to do match reports. Press boxes were very, very intimidating. I wasn't part of the male clique, wasn't part of the press pack.

'There were lots of assumptions as a woman. You'd turn up to collect your media pass and you would be directed to the catering door. Or you'd go into the press room and they'd ask: "where's the team sheet, love?", "where's the coffee?"'

Jo also recounts the sexism she experienced working in radio when she edited the BBC's flagship football phone-in 606. 'It was tough. Most of the presenters were fine with me because they knew I knew football. But there were times where I remember telling some presenters off for "banter" in the office and it didn't go down well at all. I can have a laugh outside the office, but there's certain things that I don't want in the office and it didn't go down well. I was made to feel that I was a bit of an outsider and I couldn't take it. It was personal jokes about how I looked.'

Fortunately, things have very much improved in this area, especially in recent years following campaigns such as #MeToo. 'It's changed so much,' continues Jo. 'The things that used to go on in the studio, in the workplace, when I started – you would be out immediately for stuff like that now.'

What's also changed over the decades is the presence of trailblazing women in sports media to inspire the next generation.

Julie Welch was Fleet Street's first female football reporter in 1973, and she shares many extraordinary anecdotes in her book *The Fleet Street Girls*. 'Making my first visit to White Hart Lane, the Spurs stadium, as reporter rather than a fan, I did not know where to enter the ground. I was directed to an oak-panelled hall. Spotting a door marked "Press", I pushed it open and barged in, only to be confronted by a line of my fellow reporters facing the urinals.'

She points out: 'I think we've forgotten – or are too young to have experienced – the entrenched sexism that meant it was completely normal for women to be barred from places or institutions. As the owner of a vagina, I was not allowed to join the Football

Writers' Association. This, too, was when a nice "girl" didn't go into a pub unless she was with a man.'

Asked about being a trailblazer she says: 'I feel ambivalent about the trailblazer thing because I'm being singled out. I was very matter-of-fact about it. That was my job. It was nice to be the first woman, but I was pleased when Sue Mott came along in the late 1970s for the *Sunday Times* just to be not the only one.'

Another much-respected pioneer of women's sports journalism was Vikki Orvice, who tragically died of breast cancer in February 2019. Vikki had been the first female football reporter on the staff of a tabloid newspaper in Britain. In 2016 she commented: 'I thought when I started out in tabloids in 1995, there would be a trajectory of women starting to emerge in sports writing, but it has not been the case at all. In fact, it has got worse . . . women in sports writing peaked in 2000 . . . the only females at the *Sun* are me and two secretaries.'

In the final weeks of Vikki's life, she set up an apprenticeship for a young female football reporter in her name at the *Sun*. Isabelle Barker was the first woman to take up this position and she now reports on plenty of football, including the women's game. What a fabulous legacy for Vikki to have left.

Other highly regarded female sports writers include Martha Kelner, formerly the *Guardian*'s chief sports reporter, who made the move to broadcasting and is now a sports correspondent for Sky News; Rebecca Myers at *The Times*, who is lead reporter for the *Sunday Times* Sportswomen of the Year Awards; Kate Rowan, long-established and much respected rugby reporter at the *Telegraph*; Suzy Wrack and Louise Taylor, football writers at the *Guardian*; and Fi Tomas and Molly McElwee at the *Telegraph*.

Three notable female sports writers who recently made the move from print journalism to *The Athletic*, the subscription-based sports website, are Amy Lawrence, former football writer at the *Guardian* and *Observer*; Sarah Shephard, formerly of *The Times* and *Sport* magazine; and Katie Whyatt, former football writer at the *Telegraph*.

The gender balance for sports broadcasting feels better than in print. The trailblazers in this field will be familiar to older sports fans and include Mary Raine, the first woman to cover a football match for BBC Radio *Sports Report* in the 1960s, and Sally Jones, BBC *Breakfast*'s first female sports anchor in 1986. Sally recalls how tough it was for women commentators at the time: 'If we made the slightest slip, chauvinist critics had a field day, concluding that all women must be useless sports presenters. If Steve Ryder made a blooper, no one said all men were rubbish, just that Steve was having an off-day.'

Other familiar names include the sadly departed Helen Rollason, the first female presenter of BBC's *Grandstand* in the 1990s, and the much-admired Eleanor Oldroyd. Talk to women working in sports journalism today and many will comment that they were inspired (and often supported) by the 'First Lady of Fighting Talk', BBC's Elly Oldroyd. With a career that began in commercial radio, Elly joined BBC Radio Shropshire as a Sports Producer in 1986 before joining BBC Sport in 1988. By 1995 she became the first female presenter of *Sports Report* and still hosts many weekly 5 Live shows today. In both 2014 and 2016 her brilliance was publicly recognised when she was named the Sports Journalists' Association Broadcast Presenter of the Year.

Elly was very honest when I asked her how she'd dealt with being a woman in what was a very male environment of sports media:

You had to have a thick skin. You think about the #MeToo movement now – if we'd talked about that then, I wonder whether we'd have got jobs?

I do think I've put up with things – you know – you do turn a blind eye, you do smile prettily, laugh off remarks because you don't want to make a fuss. You don't want to make a big deal about it.

You don't want to damage these fragile male egos for God's sake because you worry about your future. You worry about your job. So even though I had strong male advocates, my bosses, there were plenty of people that would have done anything to undermine me or make me feel small or just put me in my place.

In terms of TV, Sue Barker became the first female to host *A Question of Sport* in 1997. As a side note, while it's wonderful that Sue hosted 'the world's longest running TV sports quiz' for over twenty years, it's disappointing that the show has never had a female captain, apart from a guest captain appearance by Mary Peters in 1976. Perhaps that will change soon, with the announcement that this was the final series for Sue and the current captains Phil Tufnell and Matt Dawson.

In more recent years the hugely professional presenters who have become familiar faces on our screens have included the likes of Kelly Cates, Reshmin Chowdhury, Jessica Creighton, Kirsty Gallacher, Karthi Gnanasegaram, Hazel Irvine, Jacqui Oatley, Suzi Perry and Georgie Thompson.

Gabby Logan has been a particularly key figure with her superb broadcasting ability as she moves seamlessly from football to athletics or rugby union. Similarly, it's always a joy to see Clare Balding presenting, from her early days in horse racing through to the Boat Race, Wimbledon, Olympics, Paralympics and Rugby League, the last a sport that holds her in such high regard that she was recently appointed President of the RFL.

Former world-class athletes are also making names for themselves as presenters and pundits, including Isa Guha, the first female expert summariser for BBC's *Test Match Special* in 2014; Maggie Alphonsi, the first woman pundit on live men's rugby on ITV in 2015; Eniola Aluko, the first female pundit on BBC's *Match of the Day* and live men's football on ITV in 2016; and Alex Scott, the first female pundit on live Sky games in 2018.

The impact of Alex Scott has been phenomenal. Despite being repeatedly trolled on Twitter just for giving an opinion on men's football, she has remained the ultimate professional, flawless across both men's and women's football.

On radio, too, women's voices are finally being heard more. Alison Mitchell was the first woman to commentate regularly on *Test Match Special* and is Britain's leading female cricket broadcaster. A former winner of the Sports Broadcaster of the Year at the Sports Journalism Awards, she was also the first woman to commentate on international cricket for ABC Grandstand in Australia. Vicki Sparks has consistently pushed for the coverage of women's football at the BBC. She was part of the BBC's team to cover the World Cup in Russia in 2018 where she became the first ever female commentator for a live TV World Cup match.

Although the gender balance for sports broadcasting is better than in print media, women can still find it difficult to establish themselves as experts in their field. The reaction to the announcement that Jacqui Oatley was to be the first woman presenting on *Match of the Day* in 2007 showed that so much about the media's attitude to women and sport hasn't changed significantly. 'I was just a journalist and I wanted to tell the story,' Jacqui told me. 'I did not want to become part of the story and so I just wanted to seamlessly slot in, so therefore I didn't tell anyone and I just hoped it wouldn't find its way into national media.

'Unfortunately, it made its way into the *Daily Mail* on the

Tuesday before the Saturday and that's where it all started. There was this hideous build-up in which I was front-page news, back-page news. "From Motty to totty" was the headline in one paper. "Is football ready for Jacqui Oatley?" was the front page of the *Guardian*. A massive photograph on the front page of the *Telegraph* – it was enormous. I just felt this overwhelming wave of pressure and I felt extremely lonely and isolated at that time. I was single, I was living in a flat on my own, I was just practising and working the whole time. I didn't want to be a celebrity. On the contrary I really, really did not want any profile whatsoever – I just wanted to be as good a football commentator as I could.'

Does Jacqui think things are becoming more balanced for women working in the media today? 'I think it's still extremely male-dominated in local radio. I'm not too sure why, but I don't see too many women in the local radio press box or even local newspapers. So nationally broadcast wise, yes, there are a lot more women now on TV and on the radio which is absolutely brilliant, but I do worry a little bit about the supply line because really that's where you need to get your experience where there's less pressure in a regional print media and broadcast environment and you could learn from people and kick on.'

I asked Anna Kessel, Editor of Women's Sport at the *Telegraph*, about any significant moments of sexist behaviour she remembers as a young female sports reporter.

There were just so many. And at first, I was young, and there was nothing so terrible that I was traumatised by it. It was stuff that I could brush off and perhaps didn't realise really the weight of what was happening at the time. I saw it as a bit of a challenge and thought, I'll tough it out. But I think, looking back, I realise more the significance of all those – some of them were micro-aggressions as we say now.

I went to interview a couple of well-known referees and they just refused to behave and they refused to be interviewed by me on their own. They wanted to be interviewed together and then they just kind of destroyed my interview and they wanted to talk about my arse basically.

In the future Anna hopes that as well as men not acting like this, more women will feel more empowered in those situations to say 'Sorry, I'm just going to stop the interview now because you're not behaving.' She adds: 'I could have done that, but I didn't feel that I could do that. Didn't even occur to me.'

The vitriol that many female sports reporters receive from men must also be hugely off-putting to women considering journalism as a career. Social media has clearly made this worse and it seems particularly bad for women working in football. At the FIFA World Cup in 2018 there were numerous incidents recorded of fans groping, kissing or attempting to kiss female reporters. One man who shouted insults at Mexican journalist Ahtziri Cardenas while she was filming a report returned moments later and tried to grab her crotch. Another incident, widely shared across social media at the time, saw a man attempt to kiss Brazilian journalist Julia Guimaraes while she was preparing to go live for SporTV. She firmly told him: 'This is not polite. This is not right. Never do this. Never do this to a woman, OK?' and he was heard apologising in the background.

For female sports journalists in Brazil this isn't new, with more than two-thirds of female journalists saying they'd been sexually harassed on the job, according to a survey from Brazil's Investigative Journalism Association.

In 2018 the women set up a movement to call out the harassment using the hashtag #DeixaElaTrabalhar (#LetHerWork). It highlights the challenges they face working in an industry dominated by male colleagues and fans. Stories emerged of fans shouting 'prostitute' at female reporters for entire games with the authorities doing nothing to stop them. Journalist Aline Nastari says she remembers crying after one incident but did not tell anyone because she felt ashamed: 'From the moment you make it public and you feel that you're in it together, that there are a lot of people experiencing the same thing, you feel supported to fight for something. "DeixaElaTrabalhar" symbolises this. It's that moment when we're all together, we're all united.'

The women have also been working with police and prosecutors to ensure that Brazil's laws against defamation and public insult are enforced in stadiums around the country.

Something that fascinates me is why women writing or talking about sport enrages so many men. You would not generally expect to see insults on social media mocking women who present on the news, or talking about arts, medicine, travel or science, but sport generates a unique, negative reaction. It's as if men feel they 'own' sport and that women reporting on it are somehow trespassing.

When Martha Kelner was writing at the *Guardian*, she worried that social media platforms like Twitter were making things worse. 'I have been called a slag and told I don't know what I'm doing because I'm a woman. It's more common when I write about football than a sport like athletics . . . There are people in darkened rooms spoiling for a fight. We may not get more online abuse than men, but it can be more vitriolic and insulting and our gender is often the first port of call for someone sending an abusive tweet.'

In early 2021 a particularly horrible incident saw football pundit Karen Carney (a superb former professional player with 144 England caps) literally driven from Twitter by the avalanche of negativity she received from Leeds United fans. Karen had made a comment about the team's performance – part of her job as a TV pundit reporting on a match after all – and the club had clipped the comment and shared it on social media. The club's owner, Andrea Radrizzani, stoked the flames by re-sharing the tweet, saying Carney's remarks were 'completely unnecessary and disrespectful to our club'. This led to a mass of hideous, sexist trolling of Karen on social media.

I asked Ian Wright, an enthusiastic male ally for women's football and a well-known sports pundit himself, if he worried the negativity female pundits faced might put them off these roles: 'When they're on the television, if they say anything then you start seeing a stereotypical "she should be back in the kitchen" or "what's she doing here". It's horrible to see. I do feel for the ladies because they themselves have got no wiggle room. When they're on the television, they say anything wrong and they're literally taken to the cleaners. People want them cancelled and it's unfair.'

But Ian thinks things will change, especially when audiences realise how good the female pundits are: 'I was on TV with Lianne Sanderson the other day – it was a joy. She knows so much. If the men were as prepared as these women, they wouldn't get the stick the women are getting. They're more prepared than some of the blokes. They've made me up my game. When you listen to what they say, they make you have to research more. And that's what it's about. So, they shouldn't be put off by it because they're doing the work to be on there. They deserve to be on there.'

Another reason that might be putting women off from pursuing a career in sports media is the obsession from some channels with their physical appearance. Whereas male presenters are appointed for their sports knowledge, journalistic ability and skill in front of the camera, women need to have all this *and* look good in a tight dress and a pair of high heels. In 2020, it was reported that female presenters at Sky

Sports News had complained after the company sent out a survey that asked viewers to rate their appearances. The audience feedback survey gave viewers the opportunity to rate female presenters as 'sexy', 'good-looking', 'irritating', 'loveable' or 'pretentious'.

Sky vehemently deny that the women in their figure-hugging outfits on Sky Sports are there as 'window dressing' alongside their male colleagues, something that Gabby Logan claimed in 2013 when she left the station to work at the BBC. But even today, if you Google 'Sky Sports Presenters', you'll see sites for the 'Top 10 sexiest Sky Sports Presenters', 'Hottest Sky Sports Presenters Ever!' and 'Sky Sports Hotties'. Funnily enough, they're not referring to male presenters.

Elly Oldroyd reflects on how unpleasant it was for female sports presenters at sports events: 'I remember when women were first admitted to the PFA [Professional Footballers' Association] dinner and it was a really horrible atmosphere in lots of ways. It's really blokey and I remember being there with one of the very attractive female sports presenters and walking with her to the ladies' loo. I was like her wing-woman and she walked between these tables of young footballers all just leering in the most horrible way. This blokey world is changing for the better now, but throughout the nineties, and until quite recently, it was a difficult place to be in.'

Sadly, it's not just young women starting out who see gender inequality affect their careers. Anna Kessel reflects:

> I think as I got older, the stakes got higher. This was a career that I was now committing to. I got married, I started a family and I think the structural issues really kick in then. Can you be a working mum with a child? Can you be a correspondent? What about when you've got to travel the world? What about the long hours? What about breaking news stories? Can the industry accommodate working mothers?

And at the time, the answer definitely wasn't a resounding yes and it's interesting that there are still so few working mums doing the role.

What looks like a positive shift for women in sports media has been the attitude of the *Telegraph*. Both Anna, and Vicki Hodges, her deputy at the *Telegraph*, are part-time working mothers and doing a brilliant job.

———————

Another very positive sign that things might finally be changing occurred at the British Sports Journalism Awards in 2019, where, for the first time, all four key writing prizes were won by women.

One of my all-time favourite journalists, Marina Hyde from the *Guardian*, won the Sports Columnist and Sports Writer of the Year awards; Alyson Rudd at *The Times* won Sports Feature Writer of the Year; and Laura Lambert at the *Daily Mail* won the Sports Scoop prize with her colleague Matt Lawton (for their investigation revealing how Saracens had broken salary cap rules) and also won the Sports News Reporter award. Laura has since moved on to work at the BBC.

Another inaugural female win that night saw CNN anchor Christina Macfarlane named Broadcast Journalist of the Year. Christina said she was stunned to be the first woman to win this award but shared an inspiring comment on Instagram: 'for anyone who's ever experienced a serious case of imposter syndrome like me – proof – trust your instincts, follow your gut and don't take no for an answer.'

There is no doubt that the recognition of these fantastic female journalists will be a huge inspiration to younger women entering the profession today.

9

YOU CAN'T BE WHAT YOU CAN'T SEE

Athleticism in women was no longer viewed as a novelty, aberra-
tion, peculiarity of birth or threat to femininity, but simply the
fulfilment of human potential.

Ellen J. Staurowsky, 2016

One of the most satisfying elements we see with the growth of women's sport is the increased profile of amazing female athletes who are inspiring role models for women and girls. In fact, 86 per cent of girls aged eleven to twenty-one think that women in sport are good role models for young women according to the Girl-guiding Girls' Attitudes Survey 2020.

In my podcast I often ask my guests, all trailblazing women in sport, about the sporting role models they had while growing up. Many tell me that they did not have any, as so few women had any media profile at the time.

It's for this reason that Women's Sport Trust co-founder Jo Bostock says she doesn't always think the cliché 'you can't be what you can't see' is totally true, 'because somebody has to be a pioneer, break a path'.

Those pioneers aside, though, things are now changing significantly, as little girls across the world can grow up dreaming of being the next Serena Williams, Steph Houghton, Heather Knight, Sarah Hunter or Simone Biles.

One of the questions often asked is, do high-profile role models, and big sporting events, actually drive grassroots participation in sport? It's an important consideration, particularly when millions of pounds of public funds are being invested in hosting global sporting events or funding elite athletes to perform on the world stage.

Research in the past has not always shown a clear linear link between high-profile events and sporting role models. I asked Sally Munday about this. Sally was CEO at England Hockey when the GB women won gold in Rio and is now CEO at UK Sport. In her usual, very open manner, Sally says:

> There are some people that simply don't believe that the evidence is there, that international success equals more participants, and I think there are a number of sports that you could point to and say, they had success and it didn't change the dial on participation.
>
> I think if you leave it to its own devices, you're not going to change it. But if you get international success, and you *use* that to drive the visibility of the sport and *then* you make sure you've got the right interventions that are in place to make it really easy for somebody to go and pick up a hockey stick – that's what makes the difference.

Is rising up the medals table at major events important? 'I don't want us to become first on the medal table just for the sake of it. I don't want medals for medals' sake. At hockey we've always wanted medals because of what it enabled us to do to grow the sport, to grow the visibility of the game, to get more people loving our sport. And I think that's possible across a whole range of sports and if coming first on the medal table is a catalyst to enable that, then that's a fantastic thing.'

There's plenty of anecdotal evidence in the UK to suggest that witnessing elite women's sport drives increased female participation, especially the impact of major sporting events. Sally talks about how England Hockey interacted with the 630,000 people who came to watch the sport at London 2012 – half of whom probably weren't hockey players. They set up mini hockey pitches for kids to have a go as they came in to watch the games and captured contact details. Every hockey club across the country then opened its doors immediately after the games to make the sport accessible to all.

All this activity, along with the media coverage for the GB Hockey women after 2012, and then 2016, enabled hockey to double the numbers of girls playing in clubs. 'Research tells us that a lot of those young girls were inspired by watching hockey, maybe for the first time at London,' explains Sally.

Netball has also seen the impact of the England team's success, with an incredible increase in women and girls playing netball that followed England's win at the Commonwealth Games and continued through to the Vitality World Cup. A YouGov survey showed that 160,000 more British women started playing netball or played more netball because of the latter event in Liverpool in 2019. The FA experienced a similar surge, as 850,000 more women and girls started playing football after the Lionesses reached the semi-final of the World Cup in 2019.

Not all sports get it right all the time, though, when it comes to raising the profile of their female stars. When Claire Cohen from the *Telegraph* questioned the then head of marketing at England Netball, Jo Adams (now Jo Coates), about why the sport had invested in the Rose Buddies mascots in 2012 (in an article titled 'England Netball's new mascots make me want to puke') Jo told her: 'our research tells us that young girls don't identify with elite athletes. So, we've created three stylised mascots that are relevant to the things they like. They all have their own personality – for instance, one of them likes One Direction.'

Seriously? So rather than invest money and time in promoting their own incredible athletes, England Netball invested in three over-feminised mascots. With mini skirts and lots of pink. And very large heads.

As Claire Cohen concluded: 'A desire to raise the profile of netball – indeed, the profile of any sport in which women compete – is undoubtedly a good thing. But we need to get to a place where young women do look to elite athletes for inspiration. Because – far from being a gaggle of ditsy dolls, obsessed with shopping – the England women's netball team are a brainy bunch. Captain Pamela Cookey has a management degree; another is training to be a doctor; goal shooter Jo Harten has a degree in International Relations and goalkeeper Eboni Beckford-Chambers is a trainee solicitor. With such fantastic role models on the court, who needs cartoon dolls?'

I asked Jo Bostock about the importance of role models in women's sport:

> Whether it's in business, technology, science or sport, if you can see someone like you – and 'like you' might not just be your gender, it might be your social background or your ethnicity – but you see someone like you doing well, then you have evidence that it's possible.
>
> You don't have somebody saying, 'oh go on, give it a try' and you look around going, 'well, where's the proof? It doesn't seem that

anybody like me is getting on in this industry, or this sport – that looks hard.' Great role models, they're a proof point. Yes, it is absolutely possible because I've done it and you can do it too. I think they're hugely powerful.

It's important to remember that it's not just as athletes that women in sport can be powerful role models to inspire women and girls. Having more women visible as coaches and officials is also essential, as professional match official Sian Massey-Ellis told me: 'When I started I didn't know that women could be referees because there's not that many of us out there. So, the more we have out there that you can see working on the top games, the more women will come through. It's difficult to make it to the top level, but the more we have coming through at the grassroots, the more likelihood is that we will get more girls coming to the top level.'

———

When I talk to successful British sportswomen, the majority say that 'inspiring the next generation' is an absolute must for them. It does appear that for female athletes this is more of a priority than it is for men.

As I've previously mentioned, watch any women's sport event in the UK – football, rugby, netball, cricket or hockey – and at the end you'll see the female athletes spending time, in some cases hours, having selfies taken with fans, signing programmes and balls. Often in the rain. Perhaps they know what they have themselves had to overcome to get to the top in their sports when opportunities for their gender were more limited.

When it comes to being a powerful female role model, you're

unlikely to meet anyone more passionate than professional footballer-turned-professional boxer Stacey Copeland. Stacey's charity Pave the Way aims to create a world where gender is never a barrier to human potential. The charity's goals are to challenge gender stereotypes for boys, girls, men and women and work to spark a social change in attitudes so that everyone can be free to pursue their passions regardless of gender.

Stacey knows that many people struggle with boxing as a sport for men or women.

> I totally appreciate why people don't like watching it, don't like seeing it. I totally understand that. As for women boxing, it challenges society's definition of femininity almost more than any other sport.
>
> 'However, what we do know about sport, whatever form, whatever type of sport it is, is that if we see women excelling, and women portrayed in a positive light and being positive role models, it affects every other aspect of society. I know that to be true. Boxing needn't be any different.

I spoke to Lauren Steadman, a Paralympian who, along with representing ParalympicsGB at swimming and paratriathlon, also reached the semi-final of BBC's *Strictly Come Dancing* in 2018, about what it means to her to be a role model: 'What I wanted to do in my whole life, in everything I do, is inspire people and encourage them to do things that they don't think they can do because actually they can. It's just a mindset.'

It's powerful to hear Lauren talk of how things have changed for her in public. When children used to pass her in the street they would say 'Mum, that girl's got one arm.'

Now it's 'Mum, that's Lauren from *Strictly*!' And it was lovely that, all of a sudden, they didn't see it as different, it was just that Lauren was born without an arm. It wasn't unusual, and so kids see that actually there's no difference between disability and able-bodied any more.

'I think I've had so many beautiful messages. One lady messaged saying, "I've got two twin girls and we watched your first dance shown on *Strictly* where you did your waltz. And I said to them, look what Lauren's doing. There are no excuses, you girls can do anything you want to do in your life." Wow. If all I managed to achieve was just inspiring two little girls one evening, my job is done thank you.'

Lauren's comment shows that the impact of female sports role models reaches far beyond driving participation – they have the potential to inspire girls, giving them more confidence in many areas of their lives.

It's also important that our female sporting role models represent women from all backgrounds, as Maggie Alphonsi explained when I asked her about her own sporting role models: 'Growing up I would say the role model that I looked at was Denise Lewis. Back in 2000 when she won the gold medal at the Sydney Games. It was great to see someone who looked like me and came from a similar background. I knew she was from Wolverhampton, Birmingham, and I came from north London in Edmonton in quite a challenging background. To see someone like her go that far from where she came from, and then be an example for many other women, women of colour in particular. I looked up to her significantly and I still do to this day.'

I asked Maggie how it now feels to know that she is a role model inspiring young women to play rugby? 'You don't set out to be a role model. If anything, you just set out to be the best that you can be, the best version of you. And that's what I do. I go out, I played my rugby and I've played it to the best of my capability and not let anyone stop me regardless of what their perceptions may be. So being a female I wasn't going to let that stop me, being from an ethnic minority I wasn't going to let that stop me, or coming from a low social economic background, I wasn't going to let that stop me.'

A campaign that is helping more British female athletes find their voices like Denise and Maggie, is the Women's Sport Trust's Unlocked, which launched in 2019. Pairing forty-one female athletes from twenty-four sports with forty-one 'activators' from business, media and sport, the impact of the initiative is evident, with many of those involved now speaking out regularly about the issues that concern them.

So how are these amazing female sporting roles portrayed in the media? Unfortunately, often very differently from their male equivalents. I was fascinated to read more from Emma Wensing and Toni Bruce who highlight that when female athletes receive media coverage, 'extensive international research has shown that the media have historically used five techniques to represent women in line with cultural ideas about femininity'.

As I read about the five techniques, I was very aware of having seen them used in the media. Perhaps by flagging them, and calling it out, we can continue to change the way female role models are portrayed.

– In *gender marking* a gender modifier is added to a female event or team such as the Women's World Cup or England Women's Cricket Team versus the World Cup or the England Cricket Team for the men. The implication is that the women's version is inferior to the men's.

– The technique of *compulsory heterosexuality* means that journalists present female athletes as sex objects or portray them in heterosexual roles such as wife/mother/girlfriend.

– The emphasis of *appropriate femininity* focuses on traditional notions of acceptable feminine physical or emotional characteristics or behaviours.

–*Infantilisation* presents sportswomen as girls, young ladies or refers to them only by their first names, undermining their sporting achievements.

– Finally, *downplaying sport* focuses on non-sport-related aspects such as appearance, family, personal life, alternative careers and comparisons to male athletes, which demeans female performance and reinforces the idea that, for women, sports performance and success are secondary to other things, including male sporting success.

Writing more recently, Toni Bruce recognises that, while we see less of these rules being used in media coverage today, *ambivalence* remains the most common form of representation, where positive descriptions and images of women athletes are juxtaposed with descriptions and images that undermine and trivialise women's efforts and successes.

This made me think back to the cringe-worthy moment when Ada Hegerberg, the inaugural winner of the women's Ballon d'Or, was asked to twerk live on stage by the host DJ, Martin Solveig.

Hats off to Andy Murray who took to Instagram to voice his disapproval at the time: 'Another example of the ridiculous sexism that still exists in sport,' he said. 'Why do women still have to put up with that s★★t? I've been involved in sport my whole life and the level of sexism is unreal.'

Moments like these prompted the creation of the #covertheathlete campaign in 2015 with a goal to encourage the media to cover female athletes with the same professional respect that they do the men. 'Sexist commentary, inappropriate interview questions, and articles commenting on physical appearance not only trivialise a woman's accomplishments, but also send a message that a woman's value is based on her looks, not her ability – and it's much too commonplace,' said the campaign's website. 'It's time to demand media coverage that focuses on the athlete and her performance, not her hair, clothes or body.'

If you haven't seen the parody video on #covertheathlete's website created to highlight the huge gender disparity in sports coverage, I suggest you do. A reporter innocently asks Olympic swimmer Michael Phelps: 'Removing your body hair gives you an edge in the pool, but how about your love life?' He laughs and looks incredulous. Other male sports stars are asked questions about their helmet hair, figures, skimpy uniforms and one football commentator says of Wayne Rooney: 'I wonder if his dad took him aside when he was younger and told him "You're never going to be a looker, you'll never be a Beckham, so you're going to have to compensate for that"?'

It's funny until you realise these are exactly the sort of questioning and commentary that female athletes have to deal with all the time. The last comment about Rooney was a reference to John Inverdale's sexist comment on BBC's Wimbledon women's final commentary in 2013, when he questioned whether eventual winner Marion Bartoli's father had told her, when she was younger, that she was never going to be a 'looker . . . a Sharapova . . . you're never going to be 5ft 11in, you're never going to be somebody with long legs, so you have to compensate for that'.

Interestingly, Wensing and Bruce say that the media coverage of large international sporting events is less likely to be marked by gender. The 'media rules' are 'bent' when presenting international sportswomen who are representing and, more importantly, winning for the nation. Large crowds of fans displaying flags, wearing national colours and emblems, arriving with faces painted and singing national anthems 'are as easy and appropriate a setting for collective expressions of national identity as one could devise,' says Lincoln Allison in 'Sport and Nationalism', a chapter in *The Handbook of Sports Studies*. There's no doubt that the concept of our nation appears to become more 'real' in the presence of high-profile international sport.

This is certainly my impression when you consider the more positive media portrayal of England and GB women competing (and winning) at the Olympics, Paralympics, Commonwealth Games or World Championships. As our collective national identity becomes more important it overrides the usual ways in which the sports media report on female athletes. Sadly, when the women return to compete in their domestic leagues and teams the old attitudes often return. 'Nationalism trumps sexism every time,' is how Maria Bobenrieth, Executive Director of Women Win, described this phenomenon to me.

Here's hoping that in the coming years, as women's sport continues to grow, our female athletes will begin to receive more balanced media coverage year-round, not just when major, global events are taking place.

––––––––

In recent years, we've seen an enormous growth in athlete activism, especially in women's sport.

It's hard not to be in awe of the extraordinary array of strong female athlete role models dominating global sport *and* driving social change.

Global sports icon Serena Williams is not only one of the most decorated female athletes in the history of tennis, but a massive advocate for equality and motherhood. Serena has called out the inequalities in women's tennis throughout her career and, in 2019, influenced by her actions after returning from pregnancy, the WTA announced two new rule changes around women retaining their rankings and the outfits they could play in.

Following close in her footsteps is fellow tennis player Naomi Osaka, who in August 2020 brought the Western & Southern Open to a halt with her decision to stand down from her semi-final match on political grounds, alongside professionals in basketball, baseball and soccer who had postponed their matches in protest at American police brutality and racism following the shooting of Jacob Blake.

Then there is Simone Biles, one of the most successful gymnasts of all time, with fourteen World Championship and Olympic gold medals at the time of writing (the most won by any male or female gymnast in history) and an incredible four original moves named after her. She also has the most World Championship medals (twenty) won by any female gymnast.

Despite all this, Biles has remained incredibly humble about her achievements. In January 2018 she joined other brave female athletes when she released a statement confirming that former USA Gymnastics doctor Larry Nassar had sexually assaulted her. She also called out USA Gymnastics for allowing the abuse to occur and then covering it up. On 24 January 2018, Nassar was sentenced to 40–175 years in prison. Biles and the other survivors were awarded the Arthur Ashe Courage Award for speaking out.

Another courageous and much-admired role model, taking a stand on a wide array of social issues including racism, LGBTQ representation and equal pay, is US footballer Megan Rapinoe. Megan was one of the first soccer players to take a knee before games in support of the NFL's Colin Kaepernick in 2016, commenting at the time: 'Being a gay American, I know what it means to look at the flag and not have it protect all of your liberties. It was something small that I could do and something that I plan to keep doing in the future and hopefully spark some meaningful conversation around it.'

She was also one of the most outspoken of the US women's soccer team in their lawsuit against the US Soccer Federation in their fight for equal pay, telling the BBC that women 'shouldn't settle for anything less. Go for equal, go for more, don't accept any of these sort of antiquated and BS answers. Especially when it comes to sport there's been such a lack of investment for such a long period of time, so any direct comparison to the men's sports or the men's leagues is just wholly unfair. Until we have equal investment and over-investment really, because we've been so under-served for so long, we're not gonna have any sort of meaningful conversation about compensation and revenues and TV viewership.'

While we celebrate individual activists, the most powerful activism occurs when a collective unites for change. This was the case in the summer of 2020 when the WNBA dedicated the season to a narrative around social justice: all players had the name of Breonna Taylor, a black woman fatally shot by police officers in Kentucky, on the back of their shirts, 'Black Lives Matter' was visible on the floor for each game and the athletes chose only to talk about social justice issues at their press conferences.

Following the police shooting of Jacob Blake in Wisconsin, the Washington Mystics wore T-shirts with individual letters spelling out his name on the front and seven painted bullet holes on the back, a reference to how the unarmed black man was shot by police in front of his children.

'This isn't just about basketball,' said Mystics player Ariel Atkins. 'When most of us go home, we still are Black.'

Some athletes, like Natasha Cloud, the star of the Washington Mystics, even opted out of the WNBA season and gave up her salary to raise awareness for social justice issues and the fight for racial equality. Her sponsor Converse promoted her signing with her own quote: 'The biggest thing is for me to use my platform as a microphone; that's the goal, be a voice for the voiceless.' They also stepped in and covered her playing contract for the season.

I was curious to understand why we've seen so much athlete activism in the last two years and why it's women who have been so vocal. I put this question to Mary Harvey, former US Soccer player and now CEO of the Centre for Sport and Human Rights, and she answered in her usual forthright manner: 'Because we've had it, you know.'

She went on to point out that this area had also been a real unifier for men's and women's sports: 'The WNBA and the NBA, there's a lot of solidarity there. So, it's interesting. It's really cutting across. It's not us versus them. It's very much, "this is all of our problem".

'I don't know if it's cultural or it's as women. Maybe women have got to a point where we have an opportunity to say some things finally because people are now listening. We have a few things to say, and maybe it's pent up. Maybe, maybe it is we've just had it.'

Role modelling isn't just about athletes, though; it's about seeing successful women in all areas of sport.

On 2 December 2020, Stephanie Frappart became the first woman to referee a men's UEFA Champion's League match when she took charge of Juventus versus Dynamo Kyiv. In a powerful piece to camera, British sports broadcaster Kate Abdo, reporting on the UEFA Champions League for CBS Sports, questioned whether it mattered to her that Stephanie Frappart will referee a men's game on the biggest stage: 'Yes. It does. It matters to me as a woman who's looking for acceptance in men's professional sports and feeling validated by another woman being told she is amongst the best, male or female.

'It also matters to me as a woman wanting to set an example for other young girls, who love this game, and let them know that despite the fact that they may look at football's governing bodies and board rooms and not see themselves reflected, change is coming.'

Kate went on to point out that this shouldn't just matter to her because she's a woman, but that it should matter to all the fathers of daughters who want to achieve: 'not only in sport but want to achieve period. It matters that your daughters see women creating paths that will in turn make their path more walkable . . . 2020 is the year that it matters to be a girl dad.'

―――――

Storytelling is becoming ever more important, especially in an era where traditional 'match reporting' is dying out in print media. Sports stories now have more of a narrative arc, as by the time a game's being written about, most of the audience will have already seen the result or watched clips of a game.

Characters drive popularity and reach in sport and all those working in sport have a role to play in creating those female sport characters and keeping them in the public eye.

The growth of social media in the past decade means that female athletes can now *own* their media platforms.

From Instagram, Facebook and Twitter to YouTube and TikTok, female athletes are sharing content directly with their fans, by-passing the filter of the media in the process. They are attracting huge fan bases, substantially larger than the audiences they might reach via more traditional media outlets. On Instagram alone wrestler Ronda Rousey and Serena Williams each have over 13 million followers, footballer Alex Morgan has over 9 million, Indian tennis player Sania Mirza has 7 million and Simone Biles has 4 million.

The potential to monetise and mobilise this fan base is hugely powerful and something to look out for in the years ahead. Women who have been underfunded and undersponsored can now generate revenue directly for themselves and their teams. Women who have had no share of the media can now talk directly to fans. Whether earning income or driving social change, these elite female athletes are taking control of their own destinies.

Exciting times ahead.

IO

READY FOR THE BOARD GAME

The leadership and management of football, one of the most diverse games on the planet, is still controlled, fundamentally, by white men.

Dame Heather Rabbatts, November 2020

Companies that are led by diverse teams are more successful, and organisations with diverse boards have better governance and make better discussions. Diversity in an organisation also increases the talent pool, enhances productivity and innovation and improves employee retention. These are widely accepted facts in the corporate world, yet for some sports bodies, leagues and clubs, things have not really changed from the 1800s when organised sport first developed, organised for men, by men.

The world of sport has evolved, becoming more global, inclusive and commercial, yet the sports bodies themselves have been slow to modernise – perhaps unwilling to give up the power enjoyed by the few that control them. Many original leaders in the sports industry were former male athletes (when women weren't even taking part) and over time they have continued to appoint more 'people like them' and what we now consider to be an 'old boy network' has evolved across sports leadership.

In the 2015 Netflix film *Death of a Gentleman*, which depicts the corruption in world cricket, Giles Clarke, then President of the ECB, says: 'We've been involved in playing cricket and administering cricket forever.' An innocent comment perhaps, as his family have a long history of running cricket, but, in reality, it highlights a huge issue in sports governance that's finally being questioned. With many sports boards and organisations run on a voluntary basis, much of the sector has been administered by a small group who can afford to do it for free. The 'we' that Giles Clarke refers to are the white, well-off, middle-aged men.

The world is changing, though, driven in part by some shocking, high-profile governance scandals at major sports organisations in the past decade including FIFA, the FA, IAAF, the ICC, British Cycling, USA and British Gymnastics and the IOC.

I asked Jo Bostock, co-founder of the Women's Sport Trust, who also runs a leadership development business, why it's good for organisations to have a diverse and inclusive workforce:

If you want to be effective at what you do, in any kind of business, you need to have the best people giving of their best. And if you split that equation in half you need to have a great mix of people. I think talent is evenly distributed – it doesn't sit with one gender or one background – so how do you get a great bunch of people round the table?

That's your first start, but if you've got them there and then you're not giving them a chance to flourish and contribute and add value and disagree with you and bring their ideas, then you're not going to get absolutely the best performance. So, get a great mix in the room because then you have a chance of getting the right people to perform, and then create the conditions for them to give of their best, and you'll absolutely fly.

In 2016, Women in Sport published a report entitled *Trophy Women? No More Board Games*, to review the current state of equality in sports management in the UK. The then CEO Ruth Holdaway pointed out in the introduction: 'Taken at face value, the findings of this report should be cause for celebration. Following six years of research by Women in Sport into the gender diversity of sports boards, female representation on the boards of National Governing Bodies and other sports organisations funded and supported by Sport England and UK Sport is finally averaging thirty per cent. If you compare this to our first set of data in 2009, when survey findings put the proportion of women on boards at only twenty-one per cent, progress has been marked.'

Ruth went on to highlight that, despite this looking positive, further research with women and men at the top of sports organisations showed that the same barriers persisted in preventing many women from taking on leadership roles and contribute to a continued gender imbalance on boards. The result was a lack of a sustainable pipeline of female leaders rising to the top. On the ground, not much had changed and for some sports, nothing had changed.

'The next stage on the journey to equality is to mainstream and normalise senior-level female representation in sport and establish a system for recruitment and promotion based on skill, competency and meritocracy to give a fair chance to any deserving candidate,' Ruth concluded.

In 2016 there was quite a shake-up in British sport, when a new Code for Sports Governance was launched, setting out the levels of transparency, accountability and financial integrity required from anyone receiving government or National Lottery funding. The make-up of boards was a key element of this new code, with a target for all sports bodies to 'adopt a target of, and take all appropriate actions to encourage, a minimum of thirty per cent of each gender on its Board'.

For the sports bodies and organisations receiving substantial funds from Sport England who didn't have a single woman on their boards at the time, this was quite a wake-up call.

In 2019, leading sports law firm Farrer & Co. gathered data about board composition from 131 sports organisations including national governing bodies and commercial clubs. The findings were fascinating.

First the good news: across the fifty-seven national governing bodies they found an average of 35 per cent of the board members were female and that 72 per cent of the sports bodies had met the 30 per cent target. In addition, 37 per cent had a woman in a leadership position on the board. Evidently the Code for Sports Governance was having the desired impact.

The three largest participation sports, football, cricket and rugby, which had all seen considerable growth and success in their women's games in recent years, were all hitting around the 30 per cent mark. The FA led the way with four female members on a board of ten, the ECB had four out of twelve and the RFU had four out of fourteen.

This is especially good when compared to what is happening at the same time in Northern Ireland. In the summer of 2020, it was revealed that Northern Ireland's three main sporting bodies – the Irish FA, Ulster GAA and Ulster Rugby – have only one female each on their highest decision-making committees. Just three out of thirty-six positions were held by women.

Stating the blindingly obvious, Carál Ní Chuilín, the Department for Communities Minister in the Northern Ireland Assembly, said: 'It is clear there is more work to be done with governing bodies to provide opportunities for females to be appointed to the boards of the major sporting organisations.'

Reacting to the figures, Sport NI, responsible for the development of sport in the region, said it 'encourages' the appointment of more independent external members, but it's clear that verbal 'encouragement' will never be enough to drive structural change. It took the potential loss of funding from Sport England to drive many of the governance changes from the FA, RFU and ECB. Once again, money talks.

The results from the commercial clubs in the UK – over which Sport England had no financial influence – showed a very different and disappointing picture. In a sample that included clubs from the football Premier and Championship Leagues, the Rugby Premiership and the county cricket clubs, the average for board positions held by women was just 8 per cent. In fact, only 3 per cent of commercial clubs met the 30 per cent target.

In the Premier League in 2019, only one of its twenty clubs met the 30 per cent threshold and eleven clubs had no women on their boards. Not one. No women were on the boards of Arsenal, Manchester City or Liverpool, yet ironically the first two clubs mentioned are at the forefront of driving the women's professional game. How can a football club like Manchester City be taken seriously in its huge campaign to promote gender equality – Same City, Same Passion – when it doesn't have a single woman on its board? The picture in the Championship is even worse, where no club met the 30 per cent threshold and eighteen of the twenty-four clubs had no women on their boards.

In rugby union it was a similar picture with only one Premiership club meeting the 30 per cent threshold – kudos to Exeter

Chiefs who hit 50 per cent with four female board members on a board of eight. Harlequins were close, with 25 per cent female representation, but despite these two positives, across the twelve clubs the average representation of women on boards was 10 per cent. It is especially disappointing to see a club like Saracens, who were pioneers for the women's game when they established a women's team back in 1989, without a single woman on its board. Perhaps some more diverse thinking could have helped them through the decision-making around spending caps in recent years?

As you may imagine, the picture in county cricket clubs, considered by many to be the preserve of male dominance, is the worst of all. Across all the 193 board or committee positions, women make up less than 10 per cent. In fact, representation of women on boards is below 20 per cent at every club. Male decision-makers in cricket clearly feel women in the sport are better suited to making teas in the pavilion.

In total, 53 per cent of professional clubs in football, cricket and rugby have no women on boards and just 3 per cent meet the 30 per cent target.

It's the same with many global sports bodies. In 2000 the International Olympic Committee set targets of 20 per cent for women in sports leadership, yet by 2016 the average across all Olympic Committees was still only 9 per cent. Worse still, women represented only 5.7 per cent of International Federation presidents, 12.2 per cent of vice-presidents and just 13.1 per cent of committee members.

Aside from the issues of equality of opportunity and respect for women, you would think that the commercial benefits of a diverse board might appeal to those heading these sports. Studies from respected organisations such as McKinsey and Harvard Business School show that diverse boards make better decisions and are generally 10–15 per cent more profitable. Who would not want to be at least 10 per cent more profitable?

If the national governing bodies of sports like football, rugby and cricket see women as integral to the ongoing growth of their sports, then surely they recognise that it makes good sense to have more women at the top table? Similarly, if the clubs are hoping to develop strong, successful women's sides, the female representation on their boards is more than a statement of intent; it will help them achieve these goals with the viewpoint of women included in the biggest decisions for clubs.

Having a diverse board also improves the management of risk – you don't have people with the same backgrounds and opinions reinforcing decisions. There is much risk for commercial sports organisations right now – do they really believe that only men have the answers? As Tom Bruce from Farrer & Co. points out: 'Gender diversity and good governance go hand in hand. Increasing the number of women on boards is by no means a guarantee of a well-governed organisation, but it is one of the fundamental building blocks.'

Along with better governance, identifying risks and capitalising on opportunities, a gender-balanced board at the top of an organisation has also been shown to have a significant impact on the entire organisation in terms of staff recruitment, grassroots activity, marketing, advertising and the structure of competitions.

These patterns are very similar across the world. A 2016 global study on sports governance included an audit of gender ratio on boards of national sport organisations in forty-five countries. The findings show that women remain under-represented in three key areas: as board directors (19.7 per cent), board chairs (10.8 per cent) and chief executives (16.3 per cent).

Few countries have achieved the critical mass of 30 per cent representation and no continent has achieved the critical mass on any of the three indicators.

In Australia, the approach to encourage gender diversity on boards is 40:40:20. Boards need to have 40 per cent male, 40 per cent female and then 20 per cent of either gender. As a result of this, and the adoption of FIFA's 2016 gender reforms, in 2020 it was announced that Football Federation Australia had become one of very few international federations to have a 50/50 gender-balanced board. Certainly something to celebrate.

One Australian who knows all about the impact of gender reform on sports is Moya Dodd, one of the most respected women in global sports governance. I asked Moya how it felt to be one of the first women on the FIFA Council in 2013: 'It was fascinating. We were the first three women on that board in a hundred and eight years of FIFA. You got to go inside and see what it had become in those hundred and eight years.'

One of the first bits of advice Moya was given by one of the members was to say nothing in board meetings (although she imagines men who joined had been given the same advice to ensure political survival). Her interpretation was: 'Make yourself a small target and say nothing. Just be polite, small, open doors for people, come, go, don't be a spectacle.'

Moya decided that she:

hadn't come to be one of the first three women in a hundred and eight years to not say anything. I felt it was important that they got used to hearing women's voices in the room. To hear a woman speak. So, I decided at that point that I would speak at every meeting, and I would pick my topic carefully – you can't speak too often or for too long because people will find that annoying and will turn off.

It really was an environment that was quite unused to having too much diversity of thought. Diversity is important to decision-making because diverse groups just make better decisions. It is not just gender diversity that is important, it is diversity of many dimensions, but in an organisation that had actively excluded women for so long I felt gender diversity was really important and I hadn't come to sit and be silent.

Another impressive woman making waves in a very male-dominated sport is Clare Connor, former international cricketer and now Managing Director of Women's Cricket at the ECB. As mentioned in my Twelve Game-Changing Moments, in October 2021 Clare will become the first female President of Marylebone Cricket Club.

I was interested to know how she has learned to operate as a woman in such a predominantly male environment after thirteen years at the governing body: 'It's not easy. I think you learn a lot about yourself that leads to analysis about your character, how you are going to approach things. I might feel so angry or so emotional about something, and I'm not saying that can't happen in other environments regardless of gender, but it's been fascinating to reflect on how you do handle each situation. One thing is certainly presenting to the board; when the board used to be virtually all male and sort of presiding over a very male sport, it's about recognising that you've got to be really well prepared.'

This is something I often hear from senior women in sport. To be considered on a level with your male colleagues you must know even more than they do and be better briefed and prepared for meetings.

'You find a way to manage, and sometimes showing some emotion is good and sometimes it isn't. You learn how to let that manifest and when to try and suppress it. You learn when you need to be patient and when something just isn't acceptable. So, there are times when patience and the long game is what you're playing and there are sometimes when, no, this isn't OK, and you can't let something go.'

For some sports it appears to be one step forward and one back as they make strides for better female equality only to lapse into more traditional approaches. A case in point is World Rugby, who appear to have been at the forefront of driving more inclusivity across the organisation.

Katie Sadleir, General Manager of Women's Rugby at World Rugby, laughed when I asked her about how, when she'd joined, she'd been told there was no way World Rugby would ever allow women on its council. She'd arrived in an organisation where 27 per cent of the players globally were women, and yet they were governed by a board of thirty men. She thought at the time 'OK. So, there are some big changes about to happen around here.'

Katie gives full credit to the men involved in World Rugby who realised:

you can't say that you want to be world leading in sport and then not be committed to international best practice. We needed to do something significant and impactful early on if we were going to drive the transformation that needed to happen around the globe.

On the day that they signed off on the eight-year strategy, we changed the governance structure of World Rugby and brought on seventeen new woman directors. So, from zero to thirty-six per cent. Just. Like. That.

So when people say things like that can't happen, they certainly can happen.

And yet, just a few months later, in May 2020, World Rugby announced its new executive committee, and, for the second, successive term, Angela Ruggiero was the only woman on a twelve-strong board. This lack of diversity was beautifully highlighted on social media with a tweet from Alison Donnelly, the founder of Scrumqueens, who pointed out there were 'more Bretts' than women on the committee.

Fiona Hathorn, the CEO of Women on Boards, reflected: 'If World Rugby understood the benefits of diversity, they would have at least thirty per cent of their board seats taken by women. By announcing only one woman on its board, World Rugby are sending a clear message to rugby boards across the world that women don't matter as regards governance and strategic decision-making.'

I'm told to expect some significant, positive changes soon, when Hugh Robertson's independent governance review is published. First on the list of issues to be considered is 'gender balance and diversity on World Rugby boards and committees'.

FIFA, too, despite some changes to improve the gender balance in its council, still has a long way to go before the voices of women in the game are truly represented at the very top of the sport. As Moya Dodd points out: 'The electoral system at the moment is not optimal. I think that as a "quota" in those roles, it's your job to represent people who are not otherwise represented. The current electoral system doesn't really enable that to happen, because the same people who vote for "all the men", are the ones who are selecting the woman who will go to FIFA from that confederation.

'If you ask the women in football, the ones who are supposed to be being represented, who they would like, you might get a different answer. But they're not asked.'

Despite these issues, it does feel like the gender balance on major sports boards is in a much better position than it was even a decade ago; for instance, the number of women sitting on UEFA boards has increased by 50 per cent since 2019.

You're also less likely to have a Chair or CEO appoint a new board member on the basis of him being 'someone I know personally who can do that job' and more likely to see sports undertaking a rigorous, transparent, open, public recruitment process. As it should be. The running of sports is becoming ever more commercial, so the competition to find the very best people increases. Doubling the pool to recruit from must surely be an advantage.

In the summer of 2020, UK Sport and Sport England announced the first joint review of the Code for Sports Governance, identifying areas where the Code would benefit from further development. Responding to a heightened debate around racial equality in 2020, a significant focus will be the elements of the Code that support equality, diversity and inclusion – aimed at ensuring greater representation of those from ethnically diverse backgrounds, those with a disability or long-term health condition and female representation on sporting boards.

As Tim Hollingsworth, Chief Executive of Sport England, pointed out:

> The Code for Sports Governance has undoubtedly pushed the standard of sports governance to a new level and been an amazing tool for reform, particularly where bringing about greater gender parity is concerned.
>
> However, we are more aware than ever of the work that remains to be done, particularly where equality and diversity at Board and leadership level is concerned.
>
> 'With Black, Asian and Minority Ethnic numbers at Board and

leadership levels quite rightly in the spotlight at the moment, this must not be another false dawn for addressing the racial inequalities that exist within sport, and the review of the Code for Sports Governance will serve as one of the key pieces of work on this front.

Research by UK Sport and Sport England in 2019 had found that ethnically diverse people accounted for just 5.2 per cent of board members across their 130 funded organisations. More concerning was that across the major sports there was just one female Black board member, Anne Wafula Strike, from UK Athletics.

I asked Jane Purdon, a co-author of the original Code at UK Sport, and now CEO at Women in Football, if she felt the 40:40:20 governance goal for boards in Australia would have been a better target for UK Sport and Sport England back in 2016.

'I think there's a couple of things about targets looking back. I think thirty per cent was for the time, but I prefer 40:40:20 now. The bit that the Code didn't get right was on ethnic diversity . . . I think we've got to be honest, it didn't work to shift the dial enough on getting more Black and Asian people onto the boards of British sports. So, I'm very pleased it's being reviewed.'

Tanni Grey-Thompson, who won eleven Paralympic gold medals for Britain and now sits as an independent peer in the House of Lords is, as always, forthright in her opinions: '. . . we have a lack of female coaches, lack of women in leadership roles in sport, lack of female agents and the cycle perpetuates.'

I asked Tanni if she feels things are beginning to look more positive:

I do speak to more women who want to come into sport, into the admin side. I think sometimes it's hard to get your foot in the door and it's hard to challenge some of the stereotypes that exist, but this is where I think sport shouldn't think of itself as different. If businesses must have 50/50 representation on the Board, sport should be the same. And I take quite a harsh view. You know, governing bodies have had a long time to do that, lots of public money. Just do it.

We need to do more, to have more women in leadership. I think for a lot of female athletes it's hard to know what to do as they transition. There's more we can do around to help them get some more of those skills, so when they transition out of elite sport, they do have options. Because I don't want to be looking around boardrooms and be the only disabled person in the room, or the only disabled woman, or the only woman. And that is changing, but I'd just like it to be a bit quicker.

———

For all the positive changes we've seen in the governance of sport in Britain, on 10 November 2020 there was a collective sigh of frustration and disappointment, when Greg Clarke, Chair of the FA, appeared before the DCMS Select Committee to talk about the state of football.

His racially offensive, sexist and homophobic remarks were especially embarrassing for the FA, as they'd launched their Football Diversity Leadership Code just two weeks earlier. The powerful video that accompanied the launch included soundbites that seemed hollow following the comments of the FA Chair: 'Football has been great at campaigning for change, but now we need to drive that change from within.' 'We have to fight discrimination on and off the pitch.' 'We know we have diversity on the pitch, but we need to do more off it.'

Greg Clarke's subsequent resignation means that one of the

highest-profile and most influential roles in British sport is now vacant. It will be fascinating to see who is appointed and the message this sends to other sports bodies.

———

One positive to take from the Greg Clarke incident was the huge, instant reaction from the sports sector and general public – united in collectively recognising that comments like this are completely unacceptable. Similar public outrage followed the sexist remarks of eighty-three-year-old Yoshiro Mori, then head of the Tokyo Olympics organising committee who, in early 2021, reportedly commented: 'If we increase the number of female board members, we have to make sure their speaking time is restricted somewhat, as they have difficulty finishing, which is annoying. We have about seven women at the organising committee, but everyone understands their place.'

Japan's Olympic Minister Seiko Hashimoto said she wanted to hold 'thorough discussions' with Mr Mori, who was formerly Japanese Prime Minister, reflecting: 'The Olympics' fundamental principle is to promote women's advancement in sport at all levels and organisations in order to realise gender equality.'

———

In a drive to ensure better gender balance on sports boards, I personally always make an effort to encourage more women to step forward and apply to be trustees or non-executive directors. The more women we see in senior roles, the more it will encourage others to follow.

I have loved being a non-executive director on a number of boards, but, like many women, had impostor syndrome when I was invited to apply to be Chair of Get Berkshire Active, an Active Partnership. We hear so much about impostor syndrome, that belief that you don't have the necessary experience or skills for a role, and this perpetuates self-limiting behaviour. Women talk themselves out of applying for roles, which then reduces the pool of potential female applicants for senior leadership and board roles. In my case, it took the encouragement of others – women and men I knew in the sector – to persuade me I could do the job and now I feel it is my turn to persuade other women to do the same.

I was worried that I did not have the skills or manner needed to be a board Chair, which was primarily based on what I had seen myself in the past. Once in the role, I soon realised that I did not need to behave in a 'typically male' fashion – stridently taking decisions or being confrontational. I was able to be a Chair who fully supported the CEO and executive team, working in a sensitive and collaborative manner; listening to others and supporting decisions rather than needing to display my personal authority or superiority. I could lead and inspire in a fashion that worked for me *and* the organisation.

In examining gender stereotypes in the workplace, Madeline Heilman, a psychology professor at New York University, explains that bias against women in leadership is often perpetuated because typical leadership is more closely aligned to male traits and behaviours. Women are therefore seen as not capable of being successful leaders, and when they are and 'demonstrate those traits necessary to be successful leaders, they face the double bind of acting outside expectations and not being liked for doing so'.

In November 2020 Kim Ng became the first female general manager in Major League Baseball history after being employed by the Miami Marlins. At fifty-one, she had thirty years' experience in the major leagues but told the media: 'When I got into this business, it seemed unlikely a woman would lead a major league team. But I am dogged in the pursuit of my goals.'

I'd like to believe that high-profile appointments like this might signal the start of more women taking leadership roles in predominantly male-run sports. It's disappointing, though, to then look across at the US National Football League, where Susan Spencer, who took over the role at the Philadelphia Eagles in 1984, remains the only female general manager in the sport's history.

Perhaps in the future we'll see more sports following the route of the Japan Football Association (JFA) who have recently announced plans for the country's first professional women's soccer league in 2021/22. For clubs to compete in the new-look Women Empowerment League (WE League), more than 50 per cent of the club's executives and staff must be female.

Tashima Kozo, the JFA President, boldly said he hoped the new league would encourage greater female representation in Japanese football and provide a platform for gender equality and wider business opportunities: 'How we contribute to society through sports is an important mission for all of us in the sports world. We will work on establishing the career of women's professional footballer, which is the dream of many girls, and further promote women's empowerment and solve social issues.'

11

HE FOR SHE

It is by standing up for the rights of girls and women that we truly measure up as men.

Desmond Tutu, South African cleric and theologian

This book charts the unstoppable rise of women's sport, with many trailblazing, game-changing women leading the charge, but ultimately, having men onside will be essential if true equality in sport is ever to be achieved.

For the last 150 years, men have held the power in sport, whether that's making governance decisions in sports organisations, bringing money to the table as sponsors and investors or deciding what gets covered in the media. As women have discovered in many battles for equality throughout the decades, we can be hugely effective at creating change, but having men backing our cause can have an enormous impact, too.

In researching male allies in sport, I found the concept of a 'continuum of allyship' fascinating.

At one end of the scale there are those men who absolutely appreciate why gender equality in sport is good for everyone and are happy to throw their weight behind positive change in this area – to be vocal and use their influence.

Then there are men who respect women in positions of leadership, are not sexist in their behaviour and would not preclude women from opportunities, but they are unlikely to call others out or question the system.

Next are men who are just happy with the way things are, who don't want to rock the boat and think that men probably do a better job at most things than women.

Finally, at the other end of the spectrum, are what might have been known as the 'male, pale and stale brigade', the men who strongly feel that sport is a male domain and women should be excluded and prevented from progress and influence.

In any talk of male allies for women's sport the first person who often springs to mind is Andy Murray, who has constantly used his profile to publicly call out sexism when he sees it in sport.

One of my favourite clips, which received worldwide coverage at the time, is from Wimbledon in 2017. Andy has just been defeated in the quarter-final by American player Sam Querrey and is in the post-match press conference with a bank of microphones before him. A reporter wants to know what this might mean for US tennis.

'Andy, Sam is the first US player to reach a major semi-final since 2009. How would you describe . . .'

'Male player,' says Andy under his breath.

'I beg your pardon?'

'Male player, right?'

'Yes, first male player. That's for sure.'

The nervous chuckling and mutters of acknowledgement you can hear in the room are incredibly powerful. As is the fact that

Andy does not smile or offer any sympathy to the journalist for his faux pas. Judy Murray tweeted the clip that evening with the words 'That's my boy' and a heart emoji. Wonderful stuff.

Talking of casually sexist journalists, at the Rio Olympics in 2016, Murray was interviewed by broadcaster John Inverdale, who congratulated the tennis player on becoming 'the first person ever to win two Olympic tennis gold medals'. With more good humour on this occasion (he had just won Olympic gold, after all) Murray corrects Inverdale, pointing out that both Serena and Venus Williams had achieved the feat before him. 'I think Venus and Serena have won about four each,' he laughs.

In 2014, Andy chose former world number one Amélie Mauresmo to be his new coach. He said at the time: 'When I was young, every coach around me was a man. Every single one. I just looked at the positives Amélie could bring, and I couldn't see any negatives at all. Amélie was the best in the world at what she did, and whether you're a man or a woman, or in any sport or job, that's an incredibly difficult thing to do. You have to have amazing qualities to do that.'

Despite this support, Amélie received lots of sexist comments, with Australian tennis player Marinko Matosevic saying it was just a 'politically correct' decision, adding: 'Someone's got to give it a go. It won't be me.'

Andy responded with a column in *L'Équipe*, the French sports paper, where he defended his coach and declared himself a feminist. He pointed out that his former male coaches had never had to deal with the kind of scrutiny Mauresmo received, which wasn't right. 'Have I become a feminist? Well, if being a feminist is about fighting so that a woman is treated like a man then, yes, I suppose I have,' he wrote.

In a piece for the BBC in 2017 he explained: 'I've never set out to be spokesperson for women's equality. Inequality is something I started to see and become passionate about. It's opened my mind. I've actually become very passionate about getting more women in sport, giving women more opportunities.

'When I was younger, I wasn't thinking about stuff like that. But now I've seen it with my own eyes, it's quite amazing how few female coaches there are across sport.' And on top female tennis players' commitment to the sport: 'they make those same sacrifices and are as determined and committed to winning as any of the top men on the tour.'

I asked Judy Murray about her son's consistent comments and she told me: 'It makes such a big impact when he does, or when *a man* speaks out on behalf of the women. It makes much more impact than when one of the top *women* does it. Sadly, that is just the case.'

High-profile men calling out the sexism they see in sport can have a massive impact. In 2019, when Manchester City manager Pep Guardiola was interviewed ahead of a big game the journalist said: 'Tomorrow you've got the prospect of winning the first ever domestic treble in this country.'

'Men's,' Guardiola said immediately.

The reporter just continued: 'How much does that prospect of making history excite you?'

Guardiola smiled and took a breath. 'The first-time men's. Women. They won it.'

Sometimes simply giving women's sport airtime and profile can be a hugely powerful role of a male ally. When David Beckham took his daughter Harper to watch England Women, Alex Scott wrote in the *Sun*:

David Beckham took Harper to watch England in the Women's World Cup because he wanted to support Lionesses . . . not for a PR stunt. We all want to see dads at football with their daughters. And seeing David Beckham high fiving his seven-year-old Harper in the stands at Stade Océane on Thursday was so powerful. It normalises it. Beckham was there because he wanted to be, not because there was someone in his ear telling him to go. He already gets the connection with women's football. I remember meeting him while I was playing for Team GB and he would often send us good-luck messages.

The same goes for Ian Wright. We had lunch together yesterday and he's out here in France because he wants to support the Lionesses, too.

In the US, one of the highest-profile male allies for female sport was former LA Laker Kobe Bryant. His advocacy and support for future and current WNBA athletes was much celebrated in the wake of his death in January 2020. It was very common to see the five-time NBA champion sitting courtside at WNBA games with his young daughter Gianna, who also aspired to play professionally, but so tragically died in the same helicopter accident as her dad and seven others.

What Bryant did most powerfully was to give credence to the women's game. He created interest, making male sports fans curious to know why an all-time NBA star found so much joy and pleasure in women's basketball. He spent time with WNBA players and treated them as equals. He would casually mention them in media interviews and on his Twitter and Instagram feeds, which prompted fans to want to find out more about these world-class athletes.

It makes you think how powerful it would be if more high-profile Premiership footballers publicly supported the women's game and called out some of those trolls on social media.

Some male allies have chosen to do even more than calling out the sexism they see and championing women's sport – they have also helped fund it.

During the summer of 2020, when it became apparent that professional women's golf was going to suffer more than men's in the lockdown, Liz Young, a veteran of the Ladies' European Tour, decided to set up her own tournament on her course, Brokenhurst Manor. Working with Liz to build on this idea, professional golfer Justin Rose established the Justin Rose Ladies Series with his wife Kate. Their management company, Excel Sports, ran the two-month mini tour with seven tournaments for British female professionals, and they each put in £35,000 of their own money for prize funds.

'I am keenly aware that I now have the opportunity to go back to work and compete on the PGA Tour, but this is not the same for the ladies and some junior tours as well,' Rose told the *Telegraph*. 'I am sad that the Ladies European Tour has been suffering so badly and doesn't really have a start date yet from what I know. To me this seems somewhat unfair.

'My wife Kate and I felt there was an opportunity to step up and help. The prize money is modest because it is me throwing in some money and then the ladies are paying an entry fee and being able to play for a pot. We wanted to give them the opportunity to play and to be ready for when the opportunities arise later in the summer.'

Following Justin's support, other partners came on board, with American Golf and Computacenter contributing funding and Sky Sports agreeing to broadcast the series.

Formula 1 has long been seen as a traditional boys' club, with Bernie Ecclestone, the former CEO, dismissive of female drivers, once saying women 'should be dressed in white like all the other domestic appliances'. Fortunately, attitudes are now changing. Step forward former Formula 1 Grand Prix winner David Coulthard, a male ally who is making a huge contribution.

Coulthard is the advisory Board Chairman and consultant for the W Series, a ground-breaking racing series for women that launched in October 2019. The goal of the W Series is to 'shake up the industry, push aside stereotypes and change the face of motorsport'.

Believing that women can compete equally with men in motorsport, the organisers felt that an all-female series was required first to ensure greater female participation. In its first season the W Series provided identical F3 cars for eighteen female drivers who had all passed a rigorous pre-selection programme. The drivers from across the world competed on six European circuits, with the series broadcast on Channel 4 in the UK.

Coulthard has very publicly declared his unwavering support for the W Series, saying: 'I personally want to bring more women into motorsport. My sister raced, she was very good but didn't get the support because my family were supporting me and I regret that, so I want to be part of this to help support female talent and bring more women into motorsport.

'If they're good enough, they'll go to Formula 1. If they're merely good – and good is [still] good! – then they'll be in touring cars, sportscars and many other championships.'

Following the announcement that in 2021 the W Series would feature as support races for eight Formula 1 Grand Prix weekends, another male ally stepped forward. Lewis Hamilton told the BBC that this link-up was crucial to improving diversity in the sport:

When we talk about diversity, people often think we're talking about having more people of colour. It is not just that. It is having more women involved. It is a male-dominated sport and that does need to change.

I remember racing on the way up and seeing less than a handful of girls coming through. I spoke to a couple of them and knowing how difficult it was. I raced with Susie [Wolff], who was such a great talent and saw how tough it was for her in what was perceived as a man's sport.

The sport does need to do more and that is a good step in the right direction, but it needs to transcend all the way down to karting. There need to be more girls in karting with more opportunity to make their way up to that class.

They need to do more to make sure the young girls out there know it is a possible career path. And hopefully that's what W Series is going to do.

———

High-profile male athletes with influence and reach can have an immense impact in shifting the language and perception of women in sport, but it's key that male allies exist across the entire sporting landscape.

While there's a big debate to be had about parachuting men into management roles in women's sport, and how this negatively impacts the opportunities for women, there's no doubt that it can also help bring increased credibility and much-needed profile to women's sport.

Whatever your opinion of Phil Neville's appointment as manager of the Lionesses in January 2018 (and there certainly are lots of opinions), when the FA chose a well-known male professional footballer for the role, they ensured that women's football would be taken more seriously by men. We might not like that fact, but it's true.

Men in these roles can use their influence to redress the balance of gender equality. Another man leading an England women's team was Mark Robinson, the former coach of the England women's cricket team. Interviewed about his role as a man managing women, for the NatWest podcast *Championing Women's Voices*, he recalled that when England's cricket teams travelled to compete in the World T20 in India in 2016, the men flew business class while the women's squad sat in economy. The International Cricket Council had decided to pay for better seats only for the men. The following year, the England women joined their male counterparts in business class.

'Sometimes it just needs somebody else to raise the bar and shame people,' he said before sharing his shock at the inequalities faced by women cricketers when he first became coach in 2015. Kit that they received from sponsors did not fit as it was made for men. 'The shorts looked dreadful. Managers at the England and Wales Cricket Board shrugged it off. But I kicked off. That's the male ally role. If you want to create equality and respect, you need to see the world from a woman's point of view.'

Men at the very top of a sport have great power to change the game for women. The WNBA became the world's most successful women's sports league because of the likes of NBA Commissioner David Stern, who sadly died in 2020. Stern recognised the commercial potential of women's basketball and worked incredibly hard to ensure the growth and success of the WNBA, which has continued to flourish in a world where many professional women's sports leagues have failed.

Val Ackerman, the WNBA's first President, who I was lucky enough to meet at a Leaders Conference at Twickenham Stadium in 2019, said that 'the two most important figures of the second half of the twentieth century when it came to advancing and empowering female athletes were Billie Jean King . . . and David Stern'.

After Stern's retirement in 2014, Val told ESPN: 'Without his vision and engagement, the league wouldn't have gotten off the ground. He was the mastermind, and the WNBA was really in line with his vision about how sports and society are intertwined.'

The current WNBA President, Cathy Engelbert, echoed those sentiments as she commented on how saddened the organisation was by his death: 'The WNBA will be forever grateful for his exemplary leadership and vision that led to the founding of our league. His steadfast commitment to women's sports was ahead of its time and has provided countless opportunities for women and young girls who aspire to play basketball.'

Similarly, in rugby, Sir Bill Beaumont, reappointed Chair of World Rugby in 2020, has had a significant impact on the gender balance at the very top of the game and this is now filtering down to the entire sport.

Before 2017 there were no women on the global governing body's council. It was Beaumont who added the seventeen additional female posts on the World Rugby council, leading the way with such a significant change to its set-up, the first of any major sporting federation. They told unions and regions that they could have an extra seat at the council if the new member was female.

Beaumont has also been the public face of male support for women in the game. He was front and centre at World Rugby's launch of the Women in Rugby #TryAndStopUs campaign in 2019 and was also very vocal when the sport announced a move to gender-neutral titles for major events, with what was the Women's Rugby World Cup now to be known as the Rugby World Cup.

———————

It is not just those at the very top of elite sports who can have a significant impact. I have been lucky enough to meet some fantastic male allies throughout my career. Men who are happy to stand up and shout about women's sport. Who recognise that a world where women's sport thrives is better for everyone. These would include men like Tim Hollingsworth, the Chief Executive of Sport England, Brett Nicholls, CEO of Get Berkshire Active and the male trustees of the Women's Sport Trust: Tim Cozze-Young, Chris Hurst, Michael Inpong and Ben Smith.

Misha Sher, VP of Sport and Entertainment at Mediacom, has been hugely vocal about the potential for women's sport. Supportive on a very practical level, he has promoted the female athletes he represents, such as footballer Eni Aluko, and brokered deals in women's sport including Boots' sponsorship of the women's national football teams of every country in the UK and in Ireland.

Harlequins Rugby Club's passion for ensuring equality for their female team has been impressive to see – from the shared training facilities and coaches through to the women receiving equal billing in marketing materials and on signage around the Stoop. This comes from the very top of the club, with owner Charles Jillings recognising the importance of the women's game and his commitment to equality filtering down throughout the club.

Other male allies in women's rugby include Johnnie Hammond, the voice behind the *Women's Rugby Pod* podcast (with co-host Rachael Burford), rugby pundit Ugo Monye, commentator

Nick Heath, Premiership Rugby's Paul Morgan, a former editor of *Rugby World* magazine who has been a massive ally, supporting and reporting on the women's game from its earliest days in the 1990s, and Stephen Jones, Rugby Correspondent at the *Sunday Times*, appointed Director of Women's Rugby at my local club in Maidenhead in early 2021.

Male broadcasters can do much to reinforce the credibility of female sport, something that Brian Moore has always done on his *Full Contact* podcast, which regularly features female players and reports on the women's game. Will Greenwood and Rupert Cox also show great support for female players on *Will Greenwood's Rugby Podcast*.

Other men leading the way in bringing big-brand sponsorship into women's sport include Tom Corbett at Barclays and Nick Read, Kenneth Kropman and Neville Koopowitz at Vitality.

These are just some of the men I have come across in my own work, but there are thousands of others doing incredible work to drive equality, sometimes very much under the radar.

Having male allies in sports media also has a powerful impact. It was Adam Sills, Head of Sport at the *Telegraph*, who worked so hard to create Telegraph Women's Sport. As Anna Kessel, Women's Sport Editor, said:

> Everything I've asked of Adam he's said yes to. He's been an incredible boss. It was his idea. He spent eighteen months bringing this together. Finding the finance for it, getting backing from the company. He did that incredibly difficult groundwork which nobody could see, so he wasn't getting any thanks or praise.
>
> I turned up on the day that we launched it, it was my first day, stood on the stage and everyone went, this is wonderful! And I

hadn't done anything at that point. It just goes to show that when you invest in something, and you put the time into it, you care more about it. That's why it's important not just to leave that work to women but for everybody to get involved.

In terms of broadcasting, too, there are men like the BBC's Adam Mountford, working quietly behind the scenes for decades to ensure the BBC's cricket coverage now includes a host of superb female voices including Elly Oldroyd, Ebony Rainford-Brent, Alison Mitchell and Isa Guha. And former professional footballer Ian Wright, who has emerged as a very vocal supporter of women's football, both as a pundit and through his social media accounts.

It was a *Daily Record* journalist, Stan Shivas, who propelled a young Rose Reilly to a professional career in Europe. Rose told me that she used to read the back pages of her dad's newspaper and dream about Real Madrid and whether they might have women's professional teams. She saw the name of the journalist Stan Shivas who wrote the articles for the national newspaper and headed off to meet him. Unannounced. She was just sixteen.

> I went to the offices up in Glasgow, gigantic offices, and the secretary said: 'Can I help you?' and I said 'Yes, I have to speak to Stan Shivas.' She asked if I had an appointment and I said yes, which I hadn't. She took me to his office and there was this sophisticated gentleman, smoking a cigar, and he looked up and he said: 'Can I help you?' I said 'Yes, my name's Rose Reilly and I want to play professional football.'
>
> I told him my story and he said: 'I'll try to help you.'

Stan got back in touch with Rose a few weeks later to tell her he'd found a semi-professional team in France called Stade de

Reims. And that was it. Stan made the introduction to the team and the newspaper even paid for the airfares for Rose and fellow footballer Edna Neillis to fly out for trials with Stade de Reims. Rose went on to become one of the most celebrated female footballers of all time.

'I can never thank Stan enough. I kickstarted him to kickstart my career. It was amazing.'

A simple act that demonstrates the power of a male ally.

———

Male allies aren't just the high-profile athletes or senior men working in sport, though. Dads, brothers, husbands and boyfriends can all play a huge part in celebrating and normalising women's sport for the females in their lives.

It will often be my husband Matt who voices his frustration at a BBC 5 Live sports round-up that contains no mention of women's sport. I'm sure him seeing it's an issue and expressing annoyance means much more to my daughters than my pointing it out. Again.

I grew up in a very active family where sport was constantly on the television. While my dad, Roy, a physical training instructor with the Metropolitan Police, certainly held many societal views I didn't agree with, when it came to women taking part in sport I never felt that my participating and competing was any less important than that of my three brothers. He normalised women's sport, celebrating female athletes alongside males, and I'm sure that gave me the confidence to make sport a big part of my life.

What can men do to be good allies? I've learned so much from the Black Lives Matter movement recently and one of the things that's powerfully resonated is the need to be *anti*-racist rather than *non*-racist. I think it's the same for men encouraging women in sport. Good that you are *non*-sexist, but what we really need is more men in the sector who are *anti*-sexist.

The word ally should be seen as a verb rather than a noun. It is not enough to say you don't exclude women, or you would support women's sport if you saw it. Change will come when more men call out sexism when they see it; when they make a point of actively supporting women's sport. Not just ignoring the trolls on social media who make stupid remarks about female athletes or women commentating on sport but stepping in to challenge them – however exposed that makes you feel. Not settling for the inequality in funding or coverage from your organisation but asking questions and being a voice for women in sport when you are in meetings.

We live in a society which in many ways has normalised men's right to ridicule women for their performance or ability. This is hugely apparent in the world of sport where derogatory remarks about women – be they athletes or journalists – seem somehow socially acceptable. Too many men feel this is a normal thing to do and the era of social media has magnified this with thousands of anonymous men, hidden behind their keyboards, spitting out nasty comments about women.

Whenever I see mean comments from men on *The Game Changers* Facebook page, it always reassures (and surprises) me when other men step in to call out the negativity posted. It is a great reminder that there are lots of regular men out there who recognise the value of women's sport and women working in the sport sector.

So how can more men become allies in women's sport? The Tucker Center for Research on Girls and Women in Sport makes several great suggestions:

BE VOCAL

- Speak up if you see inequity.
- Celebrate female athletes and female leaders.
- Create a culture that values and supports women.

EDUCATE YOURSELF AND OTHERS

- Learn about the barriers girls and women face in sport.
- Review and question policies and practices.
- Reflect on and address your own personal bias.

PROMOTE FEMALE LEADERSHIP

- Mentor, sponsor, champion and employ women.
- Invite women to apply and communicate opportunities.
- Use your power to advocate for women.

To the men who already show their support for women's sport – we thank you.

To the others, please do stand up and use your voice and influence to help bring equality to sport, because, as Moya Dodd says: 'Our legacy is not how we're judged by our peers, but how we are judged by our grandchildren.'

12

SIDELINED WOMEN

Sports are no different from business or politics, tech, you name it. It starts at the top. People hire people who they're comfortable with, who look like them. Male boards in business hire male CEOs. And in sports, male directors hire male coaches.

Meredith Flaherty, University of Florida

Much of what I share in this chapter is relevant to women working in a variety of roles as officials, but I've focused primarily on coaches. I hope to answer three questions: why do we see so few elite female coaches? Why does it matter? What needs to change in the future?

Sport England provides some interesting background: almost half of all sports coaching is being delivered by women but less than half of them have any formal coaching qualification. Women in England are also much less likely than men to think of themselves as a 'coach'. Around a third of coaches on England's talent pathway are women, yet just 11 per cent of the coaches for Team GB at the Rio Olympics in 2016 were female.

It's not a new phenomenon. As long ago as 1982 British Sports

Councils were delivering specific interventions to increase the number of female coaches in the UK.

It is a problem the world over. In the US Title IX came onto the statute books in 1972 and transformed sports in the USA. It guaranteed no discrimination based on gender in any publicly funded institution, ensuring girls had the same opportunities as boys in everything, including sport. This meant equal treatment on the playing field and equal funding for all their sports programmes.

College or university sport in the US is like nothing we know in Europe. I remember my brother Tim studying sports medicine at the University of Virginia in the 1990s and telling us about the vast stadiums with crowds of 60,000 watching college football each week. At the time I'd thought it was a big crowd if we had more than a hundred people watching Loughborough University's men's rugby team playing on a Wednesday afternoon.

Title IX had an extraordinary impact on the access to sport for girls in colleges across the US. As Susie Petruccelli explains in her powerful autobiography *Raised a Warrior*, the thousands of sports scholarships available to young women resulted in a massive shift in participation. 'In the US between 1972, when Title IX was passed, and 1991, when FIFA held the first official women's world championship, there was a 17,000 per cent increase in girls playing soccer in high school,' she reports.

Sadly, the hugely positive impact Title IX had on sports participation did not extend to those women working in coaching, and in many cases it has had a negative impact. In the late 1970s over 90 per cent of women's sports teams at colleges and universities in the US were coached by women. As Title IX drove money into women's sports, and it became apparent that coaching staff could be well paid for their work, this shifted dramatically. Today it is only around 40 per cent. This drop occurred from the 1980s to 2000 and it has stayed at about that level since then.

With enormous crowds, TV rights and sponsors, college sports in the US is a $14 billion industry and 'Head Coach' is one of the most visible and powerful positions in sport. These people are equivalent to CEOs of big organisations, in charge of all the players and the huge backroom teams that support them. The top twenty-five head coaches in US college sport last year were paid salaries that ranged from $4.1 million to $9.3 million. Aside from the fact that women now only make up 40 per cent of the head coaches in *women's* sport, in US men's college sport only 3 per cent of head coaches are women.

In the same way that Title IX drove female sports participation in the US, globally there has been a fantastic shift in gender balance in Olympic sports, too. The IOC report that women made up less than a quarter of participants at the summer Olympics in LA in 1984 but will be just under half (48.8 per cent) in Tokyo 2020/21. Unfortunately, again this does not extend to coaching, where gender imbalance has remained static since the 2010 Winter Olympics in Vancouver, with just 10 per cent of accredited coaches now female.

So why aren't we seeing more elite female coaches and officials?

A fascinating US survey sheds light on the different beliefs in this area, which are true the world over. Male Athletic Directors (ADs) at US colleges rank the three key reasons they believe prevent more women being head coaches:

1. Time constraints due to family.

2. Failure of women to apply.

3. Lack of qualified women.

Female Athletic Directors suggest otherwise. They state the three reasons as being:

1. Success of 'old boy networks'.
2. Conscious discrimination during the hiring process.
3. Time constraints due to family.

The women believe it is structural, but the men say it is the fault of individual women.

This highlights one of the key issues in many areas where we do not see women in leadership roles. There's a drive to 'fix the women', but it turns out women are not the problem. It's the system that needs to change.

Blaming the people with no power in the system (the women) means that men don't need to question the system itself or even consider how much they personally might be a part of the problem. They just blame the women.

While it's fantastic to have programmes in place that attract and upskill female coaches and officials (and this needs to continue and receive more investment), it's not the definitive solution. You could have the greatest female coaches ever but that won't change things or create equality.

I asked Mark Gannon, the CEO at UK Coaching, what the organisation was doing to improve the numbers of elite female coaches. He told me:

In many cases women make better coaches than men. Women are generally 'people focused' first and foremost. They care about people and understand how to get the best out of them.

It's not a matter of just attracting more women into coaching, it's the environment around coaching that we need to change – it's a systematic thing.

Sports from their earliest amateur days have grown out of competition, with the development of leagues and teams. To get your club or team included you needed to step forward and get involved in the administration of these structures. It was men that took these roles because it was primarily men's sport. Many of those committees and councils and panels have remained primarily male for decades and this still impacts the appointment of coaches and managers today.

Fortunately, things are changing with positive action on gender parity from Sport England and UK Sport with the Code for Sports Governance, but this drive for diversity hasn't yet reached into professional sport. The goal moving forwards will be to break the institutional mould that we have for traditional coaches.

As Mark highlights, as with so much in life sport is run by men and they have the power to make decisions, and that includes appointing coaches and officials. One of the things that will lead to better gender balance at the top of organisations is more women involved in making decisions.

This is 'homologous reproduction', where people automatically hire other people who look like them. It means that a dominant group (in this case the men) systematically reproduces itself by employing more men than women. Similarly, white people will automatically employ more white people.

I'm familiar with the concept because, looking back, I can see it's exactly what I did in running my own sports PR agency for many years. I told myself we had a very open recruiting process, and we did interview lots of young men, but, in reality, the majority of our employees looked very much like me (or like me twenty-five years ago). For many years, my team were all women, and most had sports science degrees and a passion for communications. A number also attended the same university as me; a couple had even done the same course.

I didn't see it at the time, but, clearly, I was exhibiting my own bias about who I felt would make the best appointee, in just the same way as those appointing only male coaches and officials.

For women who do make it through to the higher levels of coaching, gaining qualifications can be daunting. Women talk of turning up to coaching courses to find they are the only female in attendance. It takes some confidence to do this, which is what Giselle Mather, Director of Rugby at Wasps Ladies, has in spades. Giselle was the first woman to earn the RFU's level-four coaching qualification and oversaw the development of players such as Marland Yarde, Jonathan Joseph and Anthony Watson during her nine-year role at the London Irish academy.

I remember Giselle sharing a story in the *Telegraph* which highlighted some of the challenges female coaches face.

When I was going for my level three, I had given birth to my daughter six weeks previously.

I knew I was ready to take the level three and I remember ringing up the RFU, telling them that I had to bring my daughter because I was feeding. When you were doing your level three then, you did twenty-four hours where you stay overnight.

So, I said: 'I need to bring her. If she screams, I will take her out. I appreciate if I fail as a result, so be it, it is my responsibility.' The RFU rang me back and said: 'As long as you are discreet.'

I loved her response: 'I was like "yeah, I'm going to go 'woohoo' in front of a hundred blokes!" But she was fantastic. I put her in the papoose when I was doing all the things on the course.'

Casey Stoney, manager at Manchester United Women, says the same: 'If I go through my experience of every coaching course I have ever been on, I am the only woman in the room. Unless you are a strong person it is daunting, it is absolutely daunting.'

Giselle and Casey are great examples of women who are unfazed by being in a room with 100 men taking their coaching qualifications. Obviously not all women feel as self-assured, though, as it was another decade, in 2018, before the next woman after Giselle achieved the RFU's level-four coaching qualification.

Another reason women haven't achieved the same levels as men in coaching is society's belief that men perform better at sport, which leads to an assumption that men are also better at being sports coaches or officials.

I'm embarrassed to admit I have been guilty of this mindset myself in the past. When I was growing up there were times when I would have chosen a male coach or trainer because I'd assumed they would somehow be 'better' than a female equivalent.

Then there's the belief that if you haven't played a sport to a certain level you won't be able to coach it. I asked Emma Hayes, the hugely successful manager of Chelsea Women, about this and was impressed by the response she says she always gives when she's asked that question:

Do you really have to have a lot of frequent air miles to be a good pilot? Do you have to be a fantastic student to be a great teacher? Do you have to be a really good patient with multiple surgeries to be a good surgeon? Do you have to be frugal with money to be a great banker?

Of course, experiencing something will offer insight, or provide a valuable reflection for players because you have been in that arena. You can relate to them, but it doesn't necessarily mean you're a great leader.

I think kinaesthetically it's important within your coaching teams to have somebody who's played the game at the same level as the players. Someone who's been in the arena is crucial. Is it a number one prerequisite to being a manager? No, I think it's desirable, but I don't think it's essential.

On the other side, there is often an assumption in sport that if you've played at an elite level you will automatically make a fantastic coach. Many female coaches in the US report that former NBA players are parachuted into the highest profile coaching roles over talented female coaches with decades of experience in women's basketball and winning records. As former WNBA coach Cheryl Reeve reflects in the documentary *Game On: Women Can Coach*: 'Your qualifications weren't viewed the same as male counterparts. There was a long time in our league that it was viewed that a former NBA player would be a better option than someone who had lived a career in women's basketball.'

The same might be said of the appointment of Phil Neville as the manager of the England Women's football team in 2018. I've been told there were some incredibly talented international female coaches who had applied but had not even been called for an interview when they heard that Phil Neville had been offered the job. Phil was a former professional footballer, whose appointment was undoubtedly good for the profile of women's football in the UK, but who had never coached a women's football team in his life. Clearly his profile helped the women's game, but was that reason enough to justify his appointment over other, potentially much better experienced women?

There's undoubtedly a huge amount of sexism in the world of coaching – both from men working in sport and inherent in the system. Women working in strength and conditioning (S&C) also face enormous barriers to working in men's sport. In the National Collegiate Athletic Association, which is the biggest employer in sport in the USA, only a tiny fraction of S&C coaches are female.

In a powerful interview on the *Pacey Performance Podcast* in 2020, Sophia Nimphius, a senior S&C coach and professor of human performance at Edith Cowan University, shared some moving insights into being a female in such a male-dominated industry:

> You have to not just be good, but you have to constantly defend yourself and constantly be on your toes. You walk in a room and the assumption is you are *not* good. And then you have to fight from the assumption of not good, to get the almost backhanded compliment of 'wow, you really surprised me. You know your stuff.'
>
> And you know how many people say that and they think they are being genuinely supportive. I'd rather you just be an asshole and say, 'there was no way I would previously have listened to you.' Just say that. Don't give me the backhanded compliment of 'wow, you surprised me.' What was surprising about that? I have no idea.

Sophia also points out that while much great work is being done to support women coming into the sector and to celebrate role models, no one is taking responsibility for the fact that we have a system that perpetuates these biases. 'They think the solution is to fix the women,' she says. 'Stop trying to fix me and start to fix the system.'

Another reason women are sometimes prevented from coaching in men's sport is the concern that the women might be 'a distraction' to male athletes.

Seriously.

This is a huge societal issue that needs to be addressed – that we excuse men for their behaviour because they cannot control their urges around women.

Is it any wonder that women are leaving coaching when a recent study on the lack of female football coaches in the UK, by Beth Clarkson at the University of Portsmouth, found that at every level women talked about football culture being male-dominated and all said they had routinely experienced sexism?

Aside from the sexist 'banter' these women experienced from men trying to 'assert their dominance', they talked of being given access to fewer resources – pitches, kit, etc. – if they coached female teams and were often appointed to less obviously desirable roles such as coaching the younger age groups.

Male-dominated coaching courses were seen as intimidating and uncomfortable, with all the women involved in the research reporting gender-stereotyping. One head coach for a men's team arrived to give a pre-game talk in her first week to be asked by players if she was there to clean their boots or wash their kit.

On a more positive note, women coaching at elite levels of senior football said the culture is improving and they felt a greater level of acceptance from male colleagues. Beth also reported a move away from a 'one-size-fits-all' approach to women's coaching, with initiatives like '21 for 21' providing tailored mentoring and support for twenty-one women ahead of the UEFA Women's Euro (now to be held in 2022).

In a similar move to help address the lack of female coaches in rugby in the elite women's and men's game, World Rugby have funded twelve coaching internships for women ahead of the Rugby World Cup in New Zealand in 2022. All nations competing in the tournament were able to nominate a coach to join their staff.

Katie Sadleir at World Rugby explained: 'At the end of the World Cup, there will be twelve more women who can say on their CV that they have coached at a World Cup. It's one of the barriers some women have in terms of getting head coach roles. You get into that chicken-and-egg situation where they can't get the job because they don't have the experience, and they can't get the experience so they can't get the job.'

With ambitious targets for the future, World Rugby hopes that 40 per cent of all coaching staff at the 2025 Women's Rugby World Cup will be female.

———

One of the main reasons women don't progress in elite coaching comes down to family life. Performance directors and high-level coaches can be away from home for weeks at a time – 300 away nights a year for some sports – travelling overseas with teams for training camps and championships. While we're definitely seeing a shift in households, with more men getting involved with childcare and housework, women still take on the majority of this work, and more women stay at home to care for their children and ageing parents.

I asked Sally Munday about this, just as she left her role as CEO of England Hockey to take on leadership of UK Sport:

From a hockey perspective we see a lot of male coaches moving into the 'talented space' and moving up the ladder when they're in their late twenties and early thirties.

And this might not be a particularly popular thing to say, but a lot of women are choosing to have children in that window. So, at the time where we're seeing a lot of men come in and move up, sometimes women are having children.

There are huge demands in elite coaching. For any woman who wants to have a demanding career, whether it is in coaching or anything else, alongside having a young family, you've got to really want to do it.

Should the sports be doing more to make this possible? 'I think we as employers and leaders have to make it as easy as possible for women to be able to do both, and not difficult. We've got to try and remove the barriers that are there. But even if you remove all the barriers, even if you do all the things around childcare and flexible time, all of that, that still doesn't make it easy. It's still tough to do.'

Creating a more family-friendly environment for coaches will ultimately be better for women and men. After all, it's not just women who want better balance in their working and family lives.

I asked Judy Murray, former Fed Cup coach and mother of Jamie and Andy, why so few of the women on the WTA Tour have female coaches:

The tennis circuit is pretty much eleven months of the year. It's tough to be on the road for that amount of time whether you're a male coach or a female coach. Traditionally, if women want to have families, it's very, very tough to leave your child at home or take your child with you. It's almost impossible.

It's also very expensive. In an individual sport you're responsible for all your own costs – so you have to pay for your coach, your coach's expenses, your fitness trainer. Very few are able to afford the entourage, but the ones at the top of the game can. If you're a player on the middle level or getting close to the top thirty, you probably haven't got the luxury financially of being able to pay for a physio, a fitness trainer and a coach on the road.

So often the choice of coach comes down to someone who can also operate as a hitting partner and do some of the fitness training as well. As a hitting partner you are far more likely to find men who have been at a reasonable level, who are closer to women at a good level. And that goes against female coaches on the road as well.

'If you asked me to go on the road with an elite female player now there is no chance I'd be able to hit with them.

I've never really considered this as a blocker for more female coaches in tennis, but Judy does think there's a solution in the WTA Tour providing a list of hitting partners at every venue: 'They could create that with local players, male or female, and you just draw from that in the way that you do from the physio rota or the lifestyle rota – it is a service that's provided. That might encourage more women to take on female coaches.'

The perception of what makes a good coach also needs to change as more women are promoted into elite roles in sport. As the sporting world reels from the stories of gymnasts, athletes and swimmers who were mistreated by dominant, aggressive, bullying coaches with a win-at-all-costs mentality, it's time we promoted a more empathetic, supportive style of leadership; a more participant-centred coaching approach that considers the wellbeing of the athlete beyond their performing lives.

That said, we also need to challenge the myth that women are 'soft, caring and maternal'. Having more women in coaching and changing what we see as best practice in coaching are interrelated, but not the same. Not all female coaches are stereotypically nurturing and feminine in their approach. Not all men are dominant and aggressive.

This common gender-stereotyping means that female coaches are seen as great for grassroots sport, especially working with young athletes, but once the job is no longer about nurturing and becomes all about performance and winning, a more masculine skill-set is called for with more authority, discipline and strategy.

Dr Nicole LaVoi, Director at the Tucker Center, says:

> When we think about what it means to coach – you're loud, you're in control, you have authority, people take your direction, you make decisions. These are behaviours that are stereotypically associated with men and masculinity so what it means to 'coach' already privileges men.
>
> So, when women 'coach' they have to have behaviours that look like men stereotypically. If you conform to a traditional female role where you are caring and kind and nurturing, then you're perceived as being too nice and incompetent. Men in the coaching profession just don't have to walk that same line in order to be perceived as competent and relevant.

Raising the profile of successful female coaches like Mel Marshall is important to encourage women to see there is a pathway in elite coaching. A highly decorated international swimmer herself, in 2018 Mel was named International Swim Coach of the Year, having coached the current Olympic, World, European and Commonwealth champion Adam Peaty.

Watching a passionate Tracey Neville coach the England women to Commonwealth gold in 2018 would have inspired thousands of young netballers to consider coaching in the future, just as the appointment of Australian Lisa Keightley as the first full-time female head coach of the England women's team will do in cricket.

In 2020, a female coach making an enormous impact was Katie Sowers, the first woman to coach at a Super Bowl, who in the process changed the perceptions of women's capabilities in the minds of millions of Americans. An offensive assistant coach with the San Francisco 49ers, Katie was the second ever full-time coach in the NFL and the first openly gay coach.

'I am willing and happy to be a trailblazer because I know that other women, other young girls, are watching this and maybe their path seems a little clearer now,' Katie said at the time. In a powerful tweet she added: 'If your daughter has a dream of being a football coach in the NFL . . . or a ballerina . . . or a professional soccer player . . . or a teacher . . . or a nurse . . . or a doctor . . . or an astronaut . . . or even PRESIDENT . . . just let her know this . . . She. Can. Do. It. And she will change the world.'

In researching the many challenges facing female sports coaches, an area that shocked me, that I'd never really considered before, was how a woman's sexual orientation could dramatically limit her opportunities. Perhaps it's an unspoken barrier in the UK, but in the more conservative US, homophobia also remains an incredibly powerful deterrent to women from joining or remaining in coaching positions. Until recently some US college sports teams had policies that banned them from recruiting coaches who weren't heterosexual.

The story of how Katie Sowers came to be coaching in the

NFL, rather than basketball, the sport she'd formerly played, is heart-breaking and yet fairly typical in the US, it turns out.

Katie asked about becoming a volunteer assistant coach at her college women's basketball team but was turned down because she was openly gay. 'With coaching being my final destination, I thought it would be natural to ask if I could be a volunteer assistant coach, and my coach called me in and he said they have a lot of parents that have been worried about their daughter being around someone who is gay . . .' she told NBC Sports Bay Area. 'So that's not something that they would want around the team. So, he asked that I would not be around the team any more.

'I was near tears. He gave me a hug and he said, "It's nothing personal," and I remember hugging him but being extremely upset. It was just something that I grieved about for a while, but I decided that I had to move on.'

As Katie's profile rocketed in 2020 as the first woman coach at a Super Bowl, the President of her former college responded: 'Sadly, in 2009, our policies and the laws of Indiana allowed for hiring decisions to consider sexual orientation. I am glad that Goshen College adopted a new non-discrimination policy in 2015.'

Even today, many women working as sports coaches feel they can't be their authentic selves and choose to hide their sexual orientation. So, while women's sport is an incredibly inclusive environment for participants, that's not the case when those same women want to progress into coaching at the end of their playing careers.

So why should sports want to encourage more women into leadership roles as coaches and officials?

As I've already said, in all areas of business, diversity leads to success. Clubs and teams that do not consider female managers are missing out on considerable talent by ignoring half the population.

In a 2019 *New York Times* article entitled 'Where Are All the Women Coaches?', Lindsay Crouse explains that, just as businesses have shown they can be more successful and profitable with diverse teams, so sports can have more success by including the other half of the population and leveraging their talents. 'Women need to be twice as good, often while working twice as hard, to stay in the game. A lot of women leave. And when you let an entire category of people disappear from your talent pool, everyone suffers.'

She continues: 'Adding women to leadership roles improves the overall performance of a team, across fields. According to a Harvard study, gender-balanced teams perform better than male-dominated teams. A 2019 *Harvard Business Review* study found that "women outscored men on 17 of the 19 capabilities that differentiate excellent leaders from average or poor ones".'

Female coaches and officials are also excellent role models for girls and boys in sport. It's inspiring for young girls to see women in positions of leadership and authority and also good for young men to have the confidence to take direction from strong women.

Edniesha Curry, the only woman coaching in US College Division 1 men's basketball, says: 'What we're doing here at the University of Maine, is really, really special. Empowering these young men to have the confidence to work with strong alpha women. When they go into the workforce, they're going to work with women. We've seen a little bit of the needle moving.'

In her book *Women in Sports Coaching*, Dr LaVoi shares the many reasons female coaches matter:

- Women in coaching roles help challenge gender stereotypes about leaders in business.
- They help other women see how to navigate the workplace as a minority.

- Women that have been coached by women are more likely to become coaches themselves.
- Women bring different perspectives to culture and decision-making.
- They advocate more for equality.
- Women coaches are visible and powerful reminders for men and boys that women can be successful leaders worthy of respect and admiration.
- Discrimination, abuse and harassment are less likely with a gender-balanced workforce.

While seeing more women coaching in men's sport is certainly something we should aspire to, it shouldn't be the only measure of success for female coaches.

This was clearly illustrated in early 2021 when the British media made much of the fact that Emma Hayes, manager of Chelsea Women, was being linked to a vacancy at AFC Wimbledon, a club in the third tier of the men's English football league system. It would have made Emma the most senior woman in a coaching role in the male football pyramid and there was an assumption by many that she would take it if offered – because it was in the men's game.

Emma, however, quickly pointed out that it was an insult to suggest it would be a 'step up' for her to take the Wimbledon role. She went on to explain that she had no intention of leaving her job at Chelsea, where, with a squad that included some of the world's finest female players, she had won three FA WSL titles and two Women's FA Cups.

Emma told the media: 'I'm in the best job in the world. No amount of money is going to tempt me away from that.'

I asked Liz Nicholl, the former CEO of UK Sport, why she thought we still have so few elite female coaches and performance directors and she was very honest in her response: 'That would be one of my disappointments. I haven't been able to crack that one. But we do know more about why.'

Liz explained that at recent World Class Performance Conferences she had invited female attendees to gather and share what they felt about the opportunities they have and what the blockers might be.

Here's what she heard: 'Firstly, they wanted to see more role models of women that have succeeded in achieving significant roles in performance sport. Secondly, they wanted more networking opportunities, to be co-ordinated and enable them to share their experiences with other women in similar circumstances. Thirdly, there was a view that some of the appointment panels, selection panels, were male-dominated and could that be addressed?'

In November 2020 UK Sport announced a new leadership programme as part of a bold plan to more than double the representation of female coaches in the Olympic and Paralympic high-performance community by Paris 2024.

The scheme will see six of the best female coaches in the UK offering support and development opportunities for the next aspiring generation of elite female coaches. Paula Dunn (para athletics), Kate Howey (judo), Mel Marshall (swimming), Bex Milnes (para triathlon) and Tracy Whittaker-Smith (trampolining) will offer a unique opportunity for coaches to observe them working and develop understanding of high-performance coaching. Karen Brown, Great Britain Hockey and England Hockey coach for fifteen years, will be a mentor for the programme.

Commenting on the plans, CEO Sally Munday said:

UK Sport is determined to see greater diversity across the high-performance community and this programme will focus on seeing more women at the top end of high performance. Coaches, alongside athletes, are at the heart of our high-performance community and we firmly believe that a more diverse cohort of highly skilled coaches will help more of our Olympic and Paralympic athletes realise their potential.

There are currently far too few female coaches operating at the highest level of performance and we are committed to addressing this reality and, working with our stakeholders, driving the change we want to see.

13

IN THE RED CORNER

Courage, sacrifice, determination, commitment, toughness, heart, talent, guts. That's what little girls are made of; the heck with sugar and spice.

Bethany Hamilton, professional surfer

If it wasn't bad enough that historically dubious medicine stopped women playing sport because of the supposed risks to their bodies and fertility, even when women have been allowed to participate the sports science has invariably assumed that women's bodies were just 'small versions of men's'.

It's ironic that it was men talking about 'women's bodies' for years that led to the banning of them from sport, but now we have men in sport who *don't* want to talk about women's bodies, and that too has a negative impact.

It is a relief, then, that this topic is finally being aired publicly. Media, coaches and sports organisations are talking openly about issues facing female athletes, including the impact of hormones on their bodies and performance, the increased prevalence of female sports injuries and the difference in the effects of concussion on the female brain.

The topic of periods and how they impact female athletes got its first big airing in 2015 when British tennis player Heather Watson blamed 'girl things' on her exit from the Australian Open. The week that followed saw huge media coverage with other female athletes coming forward to talk more openly about their monthly cycles and their effect on performance. The BBC hosted a debate to explore 'Are periods the final taboo in sport?'

While some people think talking about the issues caused by periods can be a double-edged sword, undoing all the work that's taken place to reassure men that women aren't 'less capable' once a month when they're menstruating, it's actually incredibly important that menstrual cycles become a normal part of conversation across all of society.

More research is needed in this area, but sports scientists agree that women may be more prone to injury when oestrogen is at its peak level around the time of ovulation, as the presence of the hormone can make tendons and ligaments more lax and elastic.

'The menstrual cycle is an inflammatory process and excess inflammation can result in an injury,' says Dr Georgie Bruinvels, a sports physiologist specialising in this area. 'It's not solely down to high levels of oestrogen, but tracking the cycle is also very important in terms of bone-injury risk.'

The fact that fantastic progress is being made in this area became very apparent in early 2020 when Chelsea announced that they were the first football club in the world to tailor their training to players' menstrual cycles. Manager Emma Hayes was the driving force behind the initiative, having noticed that her players' performance, mood and energy were directly impacted by where they were in their cycle.

Hayes and her team at Chelsea worked with Dr Bruinvels, who developed the FitrWoman app for the sports science company

Orreco. The app allows women to input information about their menstrual health and related symptoms, which can then be logged and monitored. With the consent of the players, Chelsea's coaches can access their information to tailor their training programmes.

'The starting point is that we are women and, ultimately, we go through something very different to men on a monthly basis,' reflected Hayes at the time.

> We have to have a better understanding of that because our education failed us at school; we didn't get taught about our reproduction systems. It comes from a place of wanting to know more about ourselves and understanding how we can improve our performance.
>
> I'm a female coach in an industry where women have always been treated like small men. The starting point is that we are women and, ultimately, we go through something very different to men on a daily basis. I think it's a subject that's been a taboo and there have been a lot of unknowns for us, so to bring that into the open and deal with it quite normally, as we do with nutrition, will be really helpful.

I love that Emma also sees that this is just the beginning of something that will become normal in the future: 'These players are going to be the first generation of women who are well educated about their menstrual cycle and they will spread that knowledge as far as they possibly can and we hope that becomes a culture within every football club in the world.'

Along with the physical impact of menstruation, for many teenage girls periods can be a significant factor in their decision to stop taking part in sport. So many considerations that boys never have to contemplate. How can I swim – what if I leak in the water? Will my pad show beneath my tight gymnastics leotard or my skimpy volleyball shorts? What if my tampon string pokes out from my tiny athletics briefs when I'm hurdling? What if I leak when I'm playing in a white tennis dress or white football shorts? What do I do with my pads or tampons if I'm in an all-male changing room with no sanitary bins?

Sport England research for 2017–18 showed that among fourteen-to sixteen-year-old girls, 42 per cent say their period prevents them from taking part in physical activity in school.

Even women at the top of their game face this issue, as was highlighted in an article in the *Telegraph* in 2020. One international rugby player told the paper that while it wasn't shocking not to have sanitary bins because it was what they were used to, it only really came home to her when she was on her period and trying to get rid of a tampon: 'Because there wasn't a bin in the loo, I got blood on my shorts. Most countries in the Six Nations play in white shorts, so I can hardly be the first women this has happened to.'

Despite the positive changes in the conversation around the impact of menstrual cycles it was shocking to read in the BBC's 2020 Elite British Sportswomen's Survey that 40 per cent of respondents said they did not feel comfortable discussing their period with coaches. That is 40 per cent of women at the very top of their game on the elite pathway who can't discuss something that has an enormous impact on their bodies and potential performance.

And this was even though 60 per cent of respondents in the survey said their performance had been affected by their period, and they had missed training or competitions because of it.

Athletes reported a whole host of practical issues they regularly faced including white clothing, no sanitary bins, wearing the same tampon or pad for hours on end, along with issues many women face each month including painful cramps and bloating. Clearly these physical symptoms present a much bigger challenge if you're an elite athlete who has to compete at her very best in front of a crowd, when perhaps all you want to do is snuggle down on the couch with a hot water bottle until the pain passes. Many young female athletes now take birth control pills to help the timings of their periods, so they don't coincide with major events, or take them all year round to avoid periods altogether.

As the BBC report pointed out: 'We live in a world largely designed by men, for men. Sporting laws and stadiums are designed with men in mind, whether or not those in charge realise it.'

Take cricket, for example.

'In the laws, you're not actually allowed to leave the field to go for a wee,' said Scotland's Katie McGill. 'In a fifty-over game, you're out there for three hours or more. A lot of us will double up with a tampon and a pad. It's not great. If you get the wrong day . . . you're running around a lot and then in the in-between bits, you're standing still a lot. You have time to think about it.'

Some of the women who responded to the survey said they would not be comfortable discussing their period with their coaches, many of whom are middle-aged men. The women were worried their period problems would be used against them in selection and they did not want to be seen as finding an excuse for underperforming.

Lack of access to period products can also be an issue that stops girls playing sport, so it is wonderful to see high-profile sporting role models like Steph Houghton, captain of the Lionesses and Manchester City, backing the Period Poverty Campaign.

I asked Steph why she became an ambassador for the charity: 'For girls who are a bit less privileged, in terms of not having access to tampons or pads, I think it's important for us to try and encourage them to continue playing sport.

'Periods shouldn't affect you playing the sport you want to do or being in school and doing PE. We should strive to encourage young girls to play. Show them that even if we do have periods, we can still do whatever we want to do, that should never stop us.'

―――――

When it comes to experts in the field of women's health in sport, there are few more knowledgeable than Dr Emma Ross. Emma led the English Institute of Sport's (EIS) Female Athlete Health team with a SmartHER initiative, encouraging athletes, coaches and support staff to have conversations and consider female physiology and psychology in training, recovery, nutrition and the coaching environment.

Emma explained to me that after the Beijing Olympics it became clear that British women weren't winning medals at the rate of men, and UK Sport was keen to understand why. Having spoken to those supporting athletes it became very apparent that for all the work on 'marginal gains' – making tiny percentage improvements with technical alterations to kit, equipment and training methods – there were some huge considerations around female physiology that were being ignored.

Emma and her team did insight work with coaches, practitioners and the athletes themselves to establish if female specific factors were being considered when training and preparing. The answer was a resounding no.

'We were training women in a way that had worked for men. We were taking programmes that had worked for men and simply transplanting them into women, ignoring the fact that women have all these very specific things that are just about being a woman. They aren't a weakness; they are just part of her – her as an athlete – but we were ignoring them,' said Emma.

The EIS set about educating everyone about these differences. It was important for the coaches and practitioners to understand why it was important. A big part of the motivation was seeing the significant improvements in performance that could result from better understanding and adaption of training.

But before they could start educating people, they needed to take a step back and ask: 'Is anyone even comfortable about having those conversations right now?' It turned out that lots of people weren't.

'We found that the male coaches, through no fault of their own, had not even factored in any of this stuff. We have created a culture in sport where women are changing who they are to try and belong. Changing to be more like men and not talk about menstrual cycles, pelvic floors or breasts, because we're going to be more like men to fit in the system,' said Emma.

The EIS work focused on menstrual cycles, breast and pelvic-floor health and considerations to reduce injuries in women that might result from female biomechanics or hormones.

'We're not going to ever be able to make it so that women don't feel the experience of their menstrual cycle – that's not what we're trying to do. We're saying if there's anything in your life as a female – and that could be your cycle, or leaking urine, or bladder or bowel problems related to pelvic health, or injuries related to your hormones, or breast health – whatever it is, we just need to address it because it hasn't even been considered up until now.'

I asked Emma about the belief that the pill was the silver bullet for sportswomen, stopping their cycles and preventing any negative impact. It turns out it's not as simple as that.

'It's not always my go-to place,' she told me. 'The menstrual cycle is a vital sign of health. Where female athletes are doing too much training and not fuelling enough the menstrual cycle disappears because of the stress that's been placed on the body. That's a really good signal. "I lost my period. I'd better adjust".'

It turns out different pills can also affect women's performance and Emma adds: 'The other thing about our female hormones is that they're amazing. They're amazing for us, our bodies, our bone strength, our cardiovascular strength, our brain health, our breast health. And again, it's educating people that's a real positive of having them.'

An area I'd not really considered was the importance of sports bras and the difference they can make to performance. I was really surprised when Emma told me: 'If you were wearing a poorly fitting sports bra, and you started on a start line of a marathon alongside a clone of you, identical in every way apart from she was wearing a brilliant fitting sports bra, she would finish a mile ahead of you.'

That's a 4 per cent improvement in performance.

Emma explained how women's breasts move when they run and this movement affects gait and running style. This can lead to a shortening of the stride, so less ground is covered. The upper body then starts to activate more muscles to try and counteract this and more energy is used. This can also affect breathing mechanics as ribs are trying to move and become tense. Some women wear compression sports bras, which can be restrictive and hinder breathing. All these small things add up over a marathon and contribute to the significant difference.

While it was fantastic to learn that changes are being made in many areas – for instance, all women in Team GB were receiving bespoke sports bras ahead of the Tokyo Games – there's still so much to be done.

No longer working at the EIS, in 2021 Emma, in partnership with Baz Moffat and Dr Bella Smith, launched The Well[HQ], a digital hub to empower active women (and the people who support them) with the knowledge needed to optimise health, happiness and performance. Hopefully, this initiative will ensure all women are able to better understand their bodies.

————

The impact of periods is not something that only affects young women starting out in sport or elite sportswomen. I didn't discover triathlon until I was forty-six but, having tried a sprint version of the event in 2012, in January 2013 I announced to my family that I wanted to qualify to represent Great Britain as an Age Group athlete. Six months later and two stone lighter, having learned to ride a racing bike and whip off a wetsuit, I did just that and proudly pulled on my GB kit to compete at the World Championships in London.

For the next two years I continued to represent my country at European and World Championships, taking part in key qualification events in the build-up to each one to gain selection. All in all, this meant that for about ten weekends every year I would be immersed in the world of competitive triathlons.

My journey into triathlon coincided with my approaching menopause, and with that came changes to my menstrual cycle that I had never anticipated. Just as it is taboo for women to talk about periods, talking about menopause can be even more of a challenge. After years of hearing disparaging remarks mocking grumpy females having hot flushes, women are hardly likely to declare to the world what is happening to their bodies.

For me, the biggest surprise was the change to my monthly cycle. I'd always been pretty regular with my periods, both in how often they occurred and how long they lasted. I'd naively assumed that as I neared menopause they would just get lighter and less frequent, until eventually they stopped completely at about fifty-three – the average age that a woman goes through the menopause.

But no. It turns out that was not the case, and nor is it for millions of women. Mother Nature has other plans as our fertility comes to an end. My periods became much heavier and much more frequent. At one point I was having extremely heavy periods almost every fortnight.

My problem, which will be familiar to many women, was how I could get through the event without the opportunity to change my tampon. When taking part in a triathlon, there is some pre-race preparation as you rack your bike and get into your wetsuit before filing down to get into the water to start your race. Even with a last-minute dash – invariably standing in a long queue for a Porta-loo before pulling up my wetsuit – this meant it could be about four hours from start to finish.

Hearing the despair in my voice as I realised I'd come on again the night before another big race, my lovely husband took it upon himself to head out to the local supermarket in search of some extra-extra-large tampons that might help me through the long 'Olympic Distance' event the next day. Now if that's not love and devotion, I'm not sure what is.

I remember one qualification race at Belvoir Castle where I genuinely thought I was going to have a *Carrie* moment (a cultural reference for those of a certain age) and that I'd be finishing the 10k with blood running down my tired legs.

I didn't, but the struggle of dealing with my periods certainly had a negative impact on my taking part in a sport I loved. When I stopped racing in 2018 it was with some relief that I wouldn't have to face the challenge of dealing with competitive sport and periods any more.

Along with all the issues associated with hormones and women's bodies, female sports science is also developing rapidly in areas such as concussion. Research indicates that in sports open to both genders, women are more prone to concussion than men, with one comprehensive study showing that girls had a concussion rate of 1.7 per 1,000 athlete exposures with boys at 1.0 per 1,000. In addition, the concussion symptoms last longer for female athletes and it also takes women and girls longer to recover.

Some believe the higher rate of concussion is because women have weaker muscles in their necks and shoulders to absorb the impact, but scientists are also exploring the reasons why women tend to have more severe symptoms and take longer to recover.

Without spending too much time on the detailed science here (it was over thirty years ago that I studied sports physiology at university, after all), it appears that it could well be to do with the difference in the tiny, fragile axons: the nerve cells in the brain – each about 100th the size of a human hair. Male axons are larger, with a more complex structure than women's. This means that when concussion occurs and the axons are damaged in the women's brains, little microtubules inside the axon are more likely to rupture, which can ultimately lead to the destruction or death of some of the axons.

So, while men's brains and nerve cells might be recovering after a concussion, given the same type of head impact, women's brain cells may be degenerating even more. With newspapers such as the *Telegraph* writing detailed reports about female concussions in 2019, it's a relief that the topic is now being widely aired.

PINK Concussions is the first ever non-profit organisation to focus on pre-injury education and post-injury medical care for women and girls with brain injury including concussion incurred from sport. It shares some stark observations on its website:

1. Women and girls sustain more concussions at a higher rate than their male counterparts in sports with similar rules.
2. Women and girls have been documented to have a higher number, and more severe, symptoms than males.
3. Women and girls tend to have longer recovery periods than males, and more post-concussion syndrome.

They also point out that since women and girls are rarely educated about female brain injury, they are not prepared to cope with the higher number and more severe symptoms as well as the longer recovery times and the risk of prolonged concussion symptoms (formerly called post-concussion syndrome).

These women and girls, along with their family, friends, teachers or employers, are often unprepared for the recovery ahead and have unrealistic expectations of the time needed to heal.

In addition to the physiological differences outlined above, another study has identified that while male concussions are generally caused by collisions between players, female players were more vulnerable to concussion while falling following contact.

Dawn Comstock, a professor in the Department of Epidemiology at the Colorado School of Public Health, flags another potential reason for the gender disparity in cases when she talks to Jessica Luther for *Loving Sports When They Don't Love You Back*. It could be the physiological reasons cited, but 'Undoubtedly there are also sociocultural issues going on. There's a ton of really good research out there that says women are just more willing to talk about their physical health than men are.'

We live in a society where girls playing sport may be more likely to report their concussions than boys, who are determined to appear more traditionally tough, shrug off any injury and get back out into the game.

'So if girls are more willing to report than boys, maybe boys are getting just as many concussions, or maybe they're getting more, but we don't capture those because they don't get reported and they don't get diagnosed.'

In 2017 a brain bank focused on women was announced with PINK Concussions and the National PTSD Brain Bank working together to actively recruit women over the age of eighteen to donate their brains for research.

In 2018, before the Winter Olympics in PyeongChang, three female Olympians announced they would donate their brains to the Concussion Legacy Foundation so that their brains could help with concussion research. They were all Winter Olympic stars: US bobsleigher Elana Meyers, Canadian ice hockey player Hayley Wickenheiser and US ice hockey player Angela Ruggiero.

The summer of 2020 saw the largest ever women-specific rugby injury research project launched by a team of researchers and practitioners from across the world of sports science and medicine. The group had identified a significant gap in research into female rugby players, and therefore set out to create an evidence base for women-specific interventions that will improve player safety in the future.

Most injury prevention techniques in rugby are based on male-specific data, so any changes to rugby laws or coaching practices to reduce injuries are more likely to help male rather than female players. The ambition is that this research project will help redress the balance.

———

Another area that is finally getting more coverage is the fact that women are known to have a higher risk of ACL (anterior cruciate ligament) injury than men. The chances of an ACL tear in female athletes are two to eight times higher than in their male counterparts.

Theories to explain this include:

- *Anatomical* differences: the width of the pelvis, the Q angle (how your quadriceps muscles in the thigh align with your kneecap), the size of the ACL and the notch where it crosses the knee joint.
- *Hormonal* differences: the ACL has hormone receptors for oestrogen and progesterone so the menstrual cycle might impact the likelihood of a tear.
- *Biomechanical* differences: knee stability depends on static ligaments such as the ACL along with dynamic stabilisers including the muscles and tendons around the joint.

All these things can be exacerbated as young female athletes go through puberty and the size and shape of their bodies change rapidly without neural pathways from brain to muscles having time to catch up.

A lack of substantial strength and conditioning in the training regimes for young females has also been an issue historically, especially when you consider the huge impact on young bodies of jumping and landing in netball and basketball or adapting to lateral contact in sports like rugby and football.

In *Women and Sport: Continuing a Journey of Liberation and Celebration*, Dr Pietro Tonino, director of sports medicine at Loyola University Medical Center, expresses concern for the rise in the number of female athletes he sees in his practice: 'Many of these injuries could be prevented with a simple warm-up program that could be done in minutes. One such program is the FIFA 11+, a warm-up that takes about twenty minutes to complete. In teams who did the warm-up twice a week, FIFA found a thirty to fifty per cent reduction in the rate of ACL injuries among players.'

Having witnessed many female athletes struggling with the physical and mental challenges of rehabilitation after ACL injuries – one of my own daughters included – it's clear that this is an area that warrants increased research. Hopefully, more work will also be done to educate female players (and their coaches and parents) about the importance of pre-habilitation and building strength around their joints as an integral part of any training programme.

––––––––

It is not all negatives for women's bodies in sport compared to men's, though. While our body size, physical strength and power mean you're unlikely to see a woman breaking the world records of Usain Bolt or Michael Phelps any time soon, when it comes to the toughest, longest, most brutal events women seem to be pulling ahead.

From swimming the English Channel four times to outrunning and outcycling men at ultra-distances, our sisters are setting some extraordinary new records.

In January 2019, thirty-five-year-old Jasmine Paris made headlines across the world when she won the Spine Race – 268 miles nonstop along the Pennine Way. Her time of 83 hours, 12 minutes and 23 seconds beat her nearest male rival by almost fifteen hours. (Oh yes, and she completed the race while expressing milk for her baby daughter at the aid stations along the route.)

Later that year, Maggie Guterl became the first ever woman to win the Big Dog Backyard Ultra in Tennessee, a bonkers race that only ends with the last person standing. Maggie covered 250 miles, running for sixty hours.

Cyclists were breaking records that year, too, when, in a watershed moment for female riders at ultra-distance, twenty-four-year-old German doctor Fiona Kolbinger won the Transcontinental Race, travelling 2,485 miles across Europe in just 10 days, 2 hours and 48 minutes.

I am a keen open-water swimmer who occasionally toys with the idea of one day swimming the Channel. Only around 1,700 people have swum it unassisted, fewer than have climbed Everest. You'll therefore appreciate why, in September 2019, I watched in awe as US swimmer Sarah Thomas completed the Channel crossing four times in a row. It took her 54 hours and 10 minutes. The Channel is only twenty miles at its narrowest point, but she actually swam closer to 130 miles because of the strong tides.

There are different views on why we are seeing this surge of women's success in ultra-races. Some believe it might be because women have physically learned to endure more pain during their lives. Most women deal with period pain each month and about 10 per cent experience severely debilitating conditions such as endometriosis. Add to that the pain of labour and childbirth, and you can see why some believe that if women develop internal coping mechanisms to deal with regular pain, the short-term pain of a race may fade in comparison.

Others believe it is women's superior ability to deal with the mental challenges of ultra-racing that gives them the advantage. Someone who knows all about this is four-times Ironman Triathlon World Champion Chrissie Wellington.

She told me:

Your success is about your ability to endure both physical and mental challenges, not to get too carried away with successes and to be able to overcome the lows. It's not just your physical prowess that's going to mean that you can succeed, it's about utilising all of the different strategies that you've got in your toolbox, mentally, to be able to override that discomfort or that self-doubt. It's as much coping with boredom or negative self-doubt as it is when you are in a state of physical discomfort.

I think the most important weapon of all is the knowledge that you have overcome in the past. In every single Ironman race I did, I wanted to quit. But I always looked back at times in training or other races that I've done, when I've wanted to quit and I think, well I didn't then, and I went on to achieve my goal. I went on to win or went on to do a PB, so grateful that I overrode that voice. So, every time I want to quit, I remember the previous times that I've wanted to.

———

There's much more to be explored around the female body and sports performance, but it does feel as if the conversation is finally moving on.

It's great to hear experts like Dr Kirsty Elliott-Sale at Nottingham Trent University saying: 'Athletes are very keen to talk about how they sleep, what they eat, how they train, what sports kit they're wearing, and yet for such a long time we've not really considered or spoken about menstrual cycles or hormonal contraceptive use.

'It's been pushed back, and I think the tide has turned. There is certainly more of an appetite now for this type of research to be implemented into elite sport.'

14

JUST ADD SEQUINS

Sportswomen must be physically and mentally strong yet also portray an image of vulnerability to be perceived as feminine. It is a 'set up'. Upon achieving a feminine appearance, women in sport are then sexualized, trivialized and devalued.

Vikki Krane, 'We Can Be Athletic and Feminine, But Do We Want To?', 2012

I have a vivid memory of coming home in tears, aged about fourteen, after a local boy had teased me, saying perhaps I was really a man because I'd just won the Middlesex County shot-put competition.

It was something I had been proud of at the time, and his comments, made in front of my friends, had left me embarrassed and sad. Seeing me in tears, my older brother Tim suggested next time I respond by asking the boy what he had ever got a county medal for . . . perhaps wanking? It made me laugh at the time, shocked at the rudeness of Tim's suggestion, but also wishing I could have made such a quick retort when the boy had mocked me.

Jump forward to my being a mother of teenage girls, and it really saddened me that, thirty years later, they, and their friends too, were called butch and dyke at school because they took part in competitive sport.

What those comments reflect, along with the vitriol that sportswomen have to endure each day on social media, is a historical, cultural belief that sport is inherently mannish and masculine and that women who want to play and excel at sport are therefore 'less feminine'.

As I explained in my opening chapter, much of what women in sport still experience today stems from Victorian pseudo-science and the assumption that physical exertion would damage women's bodies and their ability to reproduce. This is magnified by traditional views of femininity that persist in society, depicting women as soft, gentle, delicate, weak, fragile and elegant. Sport, on the other hand, requires us to be strong, powerful, aggressive, bold and skilled – traits more typically associated with men.

Many people (primarily men) also feel uncomfortable about women taking part in physical, contact sport because it challenges societal norms of what is appropriate behaviour for each gender.

The depressing thing is that this means many girls and young women stop playing sport because they worry it will make them look what society still tells them is 'unfeminine'. Girls feel forced to choose between being *either* sporty *or* feminine. We live in a world where girls are still brought up to believe they need to look a certain way to attract men. Boys can roll out of bed and head to school with barely a comb through their hair, but for many teenage girls and young women there is always huge pressure to look good. Hair, makeup, clothes and body shape are the focus of their attention. This can mean that all the joys of wonderful sweaty, competitive sport are rejected as a result of the pressures of physical appearance.

Things are changing in this space, which is positive news. In the last decade we have seen a significant shift in women's attitudes to strength and power, which are now viewed as qualities to be admired, with fewer girls wanting to be seen as frail and weak. Women's bodies are being celebrated for what they can do rather than how they look with campaigns such as Strong Is the New Skinny and movements like Girls Gone Strong.

Increased media coverage of female athletes and sporting role models can also have a significant impact. The more we can see and celebrate extraordinary sportswomen, the more we can normalise women playing and excelling at sport, being strong and powerful, having muscles, showing exertion and looking sweaty, the better.

It is sometimes a tricky path for women's sport. Some (a minority) feel that we need to 'feminise' sport itself to make it more appealing to young girls. There was much uproar in 2016 when the FA revealed its innovative ideas for attracting more girls into football, which included pink whistles, nice-smelling bibs, clothes vouchers and allowing girls breaks to stop and check their phones. Some young female football fans let the FA know what they thought about the approach: 'We aren't all brainless Barbie dolls.'

I remember a similar campaign for girls' sport a few years ago in which the then CEOs of Sport England and the charity Women in Sport talked about changing the emphasis for girls in schools to focus more on dance and Zumba – think sequins and swooshing – rather than girls needing to run about and get sweaty.

In 2014 an understandable outcry followed after the sports and equalities minister, Helen Grant, addressed women who might find traditional sports and sweating 'unfeminine'. 'You don't have to feel unfeminine,' she declared. 'There are some wonderful sports which you can do and perform to a very high level and I think those participating look absolutely radiant and very feminine such as ballet, gymnastics, cheerleading and even roller-skating.'

I feel passionately that it should not be about changing sport to make it more feminine, but society changing its views of what's appropriate for women and girls.

There's a paragraph in Anna Kessel's magnificent book *Eat Sweat Play* that completely resonated with me when I read it:

> Society's stereotypes tell us that women don't like sport, but when we really think about that it doesn't make any sense. Isn't the fundamental principle of being physically active something that comes naturally to us from the moment we start to walk? Don't we all remember our childhoods, running down a hill so fast it made us laugh until we couldn't breathe? Daring ourselves to climb a tree, to do our first cartwheel, our first handstand? What happened to us? When did we change? When did we lose our sense of fun, our sense of play? Sport is just playing, after all.

Anna's so right. Sport in its simplest format is about moving our bodies to play games. It's natural. It's fun. It's inclusive and exciting. At what point in her upbringing does a young girl who loves splashing in the pool with her brother, kicking footballs or riding a bike begin to sense that all the fun and exhilaration to be found in playing sport isn't for her? At what point are we telling our young women that it is no longer appropriate for them to be scruffy and sweaty and muddy like the boys?

I grew up with three brothers, one of whom was my twin. I don't ever remember being told I couldn't take part in any of the sports they did. My twin and I learned to swim at the same time, and I joined the athletics club with my older brother, Tim.

But I wasn't typical of the girls in my school because I loved sports so much. I went to an all-girls' school in the 1980s. The fact that I wanted to compete at athletics was something slightly alien in a school where it was more about netball, hockey or tennis. I was the only girl from my school who came in with wet hair after early morning sessions in the pool or went off to compete in athletics competitions at weekends.

——————

What does it mean to be feminine today? Are female athletes finally able to be both sporty and feminine?

Professor Mary Jo Kane, founder of the Tucker Center for Research on Girls and Women in Sport, says that when it comes to female athletes being represented historically in the media, they are much more likely to be presented off the court 'out of uniform and in sexy poses', which gives the message to society, and to female athletes themselves, that they are primarily considered in terms of how pretty and sexy they are rather than their athletic ability.

Professor Kane says this matters a great deal, because when young women see sexualised images of athletes, it tells them their bodies are just there to be consumed.

Coverage like this also implies that women do not possess the same physiological attributes as male athletes. Women are not seen as strong, powerful and competent. It makes men appear superior in sport and, by implication, superior in other aspects of life. Changing how we see female athletes can change how we see females in general.

'Sex sells sex. Sex doesn't sell women's sport' is the clear finding from many research studies talking to fans of all ages along with female sports participants. When shown a range of images of women 'in sports kit, in action and on court' through to leisure shots and then in sexy poses, it's the images of women actually playing their sport that all audiences found aspirational and most likely to encourage them to watch women's sport and recognise the competence of players. The only grouping to prefer the shots of women in fewer clothes were younger men, but even they agreed it did not make them more likely to follow women's sport – they just thought the women looked sexy.

These findings were reinforced in 2021 by research from Two Circles and Women's Sport Trust which showed that images of female athletes 'in action' were 12 per cent more likely to prompt viewers to find out more about the specific sport than images of those athletes in personal or entertainment settings.

Some people may believe that female athletes looking attractive and sexy in the media will help increase the profile of sport and potentially encourage more participation. Research, however, would suggest that *Olympic gold cyclist Victoria Pendleton loses her lycra in revealing photoshoot*, a genuine headline from the *Daily Mail* in 2009, did little to establish the credibility of elite female cyclists in the minds of its readers.

From 2002 to 2007, the Ladies Professional Golf Association attempted to increase the marketability of its players with a programme called 'The Five Points of Celebrity'. A Players' Summit included compulsory training on the elements of this plan: namely, performance, approachability, passion and joy, relevance and appearance. While players recognised the need to raise consumer awareness of the women's game (and their potential earning capacity) many were disappointed that 'appearance' was such a focus of the plan, with a pressure for them to embody femininity.

I have always felt uncomfortable with the tabloid media's desire to dress elite sportswomen up in 'glamorous' clothing to show the 'other side' of their lives. As if looking amazing in their sports kit is not enough of a reason to give them coverage in the newspaper. I remember a particular shoot the *Daily Mail* did with the GB Hockey team after they'd won gold in Rio in 2016 and the women were all in high heels and sequinned evening gowns. *And the gold for glamour goes to . . . our hockey girls: Team GB heroines swap their shin-pads for sequins as they reveal all about their Rio medal joy*, the headline read.

I was so disappointed to see it at the time. It felt belittling and demeaning to these extraordinary athletes. I am sure the GB Hockey communications team were delighted with the mainstream coverage – the *Daily Mail* again – but I always wondered how the players themselves felt about it.

All that said, even on court, you could say that the GB Hockey women are still conforming to traditional gender stereotypes . . . by playing in dresses. It's the same for netball. Female athletes do not choose to train every day in skirts or dresses, preferring more practical leggings or shorts, but when it comes to competition the rules dictate that they must wear dresses. Why?

In 2019 I had planned an April Fool campaign for a client – a rugby club playing in the Premier 15s. The April Fool hook was that we would be revealing that from next season the female rugby players would play in skirts. The press release we had drafted declared that in order to attract more women into the sport, the club was backing the idea that the women would now play rugby in skirts.

I had even included a comment that the club was taking its lead from the International Boxing Association, who, ahead of 2012, had recommended that female boxers wear skirts to differentiate themselves from the men. This bit about boxing was actually true, although thankfully the women rebelled and the ruling was overturned.

For various reasons, we didn't go ahead with the April Fool, but for me the fact that it sounded so ridiculous to suggest that these fabulous, powerful, strong female rugby players would really want to play in something as impractical as a skirt spoke volumes.

Perhaps things will change sooner than we think when it comes to women playing sport in dresses. In December 2020, Netball Australia's State of the Game report highlighted that 'young girls and women are turning their backs on the sport because of the nature of the uniforms'. It's an urgent area to address, according to Megan Maurice in the *Guardian*:

> The report canvassed opinions from across the netball community, from grassroots to elite players, and the issue of uniforms was one that echoed strongly through all levels of the game.
>
> Netball has still not confronted the female/athlete paradox, where the traditionally 'masculine' traits of strength and aggression – which are required in sport – must be balanced by femininity in appearance. This is where the dresses come in. There is an idea that the audience can feel comfortable in seeing players clash in the air, fight for the ball and be taken from the court with blood streaming from their faces as long as they do so while dressed appropriately for their gender.

———

This need to have women in sport wearing feminine clothing dates back to the 1800s, when it was a huge obstacle for women wanting to be more physically active. Restrictive corsets made it almost impossible for women to fill their lungs properly, while society considered it indecent for women to show as much as an ankle – not exactly outfits that would allow women to move freely.

In the 1890s, women wanting to take up the popular new hobby of riding a bike, and enjoy all the freedom that this provided, were hampered by the need to look 'ladylike' at all times. As a letter to US agricultural magazine *The Country Gentleman* questioned: 'What on earth the common or garden lady bicyclist wants with knickerbockers and other strange garments in the street I cannot think. No wonder the rude man in the street jeers after them. I am only saying this for your own good, dear ladies. I am too great an admirer of yours to allow you to continue your "rational" dress without a word of protest. Wear your knickerbockers by all means but let them be concealed by a skirt.'

Putting women in feminine clothes to attract crowds wasn't an April Fool for women's baseball in the 1950s, when chewing gum magnate Philip K. Wrigley, the owner of the Chicago Cubs major league franchise, drove the development of the All-American Girls Professional Baseball League, along with advertising executive Arthur Meyerhoff.

Wrigley said he was personally repelled by the 'pants-wearing, tough talking female softballer' and devised an approach that he thought would attract sponsors and spectators. He and Meyerhoff moved the sport away from softball to become 'baseball for women' but using what they termed the 'femininity principle' to ensure the league was committed to preserving feminine ideals. Even the names of the teams reflected the drive for femininity – the Daisies, Lassies, Peaches and Belles.

The women, who were chosen for their attractiveness along with their physical skills, wore makeup and short skirts. They commented on the pain of sliding into the bases without the protection of the long trousers worn by men. They received lessons on 'graceful social deportment' and players were reminded that 'boyish bobs and other imitations of masculine style and habit were taboo'. They were never allowed to appear in public in shorts or trousers. No women of colour were ever recruited.

The success of the league in the 1950s saw the 120-game schedule attract between 500,000 and 1 million spectators, but the league declined at the end of the decade in part because society began to reject gender distinctions. The story of women's baseball is a complex one. While it was positive news that highly skilled, talented female athletes could be paid to play sport just like the men, it also reinforced stereotypical views that women should always remain feminine in sport.

I am concerned that this attitude is still apparent in some sports today, among certain sports administrators who try desperately to make women's sport appear more feminine and traditionally heterosexual, which in turn can alienate women and girls who do not identify with traditional depictions of what it is to be female.

In 2011 the Badminton World Federation stated that all female players must wear skirts on the court 'to ensure attractive representation of badminton'. Players and fans were not happy and fortunately the rule was quickly overturned, despite the then Deputy President explaining: 'We just want them to look feminine and have a nice presentation so women will be more popular.'

Another example closer to home was England Netball's Netball Nails campaign in 2013, described as 'part of a campaign to help raise awareness of netball, as well as illustrating that competitive sport doesn't have to be ugly and macho – you can still be beautiful, feminine and glamorous both on and off the pitch'.

In the US, another sport that struggled with the reputation of being too 'masculine' and not suitable for feminine athletes in the 1900s was track and field athletics. Few white women chose to compete for this reason, and it was African-American women who ignored public perception and stepped into the light to lead the way in track and field, with huge international success. Their legacy continues to this day.

A little unbelievably, such was the negativity towards women competing in athletics that in the 1950s the Olympic governing bodies seriously considered eliminating several track and field events from the Games because they 'were not truly feminine'. IOC member Prince Franz Joseph of Liechtenstein even commented that reducing the number of women's athletic events would not only help solve the problem of Olympic overexpansion, but 'we would be spared the unaesthetic spectacle of women trying to look and act like men'.

As women's sport grew in prominence and popularity through the 1950s, it was still very much impacted by beliefs about women's 'weak' bodies and perceptions of femininity from earlier in the century, coupled with society's growing homophobia. As the male-dominated sports press continued to develop, male journalists celebrated the female athletes who subscribed to their feminine ideals, dressing in fashionable clothes and demonstrating grace and elegance in their play.

Over a hundred years later, as I was growing up and watching Wimbledon with my mum in the 1970s, I can remember the antagonistic comments the media made about Martina Navratilova playing in shorts versus Chris Evert in her frilly knickers and floaty dresses. Tennis at that time highlighted the conflict of athleticism versus more traditional views of femininity, with Chris Evert earning more in sponsorship despite Navratilova winning more tournaments overall.

Along with being judged for their appearance, female tennis players were also criticised for their sexuality. Here's what the *Sunday Express* reported in 1978: 'When Martina Navratilova plays at Wimbledon this week the eye of every healthy lusty male will be on her. She personifies the essence of attractive femininity. Disillusioning, isn't it, to learn that she is shacked up in the United States with the country's most aggressive lesbian? I sigh with nostalgia for the days when at tournaments like Wimbledon the greatest danger to the chastity of young lady tennis stars came from randy males. Devastating, isn't it, to learn that nowadays their greatest peril would seem to come for other lassies in frilly panties.'

I love that Martina's response was to snub the media comments by appearing even more 'traditionally masculine', wearing shorts and tops that emphasised her wonderful, strong body.

Sadly, the physical appearance and attire of female tennis players can still be an issue today. It was only in 2017 that the WTA itself courted controversy when they asked fans to vote in an online poll to choose the female player they felt was 'best dressed' at Wimbledon that year. By focusing on their appearance, the implication was that this mattered more than the players' talent and athleticism.

Similarly, it is hard to forget that horrible moment when a male TV presenter asked the world number seven, Eugenie Bouchard, to 'give us a twirl' following a convincing 6-0, 6-3 victory at the Australian Open. Rather than ask her about the win, Ian Cohen, from Channel 7, asked whether Bouchard could 'tell us about her outfit'.

'A twirl?' the twenty-year-old Canadian asked with disbelief, to which Cohen explained: 'A twirl – like a pirouette.'

Attitudes are slowly changing, but as Jaime Schultz explains in *Women's Sports* 'there are still certain sports that we think of as "feminine" and "gender appropriate." These tend to be individual sports that involve little physical contact between competitors, while emphasising grace, beauty, and artistic expression. It has therefore been less controversial for women to participate in sports such as tennis, gymnastics and figure skating.'

Of course, another factor that may drive female athletes to emphasise their femininity is that 'conventionally attractive' sportswomen have generally received more media attention and larger endorsement deals.

In what is sometimes referred to as 'the Kournikova syndrome', the Russian-born player enjoyed unprecedented profile and sponsorship during her career, despite never winning a major singles tournament. The depressing title of a cover story in *Sports Illustrated* in 2000 read, 'She Won't Win the French Open, But Who Cares? Anna Kournikova Is Living Proof That Even in This Age of Suppose Enlightenment, a Hot Body Can Count as Much as a Good Backhand.'

———————

Another unsettling trend in the sporting space is leading sportswear brands choosing to use models and celebrities to promote their products rather than female athletes.

In 2016, US Olympic ice dancer Meryl David shared three photos on Twitter of Bella Hadid wearing Nike, Kylie Jenner wearing Puma and Aly Raisman (the Olympic gymnast) wearing Reebok. Her hugely supported tweet read: 'I'll take the one promoted by the athlete please.'

Many might say that, as she had over 14 million followers on Instagram at the time, it is perhaps clear why Nike chose Bella Hadid.

The trend began back in 2014, when supermodel Gisele Bünd-chen was named as the first non-athlete to be the face of Under Armour. Despite the negative public response to this move, other sportswear brands soon followed suit, with Reebok choosing Gigi Hadid, Adidas working with Kendall Jenner and Karlie Kloss, and Cara Delevingne being a Puma ambassador since 2016.

In August 2020 sportswear company Canterbury of New Zealand made a massive faux pas in this area. In launching a new Ireland Rugby shirt, the sponsor used female models rather than members of the women's rugby squad. The image showed three airbrushed women, wearing long dark trousers rather than shorts, alongside three male members of the Irish men's squad.

Florence Williams, a Wasps player, took to Twitter to show her annoyance: 'SPOT THE DIFFERENCE. 2 jersey launches. 3 models. 3 international players. 3 profiles lifted. 1 HUGE opportunity missed. By not using the female players to market THEIR OWN KIT an opportunity to build recognition, fan bases and creating role models for future generations is lost.'

Trying to explain the decision, a helpful man on Twitter suggested that Canterbury had chosen the models as they looked more feminine than female rugby players. What followed was wonderful to witness, as my Twitter feed became flooded with hundreds of rugby-playing women calling out Canterbury (and those comments) and sharing images of them playing under the hashtag #IAMENOUGH.

The impact was fantastic and, to give them credit, Canterbury immediately contacted Williams, backed the #IAMENOUGH campaign and pledged to use real rugby players in all future kit launches. They also issued an apology for getting it so wrong.

Talking to Telegraph Women's Sport afterwards, Williams said:

'I'm sick of female athletes having to be constantly grateful. Yes, I'm grateful for the progress, but we're not at the destination yet.'

What I most admired about this rapid response was that women in sport (and male allies) saw their collective voices having immediate, significant impact.

We are over 50 per cent of the population after all. Just think how effective we could be if we work together more frequently to call out the brands and sports bodies in this way.

A disturbing move onwards from the consideration of what constitutes 'appealing and feminine' for female athletes is the notion of sex appeal. You just have to consider the variance in male and female uniforms in some sports to witness this. Male athletes wear clothes designed for comfort while completing their activity, while female athletes' clothes are often much scantier than required.

In elite track and field women compete in sports bras and short, tight bottoms with their stomachs and thighs on display. The men generally wear thigh-length lycra shorts and vest tops. Why the difference?

When considering ways to increase the popularity of women's football in 2004, Sepp Blatter, the former head of FIFA and once one of the most powerful figures in sport, incurred the wrath of many female players when he said: 'Let the women play in more feminine clothes like they do in volleyball. They could, for example, have tighter shorts. Female players are pretty if you excuse me for saying so.'

Until 2012 the female beach volleyball players to which Sepp Blatter referred were required to wear bikinis, the bottoms of which could be no more than six centimetres wide on the hip, while the men played in baggy shorts and vest tops. Not only did this clearly sexualise the sport, it made women's beach volleyball a bit of a joke, detracting from the fact that it is an incredibly tough sport.

At least these rules have now changed and in Rio it was wonderful to see Egyptian teammates Nada Meawad and Doaa Elghobashy shun the bikini in favour of long sleeves and long pants. Elghobashy also covered her hair with a hijab.

———————

It does feel that the depiction and narrative around sportswomen is at last beginning to change.

Platforms like espnW are driving this with their coverage of women's sport, and in 2019 global media coverage of the FIFA Women's World Cup also focused more on the players' skills and abilities than how they looked.

The WTA sought to raise the profile of women's tennis recently by showcasing female players on the tour as highly skilled and dedicated elite athletes. Commenting on the Strong is Beautiful campaign, CEO Stacey Allaster said: 'The unique combination of athleticism, strength and determination on the court and success, interests and inner beauty off the court is what makes women's tennis so attractive to millions around the world.'

And what is not to love about the WNBA's campaigns in recent years, 'Watch Me' and 'Watch Us Work', which highlight how extraordinary the players are in all they do.

It would be wonderful to see more sports emulate these in the future.

———————

While the primary message in this chapter is that we want to celebrate sportswomen for their accomplishments rather than their appearance, in a fascinating essay, 'New Rules for New Times: Sportswomen and Media Representation in the Third Wave', Toni Bruce asks if female athletes can be both pretty *and* powerful.

Decades of research on the media representation of sportswomen, some of which I've mentioned, reinforces the polarised debate about whether women should pose for lifestyle or sexy photoshoots or if this detracts from their status as elite athletes.

'The mismatch between femininity and athleticism has been well rehearsed in the literature since attributes associated with sport – physical strength, mental toughness, speed and muscle – are also signifiers of masculinity, so much so that the concept of the female athlete can itself be viewed as an oxymoron.'

This is changing, however, and just as many modern-day feminists are happy to embrace and celebrate their femininity, so we've seen the rise of feisty and feminine female heroes who happily 'kick ass' and look gorgeous at the same time. From movie stars Captain Marvel, Wonder Woman and Black Widow through to Daenerys Targaryen, Ayra Stark and Cersei Lannister in *Game of Thrones*, what's not to love about these magnificent, powerful women?

As Toni points out: 'Across a wide range of cultural sites, images of masculinity and femininity are now combined and recombined in different configurations that challenge traditional notions of gender difference.'

And so we see sportswomen declaring that they don't feel objectified in photoshoots but enjoy the opportunity to showcase and celebrate their fit, healthy, beautiful bodies. Perhaps it's no longer acceptable for society to dictate that sportswomen shouldn't combine their sport and athleticism with being sexy and attractive?

As Toni Bruce concludes: 'In identifying the similarities between the rise in cultural visibility of strong, tough and beautiful female movie heroes and strong, tough and beautiful athletes I suggest we are seeing the emergence of a potentially new form of femininity that refuses to cede physical strength and sporting excellence to men and thus represents an important rupture in the articulation of sport and masculinity.'

15

OH, SO YOU'RE A LESBIAN THEN?

I hate the word homophobia. It's not a phobia. You're not scared.
You're an asshole.

Attributed to Morgan Freeman, 2012

Having worked in women's sport for over thirty years, I've witnessed what a positive place it can be for the LGBTQ+ community. Sport provides an inclusive environment, enabling women and girls to feel fully accepted whatever their sexuality. Being part of a team can be a safe haven for a young woman, normalising her identity in a way she may not have experienced elsewhere.

Sadly, however, societal perception about queer women can also be the very thing that drives girls away from sport. Women who play sport have historically been stereotyped as lesbians and, at a time when young women feel the pressure to conform, inundated with messages of what a 'traditional feminine female' should look like, the perceived prevalence of queerness within women's sport can be confusing and off-putting. Deviating from what society deems to be 'the norm' can be scary for teenage girls and may lead them to reject sport entirely.

The topic itself can be hard to discuss for fear of causing offence. I'm anxious even writing this chapter, as terminology is constantly shifting and words can mean different things to different audiences. The term 'queer', for instance, has evolved from a word used to describe something odd in the 1920s, to something extremely derogatory when I was growing up, to a word that the LGBTQ+ community has now taken and made their own. When I use the word queer in this chapter I do so as an inclusive term encompassing lesbian, bisexual and gender-nonconforming women.

I know that national governing bodies, with a goal to drive increased participation, have struggled with the depiction of their sports. Will celebrating the fact that your sport is so inclusive potentially alienate young women who may be questioning whether they can find a place in a sport associated with lesbians?

Are high-profile gay athletes going to put girls off, or are parents less likely to encourage their daughters to play sport if they think they might be 'exposed' to lesbians? As ridiculous as this sounds, it's a genuine concern for some, especially in the historically homophobic conservative states of the US.

I've witnessed first-hand the positive impact sport had on my own daughter – both her sense of identity and her happiness.

Even in a Western society that is more accepting than ever before in our history, coming out at fifteen was tough for Molly. Rugby provided her with an open and accepting place where she could be herself, no longer needing to hide or question who she was. In her own words it was 'freeing and refreshing to be part of a team where I didn't need to think twice about my sexuality'.

I was interested in understanding more of the history around lesbianism in sport. How did it start and why has it been seen as something so negative in the past?

As I researched the topic, it's clear that the US has a much richer written history around sexuality and women's sport than we have in the UK. What follows, therefore, is not a definitive record, but my own commentary on the elements that resonated with me as I look back through the lens of sport.

Linking 'mannish' female athletes to lesbianism goes back to the 1880s when the medical community was exploring sexuality. Attraction to women was considered an entirely male trait. If a woman was attracted to another woman, it was seen as the total inversion of gender identity – 'a biological tragedy in which a male soul existed in a woman's body', according to sexologists at the time. They also noted that lesbians 'preferred masculine sports and labour' and that among lesbians 'there is often some capacity for athletics'.

It was primarily with shifts in culture and attitudes to sex in the 1920s and 1930s that the association between lesbianism and sport took hold. Until that time, society had worried that sport would negatively affect female sexuality in two ways. First, it would impair a women's fertility and her ability to have children, and second, it would make her into a 'muscle moll', a woman who lost her physical and moral control because of the powerful impulses of sport.

As views on morality changed in the 1920s, it was recognised that women did have sexual desires. The previous Victorian ideal of a passionless wife evolved into the confident, sexually liberated flappers of the Jazz Age. It was from this point that sexuality became central to consumer culture and the vision of modern femininity was established. An advertisement at the time stated simply: 'The first duty of a woman is to attract.' While it was recognised that women could now be sexually active and attractive ... this was only if they were attracting men.

It was at this time of sexual liberation for women, with a growing presence of lesbians in society, that the public began to show concern about 'mannish lesbians'. During the hard years of the Depression, there was a hostile backlash against strong, independent women in society including feminists, career women and lesbians.

Critics claimed that sport would make women more 'mannish' and therefore unlikely to find heterosexual love in the future. In the US, PE colleges and the women's sports departments at universities became concerned that too much female companionship might have a negative impact on the sexual desires of their students. They organised 'co-ed' events to redress the balance, along with activities to emphasise the grace and beauty of their students.

The stigma of lesbianism became more explicit after the Second World War. Society became hostile towards anyone who did not conform to traditional gender norms, and women in physical education and working-class sports became an easy target for homophobic condemnation.

LGBTQ+ communities began to grow in major US cities such as San Francisco, Los Angeles and New York in the 1940s, attracting thousands of gay and lesbian migrants who felt safe and accepted in these places as the growth in bars, nightclubs and networks expanded. But, sadly, the very presence of the queer community stirred up fear and hatred in society.

It is shocking to learn more of how Western society treated homosexuals in the 1950s. LGBTQ+ people were seen by some as diseased or mentally unsound. Reformers thought they could somehow be cured, and gay men were often 'treated' with castration, lobotomies, nerve surgery and electroshock treatment in psychiatric institutions.

As a 'homosexual panic' spread, promoting mass fear and loathing of the LGBTQ+ community, the US government purged itself of gay men or lesbians from any government or military post and encouraged the police to crack down on gay bars and communities. Queer people lost their jobs, their homes and their families. Many took their own lives.

For young gay women growing up at this time it must have been a terrifying experience to realise you were attracted to someone of the same sex. Women were unable to share their feelings with friends and family, and there was no reassuring depiction of gay people in books, or any role models in the media. Queer women felt lonely and isolated as they hid their sexuality in everyday life. Sport therefore became an important sanctuary, one of the few places where women could be themselves and socialise with other lesbians.

From the 1930s through to the 1960s many LGBTQ+ women across the world found competitive sports such as hockey, basketball, football, athletics, bowling and softball an ideal place to form friendships and create a shared culture. Sports gave women the opportunity to bond with other women as teammates, friends and partners. They met others like them and felt accepted and included in a group. Sport provided one of the few social spaces where gay women could relax with freedom to live their lives without judgement. That said, their relationships were still discreet and secretive.

Meanwhile, any female athletes noted for their masculine bodies and displaying male attributes of strength, power and speed became targets for anti-homosexual attacks. Male writers mocked female sport, portraying all female athletes as 'mannish types who disdained men and desired women'.

This meant that any sports wanting to attract a paying audience at that time had to 'feminise' themselves to counter any negativity associated with lesbianism. As previously mentioned, in the US, basketball and softball competitions added beauty pageants to their events and women were banned from wearing clothes that might make them look 'mannish'. Sportswomen could be sacked from the professional teams simply for having short, bobbed haircuts.

Unfortunately, the leaders in women's sport, while trying to protect the reputation of women's sport from the negative perceptions of society, only made things worse for LGBTQ+ athletes. In an attempt to ensure their events and programmes conformed with the new 'feminine heterosexual ideal' of the time, they just reinforced the public's views that celebrated heterosexuality and condemned lesbianism.

The Netflix documentary *Secret Love* is a moving depiction of the challenge some female athletes faced in hiding their true selves for generations. It tells the story of Terry Donahue and Pat Henschel, two former professional baseball players who kept their relationship a secret for seventy years.

It appears that the same opportunities for female intimacy that drew the queer community to sport during these decades may also have pushed other women away. In the US, by the mid-1950s the majority of American women showed little interest in competitive sport, mainly because of its off-putting reputation for being too masculine and a place for lesbians.

This attitude of non-sporty girls who don't want to look 'mannish' or be accused of being gay is still apparent today, but fortunately times are changing.

———

Things feel much more positive today as wider societal attitudes to the LGBTQ+ community evolve and the presence of gay women in sport is more accepted than ever before. With increased tolerance and acceptance of diversity we have seen same-sex marriage legalised in twenty-nine countries and the emergence of high-profile queer women including global celebrities such as Lady Gaga, Jodie Foster, Kristen Stewart, Angelina Jolie, Miley Cyrus and Cara Delevingne, along with our home-grown entertainers such as Clare Balding, Sue Perkins, Sandi Toksvig and Rita Ora.

In 2020, former GB boxer and Olympic champion Nicola Adams took part in BBC's *Strictly Come Dancing* with a female professional, the first time the show had had same-sex partners competing. It was such a shame that they had to leave the show early after Katya Jones, Nicola's dance partner, tested positive for COVID-19. Here's hoping Nicola may be back on the show in 2021.

It is also wonderful to reflect that at the 2019 FIFA Women's World Cup there were forty out LGBTQ+ participants – thirty-eight players along with one coach and a trainer. Clearly the numbers may well have been higher than this, with teams competing from countries such as Nigeria, Cameroon and Jamaica where homosexuality is still punishable with a prison sentence, and other countries whose levels of societal homophobia may keep many players closeted.

Possibly the most famous lesbian in women's sport today is Megan Rapinoe, vice-captain of the US Women's Soccer team, who became a global icon for tolerance in 2019, campaigning on a raft of important issues. Her fiancée, Sue Bird, is a leading WNBA player who is having a similar impact. With Rapinoe attracting huge commercial sponsorships from brands including Nike, Samsung and Budweiser, and Sue and Megan featuring together in advertisements for Symetra Life Insurance, it's a relief to be living in a time when her sexuality hasn't damaged her commercial standing in the way it did for Martina

Navratilova in the 1970s. After Martina was forced to acknowledge being a lesbian, her image suffered, and she reportedly lost millions of dollars of endorsement as a result.

In August 2016, two of our very own gay sporting icons, Kate and Helen Richardson-Walsh, became the first ever same-sex couple to play together on the same team at an Olympics when the GB Women's Hockey team won gold in Rio.

It was a momentous moment for the LGBTQ+ community, but I was interested to know whether they were worried that the news of their relationship might overshadow the team's incredible achievements on the pitch.

'I don't think it concerned us at the time because we were very aware of the magnitude of it. There are still, today, people living in the world who will be killed or jailed because of their sexuality, so actually, two people just talking about it, in an open way, was important,' explains Kate. 'However, I think some of our team-mates were understandably concerned, and I know Danny [the GB coach] said the first thing he got asked walking into the media zone after we'd just won that gold medal was, "isn't it great Kate and Helen have won as the first same-sex couple?"

'He was angry, and it's really hard because he's not angry that we are a couple, but there was so much more to it than that. There have been moments like that when it's really uncomfortable,' says Kate, who hopes the media might do better and look at the wider story in the future.

I've always felt that team sport is a place where women can very comfortably be themselves – whether that be straight, lesbian, bisexual – especially in comparison to men's sport, but Kate doesn't feel the landscape is quite as positive as I've painted it. 'There are still lots of women living a double life and that's completely up to them of course. Nobody has to be open with their private lives, it's their private life.'

It's incredibly sad, I reflect, that they can't be themselves in a sport they love. 'It is,' Kate replies. 'If you feel you can't be yourself then things need to be looked at. So, I think women's sport is better, particularly at grassroots level, I think it's much better than for men, but I think at elite level it's still quite closeted actually.'

I ask Kate why she thinks that is. Are these women worried that it might impact their sponsorship deals, their profile or media opportunities? 'Yes, and maybe they don't want the whole focus to be about the fact that they're bisexual or lesbian and actually just want to talk about sport. And I think that's probably quite a big fear and a real fear. And then for men there is that, *plus* the stereotypical traditions of what it means to be a man. And what it means to be a man that plays sport.'

Kate thinks that the next generation coming through will demand that those traditions and stereotypes are broken. 'Unfortunately, it just takes time. I think people are beginning to be more well educated, but that's why education in schools is so important. In order to accept difference, you have to learn about it and understand it. And I think that has to start at the youngest age.'

It's perhaps not surprising that some gay women in sport are reticent to go public about their sexuality when researchers still talk of the dominance of 'heterosexism' in sport and the homophobia that exists among coaches, players, parents and administrators. Studies also show that lesbian athletes have historically been devalued in the commercial marketplace and are less likely to receive sponsorships or endorsements than heterosexual teammates.

There is clearly a higher proportion of LGBTQ+ women playing sport than in the general population. Much of this has evolved historically, as we have seen, because women's sports have been, and still are, such an inclusive and supportive environment for queer women. The bigger issue, of course, is why an individual's sexuality should be an issue at all.

David Stern, the NBA Commissioner who championed the creation of the WNBA, knew that in the US homophobia (along with racism and sexism) was part of the reason the WNBA met with such resistance. He saw the power of sport and the growth of the WNBA to break down some of those barriers.

Stern told a story about a conversation he once had with an NBA/WNBA team owner whom he described as 'very conservative'. The owner had been approached by a fan who told him she was a lesbian and lifelong women's sports fan. She thanked him for providing a place for women to play where she also felt welcome. 'Now, I happened to know his views were probably not very consistent with that fan's views on a lot of things,' Stern said. 'So, I asked him, "What did you say?" And he said, "I said thank you too." So, I knew there were some broader societal issues that were at work there that the WNBA could impact in a positive way.'

———

Being open about your sexuality can be a challenge, especially when you are a high-profile athlete. When Casey Stoney, then captain of the England women's football team, came out in 2015 she said she was a gay woman in football, but that did not mean to say that every woman playing football is gay. I asked her why she felt it was so important to make that point: 'I hate stereotypes and that's one of the reasons I didn't come out for so long, because of the whole "oh of course she is gay, she plays football".

'Half of my friends in football are married to men. I hate

pigeon-holing and I hate stereotypes, that was why it was so important to me to say right, yeah, I am gay, but it is not because I play football, and I didn't want that stereotype for the rest of my friends in football.'

Was she scared about coming out when she did? 'It felt it was the right time, in terms of being England captain, using my platform for a positive. Was I petrified? Absolutely. Did I know what was going to happen? No. Probably about ninety-eight per cent was so positive with many people reaching out to me and to say thank you.'

You can understand the impact that Casey's decision had when she shares a memory from that time: 'I remember one specific parent messaged me to say, "thanks so much. My daughter came down last night and had a conversation with me, and that was really, really nice." There are moments where you go, that is why I did it. Because it made that young girl have the courage to go and speak to her mum, and not live in fear.

'As a parent I don't want to know *half* of my little girl, I want to know *all* of her. Being able to influence someone like that was quite a thing for me.'

I asked Casey if she is worried that the homophobia that still surrounds women's sport could put teenage girls off at a time when they are very sensitive to what people think about them.

Yes. I do. I think if you are thirteen or fourteen there is a stereotype. You think I do not want to be called a lesbian, so you don't do the sport, and it is unfair.

There are a lot of gay women in sport, there are statistically because it is more accepting. But it doesn't mean that there aren't a lot of heterosexual women, there are, an awful lot. But you're right, I think the stereotype of being butch can put people off. I think the stereotypes of being gay put people off.

It's more so in football and rugby. There are a lot of gay women in tennis that don't have the same stereotype of being butch because they wear a white dress and they go out on a court and play tennis, but they are still strong athletic women.

I hate the stereotypes. Just let people do their jobs. It is about changing societal attitudes about what is feminine and strong. Yes, you can be strong and athletic, and you can still look beautiful in a dress.

———————

I was reticent about including the subject of trans women in sport in this book, not because I don't think it's something that warrants discussion, but because of the levels of anger the topic can generate on both sides of the debate.

In 2019, when I asked Anna Kessel if there were any topics she was wary of covering in the paper, she said:

I suppose the one biggest issue that I don't know what the answer to it is trans and how do we approach that, how do we solve it? I don't know.

I think even when people have been well-meaning, someone like Martina Navratilova, who I respect hugely, when she came out and wrote that opinion piece – I hate to say anything negative about her because I just think she's incredible – but the language that she used was so disrespectful.

I think, no matter where you sit on the spectrum, you have to come with respect when you talk about it and if you don't, a) no one's going to listen, you're going to get everyone's backs up, but b) I just can't take your point of view seriously unless you are able to discuss it in a dispassionate way, in a calmer, dispassionate way.

Like Anna, I do not have the answers to the issues raised by trans women competing in elite sport.

I feel very strongly about the overriding importance of inclusivity. Trans women are women, and therefore, they should be included in the realm of women's sport. It is about dignity and respect and not denying those who identify as women any of the incredible benefits that we know sport offers.

I do appreciate that trans women's inherent strength and power could become an issue in competitive sport. Most trans women who have gone through male puberty will have larger lungs, hearts, limbs, etc., a physiological legacy that cannot be nullified with hormone treatments or surgery. Reducing testosterone levels now will not eradicate those advantages. (And then, of course, there is the ethical issue of forcing anyone to have hormone treatment just to do what they love.)

Whatever various sporting bodies like the IOC decide in terms of the treatments required to compete, those born as males who have gone through puberty will generally remain bigger and more powerful than those born as females, and in the majority of competitive sport speed and strength and power are advantages.

Should this matter, though? Transgender female athletes will have physiological advantages, but I have heard people argue the case that this is one of the key features of competitive sport. Elite male and female athletes may have 'abnormal' physical traits, the very thing that contributes to making them extraordinary in their sports. The height of NBA basketballers for instance: in 2018, an incredible forty-eight of them were over 7ft tall. Or the lung capacity of Michael Phelps – reportedly twice that of the average human at 12 litres. Those using this argument are keen to point out that we don't see other male athletes complaining about these physical advantages.

On the other side, scaremongers would have us believe that we are about to see a massive onslaught of male athletes now identifying as women to win US university scholarships or Olympic medals and enjoy the subsequent commercial sponsorship this might bring. They believe female athletes will miss out having fought so hard for equality in sport and that's not fair or just.

I am not sure this is the case.

What I would hate to see is an outright blanket ban of all trans women in sport at every level. That feels too draconian. The FA currently considers each person on a case-by-case basis, which might be a potential approach.

In 2020, World Rugby became the first international federation to consider the issue of trans women in the game and I asked Katie Sadleir to tell me about that process when they were in the consultation mode: 'World Rugby doesn't just make calls without consulting its members and this is incredibly tricky and difficult, a challenge for any sport to address.'

Katie outlined the comprehensive review group chaired by a psychiatrist that includes doctors, coaches, legal experts and players who considered if the current policy is fit for purpose. 'There were question marks about the policy that the IOC had, particularly in terms of how it applied to rugby, and it would have been professionally inept of us to just pretend that that didn't exist.'

The research cited by World Rugby showed that a reduction of testosterone 'does not lead to a proportionate reduction in mass, muscle mass, strength or power' and presents a 'clear safety risk'. It calculated that players who are born as men 'are stronger by twenty-five to fifty per cent, are thirty per cent more powerful, forty per cent heavier and about fifteen per cent faster' than women playing in the same competitive matches and estimates 'at least a twenty to thirty per cent greater risk' of a female player being injured if tackled by a biological male.

'The real challenge when you looked at all the research that was put in front of that group was that we are a sport that prides itself on inclusivity and diversity, and inclusion is really, really important. But we also put player welfare as our number one priority and there were challenges that were coming from the wider community about whether or not this was fair,' says Katie.

'World Rugby is committed to making sure that it remains itself an inclusive sport. It may very well be that we need to just think about how that happens in a different way but there have been no decisions made at this stage.

'I know that there have been some absolutely passionate women players that have come back and said that they think this is atrocious that we are looking at this. I think it would be professionally irresponsible for us to not look at it.'

Following this comprehensive review, at the end of 2020 World Rugby updated its transgender participation guidelines. The new guidelines 'do not recommend that trans women play women's contact rugby on safety grounds at the international level of the game where size, strength, power and speed are crucial for both risk and performance'.

An important caveat, though, was that World Rugby 'do not preclude national unions from flexibility in their application of the guidelines at the domestic/community level of the game'.

Chair of the review panel, Dr Araba Chintoh, went on to explain: 'Unions will be able to exercise flexibility on a case-by-case basis at the community level of the game, for which the unions are responsible, while World Rugby will continue to prioritise inclusion strategies to ensure that the trans community remain an active, welcome and important member of the rugby family.'

To conclude the announcement, World Rugby Chairman Sir Bill

Beaumont added: 'Rugby is a welcoming and inclusive sport and, while this has been a difficult decision to make, it has been taken following comprehensive consultation and engagement and for the right reasons, given the risk of injury. That said, we recognise that the science continues to evolve, and we are committed to regularly reviewing these guidelines, always seeking to be inclusive.'

I welcome World Rugby's openness to addressing the challenge, because the biggest issue for me right now is that we're not able to talk about the topic calmly. Any debate on the subject is immediately shut down by both sides, whatever your opinion, even if you're just open to finding out more. The Twittersphere is this hotbed of vitriol, anger and hatred. You're either a transphobe or TERF (trans-exclusionary radical feminist) or you're going to be cancelled by others for supporting – or not supporting – the trans community.

I desperately hope that in the future we might all be kinder and more open-minded in order to explore what is a complex and emotive issue for everyone.

———

In closing this chapter, I circle back to where I started.

Let's celebrate women's sport. It's a remarkable place where women can truly and authentically be themselves, regardless of their sexual orientation.

Who wouldn't want that for their daughters? Who wouldn't want that for all women and girls?

16

RACE FOR EQUALITY

Maybe it doesn't get better in time for me, but someone in my position can show women and people of colour that we have a voice, because Lord knows I use mine

Serena Williams, 2020

Tuesday 29 August 2017 was a special day for women's sport in England, when our national women's rugby team and women's cricket team were hosted in a reception at 10 Downing Street by the then Prime Minister Theresa May. Whatever your political leanings, it was great to see these elite female athletes being celebrated and recognised by the most powerful woman in the country.

The cricketers had won the World Cup the previous month in front of packed stands at Lord's, and the rugby team had just lost out to New Zealand in a dramatic World Cup final in Ireland.

My own memory of that day was, first, the pleasure that it had brought about, followed by shock at the images that were shared. When the two teams lined up together, it was suddenly, glaringly obvious that you could only see white women. If you had added the GB hockey team to that mix, Olympic champions from the previous year, it would have been much the same.

I was embarrassed I had not 'seen' it before.

The whiteness of those elite teams reflects the entire system for many sports, where the school you attend, and where you live, are still likely to be the largest influences as to whether or not you make it onto the England pathway. However well you play at school or in street games, it can be a huge challenge to progress to a club or county set-up.

Ebony Rainford-Brent, the first Black woman to play cricket for England, says it was the support of one woman, Jenny Wostrack, who enabled her to progress in the sport. Jenny helped Ebony's mother by taking her to training and getting her into the Surrey system.

'If you look at the pathways, which I'm starting to do a lot more now, it's not connected from inner city to our traditional game. It's not at all,' declares Ebony. 'The kids are playing street projects, but there aren't talent ID processes, there aren't academies which will help those kids move from soft ball to hard ball. There's not enough investment. There's investment in grassroots programmes in those areas, but the pathway is not linked up.'

The same can be said for sports like hockey and rugby, which for many years have been very white and middle-class.

The failure of national sports teams to reflect the diversity of the population is also something that occurs in women's sport in the US. I asked Mary Harvey, former goalkeeper for the US Women's Soccer team and now CEO of the Centre for Sport and Human Rights, about the lack of diversity in the current US women's soccer team.

'Let's talk about the player pool which leads into the national team in the United States, which is not the way it is in the rest of the world,' said Mary. 'It's very much an upper-middle-class-type sport, which is probably what you're getting at. So, yes, that's a known issue.

'In every other part of the world, football is the game that is accessible to everyone. But in the US, it has become something that is accessible to people who have the money to participate. And that's going to be a natural funnel if that is then what leads into your elite programs. So, is the women's national team as diverse they could be? No, for that very reason. Because it's not reflective of the entire population that probably would want to participate if they could.'

Rimla Akhtar, former Chair of the Muslim Women's Sport Foundation and the first Muslim woman to sit on the FA Council, has done a huge amount to support British sports in making their pathways more inclusive. She told me:

I have gone across all sorts of talent centres for different sports, across the UK, and I am still seeing the same people. A lot of the sports, when it comes to the female side of things, are very white middle class, and that has to change. It has to change in terms of where you are going to access the talent, and how easy you are making it for those girls to actually come to sessions.

Barriers still lie in terms of the pathways to the elite level. We're seeing more Muslim and Asian girls across sports media and we are starting to see a few more in the coaching space, but not so many are able to make it up that pathway to the highest levels of being a performance athlete.

That is partly due to that belief that sport is not a career and because we don't have the role models, it's the chicken and egg situation. Can I really make a career of this?

But mainly I think it's because the pathways aren't inclusive enough, so the way the sports access their talents – where they choose which pool of talent they go to – that's a massive issue that still needs to be dealt with. The elite performance pathway is still a massive issue.

What's being done to change this situation? It's fantastic to see powerful influencers like Ebony leading the way with projects such as the African-Caribbean Engagement Programme (ACE) at Surrey County Cricket Club. The scholarship programme creates new opportunities for young African-Caribbean cricketers to enter the club's performance pathway, targeting eleven- to eighteen-year-old boys and girls with sporting potential. The programme will also support local African-Caribbean clubs in developing a sustainable infrastructure and in building strong links with a range of community schemes.

Ultimately, though, it's about all those involved in women's sport seeing the issues around diversity and inclusion and working to offer an alternative that's accessible for all.

———

Role models for women and girls of colour can have a powerful impact. It was wonderful to see eighteen-year-old Khadijah Mellah become the first British Muslim woman to ride in a horse race, the first jockey to compete wearing a hijab, when she won the Magnolia Cup at Goodwood in 2019. It was just three months after she'd first ridden a racehorse and she'd been studying for her A-levels as she trained.

Khadijah, a student from Peckham in south-east London, had learned to ride at a charity stables for inner-city kids. You can see her story in the excellent ITV documentary *Riding a Dream*, which finishes with Khadijah commenting: 'My story has changed the perception nationally about Muslim women, and also, the perception of Islam. All we ever hear about is the negatives, so I am just so glad that I have made it in the news as a positive Islamic story.'

I was lucky enough to be present when Khadijah collected the Young Sportswoman of the Year Award at the *Sunday Times* Sportswomen of the Year Awards in 2019. An inspirational woman in person, too.

Another young woman proving to be an extraordinary role model is Alice Dearing, Britain's only Black elite swimmer. Shocking research from Swim England shows that 95 per cent of Black adults in Britain do not swim and neither do 80 per cent of Black children. Less than 1 per cent of competitive swimmers in 2018 identified as Black or mixed race.

Alice, an athlete on the Women's Sport Trust's Unlocked programme in 2020, helped found the Black Swimming Association, with an ambition to challenge the many myths that exist around Black people swimming. She's been very vocal about the topic, calling out the issues across the media and social media.

Talking to Sky Sports, Arun Kang, the CEO of Sporting Equals, which promotes ethnic diversity in sport and physical activity, said: 'Alice Dearing has been a trailblazer in the world of British swimming, breaking stereotypes and being a relatable role model for the British Black community. She has proven that with dedication, hard work and focus anything is possible, but she has also used her platform to highlight what a struggle it is for members of the Black community to reach such status.'

And it's not just on the field of play or in the board room that we want to see more diversity, but across sport. That's why it's important to celebrate trailblazing women like football coach Manisha Taylor, who commented to the BBC in 2020: 'It is ludicrous that I'm the only south Asian female in the role that I'm in, in ninety-two clubs [. . .] because there are others who have a similar background to me who are equally qualified.'

Or Isa Guha, the retired English cricketer, who represented her country 113 times during a spectacular ten-year career before her enormously successful broadcasting career, and lawyer Shehneela Ahmed, the first Asian female football agent in the world to be recognised by the FA.

———

Regrettably, though, when the media could be helping to promote incredible ethnically diverse female athletes, it reverts to what it thinks its audience wants. Megan Rapinoe called this out in 2020, in an article for *The Players' Tribune*:

> . . . I think we need to be careful about calling the support that we got a 'feminist' breakthrough, when it's only part of the way there. Because when the support only extends to 'white girls next door' sports? That's not feminism – or at least it's not the kind of feminism that I'm here for. I don't have time for any kind of feminism that's not real and total – from race to class to religion to gender identity to sexual orientation to everything in between.
>
> When it comes to U.S. women's soccer, the general perception is that – let's face it – we're the white girls next door. The straight, 'cute,' 'unthreatening,' 'suburban' white girls next door. It's not actually who we are – the WNT's racial diversity, though not yet where it needs to be, is improving every year. And, you know, breaking news . . . I'm gay. But by and large, that's the perception. And it's certainly how we're marketed to a lot of people.

And I guess I just have to wonder, when I see the millions of viewers we're getting, and the shine on *SportsCenter*, and the talk show appearances and the endorsement deals and all of that . . .

Where's that same energy for the best women's basketball players on the planet?? Where's that energy for the women's sports that – instead of scanning cute and white and straight – scan tall and Black and queer??

Where's that conversation? As far as I'm concerned, there's no conversation worth having without it.

Megan called this out at such an important time, with huge impetus for the Black Lives Matter movement in the summer of 2020. It seems that finally people are waking up to the inherent racism that has existed in all areas of society for so long. Sport is just one of those areas, but an important one as it has so much impact on our lives and attitudes.

———

Clothing can also provide a significant barrier to women from diverse communities taking part in sport, as Rimla Akhtar highlighted when she told me more about the FIFA hijab ban in 2007.

It began with a young girl about to play football with her team in Canada, when the referee told her she had to remove her hijab as he felt there was a safety issue. Understandably, the girl said no and so the referee gave her a red card, sending her off because she refused to remove her hijab.

'That obviously created uproar and it went from being a local Canadian issue to a national and then an international issue,' says Rimla. 'It just so happened that at about the same time there was a meeting of IFAB in Manchester.' IFAB sets the laws of the game for FIFA.

'At that point there was no specific law which prevented the hijab from being worn, but this group of eight individuals (and you can imagine the demographic of those individuals), decided in their wisdom to say that the hijab wasn't allowed on the pitch, on the field of play.'

It turns out it wasn't just the hijab that was banned, it was any form of religious statement or expression on the field of play. Other items banned along with the hijab that day were the turban and the yarmulke or kippah, the skullcap worn in public by Orthodox Jewish men.

'Clearly, the greatest impact would be on Muslim women because there were many, many more Muslim women playing football, than there are Sikh men playing with the turban,' says Rimla.

'Long story short, it took us seven years, seven whole years to overturn that ban.

'And then what was a shame it was that just as it had been overturned, in their wisdom FIBA, the basketball equivalent of FIFA, decided to ban the hijab themselves in 2014.'

Rimla feels it needs a full-scale review of hijab and clothing bans across sports, which is something she has been working on for a while.

'That is why leadership, and diversity in leadership and governance, is so, so important. Otherwise, you have unnecessary laws put in by people who don't understand the impact of them.'

———

Long before the success of the WNBA, basketball in the US was a sport where Black women had a great deal of success. It provided an alternative for those who didn't have access to develop their sporting skills in the exclusive country clubs or university athletic associations in the last century – primarily reserved for privileged white middle- or upper-class women. Women's basketball flourished in Black colleges, of which only 25 per cent objected to intercollegiate sport in 1939, versus 83 per cent of mainly white institutions.

'Let's encourage our girls to be "tomboys." Let them enter any game of sport and recreation that the boy enters. Let's teach them to be real girls,' was the powerful call from Black recreation leader Ruth Arnett in 1921.

Similarly, as white American women moved away from track and field in the mid-twentieth century, concerned by the stigma associated with athletic females, Black women began to blaze a trail with huge national and international success. Throughout the 1950s Black women made up more than two-thirds of American women chosen to compete at track and field in major championships, including the Olympic Games.

As Susan Cahn points out in *Coming on Strong*, however, there was a double edge to their pre-eminent position in the sport: 'On a personal level success meant opportunities for education, travel, upward mobility and national or even international recognition . . . viewed through the lens of commonplace racial prejudices, African American women's achievements in a "mannish" sport also reinforced disparaging stereotypes of Black women as less womanly or feminine than white women.'

This misperception of the Black woman being somehow 'less feminine' than the blonde, white female is something that has been very evident in the world of tennis in the past decade. For the majority of Serena Williams's career, she made less money than Maria Sharapova, despite being by far the better player. The two played each other twenty-two times in their careers and Serena won nineteen times.

Examining Serena's place in American culture in 2015, former player Chris Evert commented on Sharapova's commercial advantage: 'I think the corporate world still loves the good-looking blonde girls.'

Jessica Luther and Kavitha Davidson reflect on this in their book *Loving Sports When They Don't Love You Back*: 'It's no stretch to say that marketers believe their consumers are more interested in worshipping the beauty of tall, skinny white women over and above well-built muscled Black ones.'

Despite being an adored icon and inspiration for millions of women, Serena has faced outrageous racism throughout her career. After a particularly hideous incident at Indian Wells in 2001 when she was just nineteen – her father, who was her coach, reported one person saying: 'I wish it was '75; we'd skin you alive' – she and her sister Venus withdrew from the tournament for the next fourteen years.

So much about her has been critiqued by others: her body, her strength, her hair and her clothes. Around the time of her win at the French Open in 2015 she was compared to an animal and likened to a man. After an outburst during the final of the US Open in 2019 a racist cartoon in Australian daily newspaper the *Herald Sun* depicted Serena as an exaggerated stereotype of African-Americans – large lips, broad, flat nose and wild afro-styled ponytail – contrasted with the image of Naomi Osaka, a Japanese-Haitian, who was shown as a white woman with blonde hair and no exaggerated features.

Bernice King, daughter of Martin Luther King Jr, said the *Herald Sun*'s stance was 'without consideration for the painful historical context of such imagery and how it can support biases and racism today'.

Female British athletes have also experienced racism from fans, though as England and Arsenal footballing legend Rachel Yankey told me, it was quite rare and happened more when she played in Europe. She remembers an incident during a European game at Real Valladolid in Spain: 'There was one person making monkey noises and shouting at me every time I got the football. I think I was just more astonished to be honest because I've read about it, I've heard people talk about it, but I couldn't relate to that. You can't ever really relate to it until it actually happens.

'I remember one time when Danielle Carter was warming up and people were throwing coins at her. Just ridiculous. That's just so dangerous anyway. But people spitting. You can't believe what some people do.'

There's also the unconscious bias of teammates, says Rachel: 'I've had comments from players, which you will put down as banter, when actually it does come down to sort of racial bias.'

Rachel relays the time she was running coaching sessions in schools and didn't want to put her own phone number on a promotional leaflet. She bought another phone and therefore sometimes carried two. About the same time, she'd bought a new car and a teammate said: 'Oh what, are you a drug dealer now?'

'And that's one of my teammates. And you can take it and you can laugh it off, but, well, you know. It's a hard one to call out and say "Oh, you wouldn't say that to another player" because then people ask why are you getting on the defensive? I think my look at the time said it all. My unimpressed look. We left it there because there's just no need for that, no need for it at all.'

Rachel goes on to explain that what was really needed at that point was for another player to step in and call it out:

It wasn't just me and my mate that were there. There were other people, but no one said anything. It was only me that looked and just gave them an angry look and thought, you know what, I'm not even going to get started here, I'm just going to walk off. I'm just going to leave it.

Was that the right thing to do? I don't know. Possibly not.

If we're going to change something then we need not just the person – whether it's the victim or another Black person – to say something, but we need everybody that actually finds that wrong to say 'do you know what, that's wrong'.

And then the person asks: 'why is it wrong?', and then you have a conversation, a debate, you find out 'oh, I didn't really understand that'. Then you can argue the points over it, and the malice over it. I don't believe that there was any malice in what was said to me. I just believe that it was a stupid thing to say and quite ignorant.

But nobody stood up. And that's where I think we all need to stand up, if we're going to overcome racism, we all need to stand up.

———

On a more positive note, we are seeing change and it's fantastic that ethnically diverse sportswomen now feature in mainstream advertising campaigns in the UK.

Long-jumper Jazmin Sawyers became the face of Olay in the UK in 2019, as Dina Asher-Smith appeared on the front cover of numerous glossy magazines and was also joined by heptathlete Katarina Johnson-Thompson in TV ads for Müller products. It was also great in 2019 to see *Elle* magazine feature Dina along with netballers Serena Guthrie and Jodie Gibson, Katarina Johnson-Thompson, track and field athlete Morgan Lake and boxers Ramla Ali and Caroline Dubois.

Talking on *The Mid-Point* podcast with Gabby Logan in 2020, Olympic gold medallist Denise Lewis said that appearing on the front of magazines at the height of her career in 2000 was something that would never have happened: 'I was told "you're not relatable. Your body, your face wouldn't sell magazines." At the time it felt very much like "I accept what you're saying and I can't do anything about it."

'So, for me to now see the likes of Dina Asher-Smith, and so many other women of colour, really owning the shelves, it's progress for the generations to follow. You shouldn't be told no.'

——————

Change comes from the top, and just as my chapter on governance called for great female representation on the boards of our sports bodies, so ethnicity should be a consideration, too. An investigation by Telegraph Women's Sport in June 2020 found that of the more than 400 board members of leading bodies in the sector, only five were Black and female.

The report analysed the boards of thirty-eight UK sports organisations, which between them have 415 directors. Almost 90 per cent of them (thirty-four) did not have a Black woman on their boards. Of the national governing bodies of the twenty Olympic sports funded by UK Sport, only one Black woman was a board member: Anne Wafula Strike, a former Paralympic wheelchair racer, who sits on the board of UK Athletics.

Just as there are different approaches to ensure better gender balance, the same follows for diversity. Some feel that the Code for Sports Governance should have included targets for diversity.

'I was disappointed that there weren't targets,' says Rimla Akhtar. 'If you are going to set a target for gender, then as far as I am concerned you need to set a target across diversity, different strands of diversity. I was really disappointed, particularly considering there is such a small number of ethnic minorities on sports boards even when the code was being put together, and even now.'

This is something Sport England and UK Sport are addressing, with programmes now in place to prepare 'board-ready' candidates from diverse backgrounds and talk of targets to be included in the updated Governance Code in 2021.

Besides a board quota, Rimla also suggests other approaches should be considered, such as more education for the sports sector – helping directors recognise and address their conscious and unconscious bias – and the provision of more mentoring, support and guidance for women of colour.

———

The murder of George Floyd in Minneapolis in May 2020 sparked a societal movement unlike any we've seen in recent years. It was a turning point for me personally, in my recognition and understanding of the oppression faced by ethnically diverse people across the world.

I recognise that I have an ongoing journey of unlearning a lifetime of biases and misinformation to ensure that the work I do can positively impact the lives of all women in sport, not just those who look like me.

We can all be more intersectional in our approach. Just as we call for more women on sports boards, women in sports media and women in elite coaching, so we must ensure those women who have been excluded in the past are also at the table, and that our pathways to elite sport are open to all young women, whatever their race or ethnicity.

17

IT'S A MASS MOVEMENT

My coach said I run like a girl and I said if he trained a little harder, he could, too.

Mia Hamm

Much of this book has focused on elite women's sport, but women have been missing out on sport across all ages and abilities for decades, too.

From little girls not allowed to join the boys playing football in the school playground, teenage girls unable to play a sport they love because local clubs don't offer girls' teams, through to older women uncomfortable about exercising in public for fear of ridicule and abuse – in every age band women have less opportunity to participate in sport and enjoy all the amazing benefits it offers.

It is shocking to note that by the age of seven girls are already less active than boys and this difference widens as they move from childhood into adolescence. Secondary school-age girls are more likely to experience participation barriers than boys, with the biggest drop-off occurring as girls move from primary to secondary schools. This is partly because of disruption to friendship groups, but often also because of their declining body confidence.

Over 40 per cent of fourteen- to sixteen-year-old girls say their period prevents them from taking part in PE and sport at school. A quarter of girls this age say that a lack of confidence stops them taking part compared to just 9 per cent of boys, according to research from Women in Sport and the Youth Sport Trust. And according to the Sport England Active Lives survey in 2017–18, there were 115,400 *more* primary-aged boys than girls meeting the Chief Medical Officers' guidelines of sixty minutes of moderate to vigorous activity a day across the week.

While this is disappointing, it is great to see that positive change is happening with much great work driven by the Youth Sport Trust, Women in Sport and Sport England. Starting in schools there are now lots of initiatives that are highlighting these gender inequalities and making a difference from the ground up.

One of these is the Barclays-supported FA Girls' Football School Partnerships programme, which aims to give every young girl the opportunity to play football in school by 2024. The scheme sees hundreds of primary schools receiving teacher training, practical resources and equipment, along with the opportunity to engage with positive role models and attend high-profile women's football matches.

The Youth Sport Trust, which partners with the FA in delivering the Girls' Football School Partnerships, has also made huge strides to change the way PE and sport are taught in primary and secondary schools with their Girls Active programme. Since 2015, 82,000 girls have been involved in the scheme at 727 primary and secondary schools across England and Northern Ireland. Working directly with secondary school girls to help them shape the PE curriculum for their own schools, Girls Active is diversifying the options on offer and in turn making lessons more relevant and attractive. The programme also helps develop skills and confidence.

One of my slight concerns about the influential work of the Youth Sport Trust is that in creating campaigns to make physical activity more appealing to schoolgirls we risk 'overfeminising' physical activity and moving away from traditional sport. So rather than encouraging schools to challenge the long-established societal views that girls should not be sweaty and sporty and strong like the boys, we instead add Zumba to the curriculum and hairdryers to changing rooms. I put this point to Alison Oliver, CEO at the Youth Sport Trust, who agreed: 'It was a huge worry to me actually at one point because I came from team sports. I was a team sport player and I could see us being part of a shift that started to say team sports isn't what girls want and isn't right for girls and we need to kind of move away from it and find these alternative things. And actually, when you talk to girls, again the research bears it out. Girls love team sport. They want to play. They just don't want to be in the team that someone's told them they have to be in. They want to work out their own team.'

As Ali points out, girls are now flooding into team sports traditionally considered to be just for boys. Many international federations for sports including cricket, football, rugby union, rugby league and Australian rules football are working hard to evolve their sports for women, having witnessed a massive influx at grassroots level in recent years. In many sports, females are now the fastest growing demographic and, in some cases, already make up more than 30 per cent of the playing population.

Once girls leave school, these gender differences continue into adulthood, where 39 per cent of women aged sixteen and over are not active enough to enjoy the full health benefits of sport and physical activity, compared to 35 per cent of men.

Fortunately, we are seeing positive change with powerful campaigns like This Girl Can.

Sport England invests National Lottery and government funding to ensure everyone can experience the benefits of sport and physical activity, but for many years women had been persistently less active than men. This was even though an incredible 75 per cent of women said they would like to do more – they recognised the benefits, but something was stopping them.

When Sport England looked at women's barriers to sport and exercise, they all led back to one main factor – the 'fear of judgement'. It was primarily fear that was stopping women from exercising. Women worried about being judged for their appearance during and after exercise; on their ability, if they weren't good enough as a beginner or were seen to be 'too good'; and also, if others would judge them for spending too much time exercising rather than prioritising their children, family or work.

It is fascinating to review the very honest reasons given by women, many of which I have felt myself in the past, despite being a confident sportswoman familiar with working out in a gym or pool. What was so refreshing about this research is that for the very first time it really got to the heart of the issue for women. For decades I have seen research carried out for the fitness industry that had tried to identify why women didn't exercise and join gyms, with the reasons most frequently cited being lack of time, lack of money or family commitments. These slightly superficial responses never recognised the authentic reasons in the way that the new qualitative research from Sport England did.

Women voiced very honest and personal concerns about their appearance. They were worried about being sweaty; having a red face; not looking like they usually do (no makeup); having to wear tight clothing; how their bodies look during exercise (jiggling and wobbling); not appearing feminine or developing too many muscles. Women were also concerned about having to get changed in front of other women and having their bodies on display in changing rooms and showers.

Getting things wrong was also a big concern; would they wear the wrong clothing or kit; not know the rules or bring the wrong equipment? Would they not be fit enough or not good enough or not serious enough to play sport with other women and therefore hold others back? Others were concerned they would be seen as too competitive.

Having considered all these barriers, the main goal of This Girl Can was to help free women from the judgements that held them back. They launched with a simple but very powerful manifesto that resonated with millions of women who had previously felt distanced from sport and exercise because of how it had been portrayed in the past.

'Women come in all shapes and sizes and all levels of ability. It doesn't matter if you're rubbish or an expert. The brilliant thing is you're a woman and you're doing something.'

Helping women to realise they were not alone was at the very foundation of this powerful campaign. Huge spending went into ensuring This Girl Can had enormous reach, with everything from the creation of content for short films, billboards and apps; extensive advertising and public relations across TV, print and cinema; and plenty of engagement on social media.

It was a brave decision by the Sport England team to invest so much in this way – something I'd never witnessed before in my lifetime – but it was necessary to completely normalise the messages and reach the mass of everyday women.

An extraordinary 70 per cent of women aged fourteen to forty said they felt motivated by This Girl Can, which had incredible reach and went on to win many awards. The real success of the campaign was that since its launch in 2015 it has persuaded nearly three million women to get more active – trying a new type of activity or increasing the amount of time spent exercising. The number of women playing sport and getting active once a week, every week, also increased by 250,000, while men's activity levels remained the same – so that gender gap has been substantially narrowed.

The next phase of the campaign broadened the target audience slightly to reach women aged forty-one to sixty, but Sport England still saw less engagement with women with lower incomes and from some specific ethnic groups – the same groups that are also less likely to be active. Significantly more Black and South Asian women don't meet weekly guidelines compared to white women and almost half of lower-income women don't meet the recommended physical activity guidelines, compared to a third of women with higher incomes.

Research showed that, along with the fear of judgement, there were more practical challenges faced by these women including lack of time, feeling tired or not having the money to afford gym memberships. They liked the campaign but didn't think the women faced the same challenges as them.

The final phase of the campaign has therefore addressed the stark inequalities in exercise levels between different groups of women. It encouraged these women to overcome the social, cultural and economic barriers that were stopping them from having the confidence to begin regular exercise.

The new Fit Got Real campaign showed 'real women' of different ages and ethnicities doing exercise their own way – running around a park, pushing a baby in a pram, hula-hooping at home and learning how to swim via YouTube.

I was lucky enough to be a guest at the launch of the Fit Got Real campaign in 2019 but felt a little disappointed when the new advert didn't give me goosebumps in the way the first one had five years before. It took a moment for the penny to drop. I wasn't in the target audience for this iteration, so it was probably OK.

———

In the US it was Title IX that had the biggest impact in getting more young women into sport. The conversion from a nation that had told its young women 'sport is not for you' to what we see today has been extraordinary, with a huge gender transformation in sports, and millions of girls flooding into sports such as football and basketball.

Also fuelling this dramatic increase in women taking part in more sport and physical activity across the world over the past thirty years has been the development of women-only events.

Sports bodies like USA Triathlon have seen a massive growth in female membership. They say this growth is due to 'society's acceptance of "active" women, women feeling more comfortable living an active lifestyle, the growth of women-only events like the Danskin and Iron Girl series and races focusing on charity involvement and fundraising'.

Whereas running clubs and events were once male-dominated, today it's women who make up over 60 per cent of race entries, according to Running USA's national survey.

Positive impact from popular women-only events has been seen in studies from New Zealand, where researchers looked at how event participation affected long-term physical activity and found that even those who were less active before the event continued to rate themselves as 'active' six months after the event.

Dr Brianna L. Newland's research with event directors of women-only events across the USA found four overarching themes that will be universal across the world.

INTIMIDATION FACTOR

All the event directors said that they started hosting women-only events because they found women were intimidated by the sport itself or by the thought of competing alongside men. Women, many of whom were returning after having children or many years away from sport, said they were scared to know what to do, or how to train for the sport, but excited to get involved. Making the events entry level to start with and providing lots of reassurance and guidance were key to overcoming this.

SOCIAL COMMUNITY

The event directors had all witnessed an increased interest in women-only training groups and wanted to translate this interest to events. The goal of the events was generally to reduce the anxiety, mitigate the barriers and create safe, fun environments.

Women also gravitated towards the women-only merchandise because wearing it made them feel part of the club or community.

ADVOCACY

Advocacy was shown in two ways by the women: personal advocacy and philanthropy.

Race directors witnessed support and encouragement among the women, with women at the start line giving last-minute advice and pep talks or sharing a laugh together. They said this was very different from the atmosphere of mixed events, something I have witnessed myself attending women's triathlon and running events.

It resonated with me personally as I had been surprised, but delighted, in my early triathlons, to see more experienced female triathletes happily sharing advice on transition set-up with newbies, showing us how to rack our bikes properly or offering talc to put in running shoes. I went on to do the same as my experience in the sport grew.

The other area was around advocacy for health and wellness through charity support, with women more likely than men to want to raise funds to help others as part of the events.

PROMOTION

The final theme was around how women-only events should be promoted. Everyone agreed that messaging should show that the event was a safe space in which women would be introduced to sport in a friendly, welcoming way that wasn't intimidating. It was important to let women know there was a community feel with opportunities for social interaction, and that they could support each other, their own health and wellbeing.

Other noteworthy elements were a recognition that women-only events were not about running events 'the same old way' minus the men. They provided the opportunity for race directors to rethink the set-up of sporting events, with alternative marketing, a different, fun, inclusive atmosphere, and a focus on participation rather than podiums.

And finally, a move away from the 'pink' or 'princess' approach, which, while popular in the past, many felt was now seen as stereotyping and misogynistic and potentially alienating women of colour.

————

We have seen the proliferation of women-only charity events in the UK, with one of the first, Race for Life, starting twenty-five years ago. Since that first race in Battersea in 1994, where 750 participants raised £48,000, Race for Life has grown into a series of hundreds of events across the country, raising nearly £500 million towards beating cancer.

Around the same time, in 1996, Nina Barough and thirteen brave women decided to power-walk the New York City Marathon in decorated bras and raised £25,000 for the charity that today is Breast Cancer Now. In 1998, Nina organised the first MoonWalk, which took place before the London Marathon, and since that time the charity has encouraged over 450,000 people to take on a walking challenge and raised more than £100 million for breast cancer causes.

In a similar vein, I loved working with Women V Cancer's Ride the Night, an event which sees thousands of women cycling through the centre of London raising money for three charities, Ovarian Cancer Action, Breast Cancer Now and Jo's Cervical Cancer Trust. The joy and camaraderie of the event was incredibly inspiring, with many stories of women encouraged back onto their bikes for the first time in years to take part in the challenge.

In the UK the flood of women into sport and activity has been especially apparent in running, where England Athletics' initiatives including This Girl Can Run and RunTogether have seen hundreds of female running groups created across the country.

We've also seen the emergence of powerful women-only running communities such as This Mum Runs, with its online community of over 100,000 women enjoying 500 free runs a month within sixty communities, and Run Mummy Run with a Facebook group of 65,000.

CrossFit has transformed the perception of women in the fitness arena with no more pink weights or high rep/low weight female workouts. In the CrossFit Box it's the same exercises for everyone. In fact, since its launch in 2000, over 50 per cent of CrossFit participants globally are women.

Finally, where 'weight training' was classed as primarily a male activity when I grew up – Arnold Schwarzenegger in *Pumping Iron* was a family favourite in our house in 1977 – millions of strong, confident women are now flocking to this space.

———

Personally, I've seen my own participation in sport change over the decades, and as I've moved into middle age and experienced all the joys of menopause. Sport for me today means joining great friends for year-round open water swimming sessions at Bray Lake, along with indoor rowing, bike rides and gym sessions.

I am conscious that 'older women' can be neglected in the drive to get younger women and girls active. It is an important demographic though, especially as people are living (and working) longer and the cost of caring for the elderly is becoming such a burden. While women make up the largest proportion of the older population, they are less likely than men to take part in physical activity and rank lower on measures such as aerobic and muscle-strengthening activity.

It's an age group that could massively benefit from sport in terms of the physical and mental benefits, but many women in this generation haven't experienced a grounding in sports so are scared to start, feeling unfamiliar with the rules and regulations.

Research shows that a third of British women say they are less active while experiencing the symptoms of menopause, but 71 per cent of those experiencing menopause want to be more active.

National governing bodies of sport have done a great job in this space in the past decade with initiatives like Back to Netball, Back to Hockey and Walking Football attracting women who thought their sporting days were behind them.

I played netball regularly until I was forty-six and then stopped when I took up triathlon. I've never gone back, but many of my friends and former teammates are still playing competitively now in their mid- to late fifties and will no doubt continue to do so. I am excited that walking netball is now an option for me to come back to and perhaps we can keep playing into our seventies.

The last decade has also seen massive growth in Masters events for swimming, athletics and triathlon, along with new walking formats.

———

A wonderful example of a club that has done a great deal to encourage 'older' women in sport is the multi-award-winning Crawley Old Girls (COGs).

Carol Bates had always wanted to play football. She'd spent years watching from the sidelines, first as a child watching her dad and then her two sons, and in the 1990s she had also managed a team of men in the Redhill & District League.

Like me, and most women growing up in the 1970s, Carol hadn't been able to play the sport, and so joined, in her own words, 'the generation of women that football missed'.

In February 2015 Carol responded to a tweet from Crawley Town Community Foundation (CTFC) about a girls' football session. She fancied the idea of a kickabout with other women but was disappointed to find the maximum age was twenty-five. In an exchange of friendly tweets with the CTFC, Carol suggested that if she could find enough women to start a new session, perhaps they could set up something for more mature women.

The sessions, promoted as 'no experience necessary, come and have some fun', launched with an hour a week for ten weeks and were attended by ten women. Since that time, COGs has grown into a hugely successful club, winning many awards and in the process inspiring the creation of hundreds more places for older women to play across the UK.

'When we entered the FA People's Cup that first year there were just four teams in the country for over thirty-fives,' says Carol. 'By 2019 there were sixty-two teams in that category along with more than fifteen walking football teams, too.'

The impact of more older women playing the game also means more women are now watching football, and want to get involved as coaches and officials. Carol says the FA have been hugely supportive as the category of 'women's recreational football' has exploded, with 460,000 more women aged twenty-five plus playing football after the 2019 World Cup than before – the biggest increase of any age group.

It's become so popular that in 2020 Sport England awarded £1 million of National Lottery funding across the nine cities hosting the UEFA European Women's Championship in 2022. Part of this will be used to create a local recreational women's football offer so that more women, like Carol, will finally have the opportunity to enjoy that 'kickabout'.

18

THE GIRL EFFECT

The difference between a broken community and a thriving one is the presence of women who are valued.

Michelle Obama

This is such an important chapter, but I found the thought of writing it more daunting than the others. It's a vast topic and not an area I've worked in directly, so I don't have the personal experience to draw on as I have with other areas of women's sport.

There are lots of extraordinary programmes taking place across the world and the subject of how sport for development can change the lives of women and girls could make up many books in itself. I was keen to consider the powerful impact sport can have on some of the most prevalent global problems affecting women and girls in the global south such as gender-based violence, childhood marriage and lack of education opportunities.

To start with I felt it was important to establish what we mean by 'sport for development' rather than 'sports development'. Until I began writing this book I certainly could not have told you the difference.

Sports development mainly focuses on developing a sport – usually to increase participation – and is often carried out by national and international sports bodies, clubs and charities. Development takes place by investing in publicity, along with the provision of equipment, instruction, coaches and access to facilities in order to introduce a sport to more people, be that as players, fans or coaches. This work can be beneficial for communities, often enabling more girls and young women to get involved in sport and enjoy all its benefits in terms of confidence, teamwork, resilience, happiness and a sense of purpose.

Some fantastic sports development programmes for women and girls have been delivered globally in recent years with substantial investments from the likes of FIFA, World Rugby and the ICC.

Katie Sadleir talks passionately about some of the impressive work World Rugby has delivered for women across the world, such as its 'Try and Stop Us: Start Rugby. Become Unstoppable' campaign, launched in 2019.

'It particularly picked out some of the places where we know women have more challenges and used women who had excelled through rugby to be inspirational role models to drive significant social change in those countries,' Katie told me. 'Iran went from 3,500 women participating in rugby pre our campaign to well over 10,000, in just that period of time.

'It's fantastic when I look at the photos that get sent from countries like Iran, or from Pakistan, or from Syria, or from Uganda, and you look at these women playing, and you know how physically challenging it is. It just makes you able to stand up for anything. On the field and off the field.'

Katie also told me how World Rugby has also made substantial investment into leadership: 'You invest in a leader and that woman changes the lives of others and then those women change the lives of others and those women change the lives of others. If I can do more to support the potential of women that want to lead, then that is just such a gift.'

It is wonderful to hear about the impact women's rugby is having across the world, and there's no doubt this work is changing the lives of the women who take part and those in their communities.

———

Sport *for* development is about using sport more directly as a 'tool' to generate social change. It traditionally works in one of three ways: supporting individuals to learn, grow and build confidence; helping a community to change its attitudes or improve its living conditions; and potentially helping a nation to overcome conflict or its effects.

It is also worth clarifying what we mean by 'sport' in the case of sport for development. A useful description from the United Nations describes it as 'all forms of physical activity that contribute to physical fitness, mental well-being and social interaction, such as play, recreation, organized or competitive sport, and indigenous sports and games'.

Evidently there are lots of ways in which organisations are helping to drive social change in communities across the world, so why is sport so powerful?

One of the key reasons is its popularity. Whether as participants, spectators or volunteers, people are attracted to sport, in many cases more than any other activity. Sport is popular in almost every community in the world, mainly because when it is delivered well it can be fun and enjoyable for everyone involved – from those taking part through to those watching and supporting.

Even in environments where people face horrible challenges in their everyday lives, the fact that sport can bring joy, fun and happiness should not be underestimated.

Sport's role as a connector is also key as it can unite people and communities. By its very nature sport is social, bringing together players, teams, coaches, volunteers and spectators. That is a large part of what we love about sport.

The networks which develop through sport can be hugely inclusive, helping to combat exclusion and enabling communities to work together to address the challenges they face.

The values we see in sport can also be powerful, including collaboration, respect for others, inclusion, teamwork and mutual support. These can be especially powerful in communities where women and girls may traditionally be excluded from much of society.

In the past thirty years sport has also emerged as global mass entertainment and in the process has become one of the world's most far-reaching communications platforms. Global sports events now reach millions and elite athletes have become influential ambassadors and role models for social development.

Finally, and this is particularly powerful for women and girls, sport has the potential to empower, motivate and inspire. Sport develops and showcases people's strengths and capacities. It highlights what people can do and, in many cases, it can change gender perceptions.

To understand more about sport for development and its potential, I spoke to Alexandra Chalat and Radha Balani from Beyond Sport, a global organisation that seeks to promote the role sport can play in creating sustainable social change. Alexandra points out that many people really don't understand sport for development or how it uses sport as a catalyst for change.

'Some of the biggest issues women are facing in the world right now are female-based violence, child marriage, payment in the workplace – serious issues. Sport is doing a lot to address that on the ground through amazing organisations and that's where sport for development, specifically with women, lies. Sport, at a community-based level, is helping to address some of the biggest issues facing women.'

Radha goes on to explain that it is the 'intentional use of sport' that enables it to be so impactful. It's not enough to bring a sporting programme or ambassador into a community and expect it to just change lives, as I'd often heard about, with well-intentioned programmes taking kit and coaches out to women and girls in the global south.

Apparently, one of the biggest mistakes people make when thinking about gender equality in the sport for development context is believing that, just because they are getting girls to play sport, this will automatically empower them to be equal in other ways. According to Radha this is just not true.

She tells me there's a misconception that sport is somehow magic and can solve societal issues. In fact, it only really works with the best programming and the right people, in the right place, at the right time. 'Many sports believe that "sport builds character". Indeed, some sports to this day purport that the very nature of their sport builds character and that those that play it are better people as a result. Quite frankly it's utter nonsense. For there to be sustained change, the use of sport, and those traits that it does engender, need to be intentionally programmed and drawn out, made relevant to life and done in safe spaces if we are to see changes in knowledge, in skills, in confidence, behaviours and beliefs in both individuals and communities.'

Radha talks about the powerful commodity of sport which 'if deployed appropriately will genuinely challenge things that we might never, ever talk about. That could be female genital mutilation or the shame of menstruation, which in some societies has the secondary impact of girls not going into or continuing their education.'

It is sobering to think that a sport for development programme might enable a young woman to get an education or bear children or feed their family. 'The world could come out of poverty if only women were empowered to work and contribute and be part of that,' says Radha.

This final point that Radha makes is highlighted by Women Win, a global women's fund that envisages a world where every adolescent girl and young woman exercises her rights: 'International authorities from the World Bank to the United Nations agree that the most effective way to fight poverty in the world is to help girls and women. Research has shown that if you invest in girls you invest in society because the education, increased earnings and human development of adolescent girls has a direct impact on their families. It's becoming known as "the girl effect". And because women often serve as primary care-takers, every dollar invested in a girl also benefits her family and the community.'

It's clearly not enough, then, just to encourage girls to start playing football or rugby or netball and assume that the confidence this brings will automatically transfer to other areas of their lives, as many sport development programmes do.

Maria Bobenrieth, Executive Director of Women Win, explained to me what they'd discovered when Nike first began investing in this area about twenty years ago: 'What we saw was that the same issues that were keeping girls from the playing field were keeping them out of society. Things like period poverty. So if you don't have a way to manage your menstrual period one week a month it's not that you only don't play sports. You don't go to school and over time you drop out.

What we saw where girls were playing on teams, they were helping each other deal with this because they didn't want any of the players to miss any of the matches.'

Maria explains they discovered many other issues that prevented adolescent girls from accessing sport. A lack of female coaches meant parents were worried about safeguarding, concerned for their daughters playing sport and travelling to venues with men. A lack of changing rooms with nowhere for girls to use the toilet and change. Girls not having any bras or underwear.

'And as we worked with sports institutions and other women's rights organisations to address these issues, we saw not only the girls participated better in sports, but they were able to develop agency. They were able to develop access to networks of friends. They did better in school.

'Participation of girls made programmes and communities better. This was transformative and at that time was a radical idea.'

An example of how the impact of sport can change the lives of the most marginalised girls and young women is One Win Leads to Another, a joint partnership between UN Women and the International Olympic Committee, a legacy of the 2016 Rio Olympics.

The programme combined sport with life-skills education for vulnerable girls in often violent communities, and what is most fascinating is the transformation that resulted. By time the girls left the programme in Brazil:

– 89 per cent said they were a leader, compared to 46 per cent before the programme.

- 93 per cent knew where to report violence.
- 79 per cent knew how safe sex would reduce the likelihood of pregnancy, compared to 25 per cent before.
- 77 per cent knew safe sex could prevent sexually transmitted infections, compared to 21 per cent before.
- 99 per cent believed that they would one day get a job.

Extraordinary changes that will transform the lives of these young women and their communities.

———

HODI is a charity founded by Fatuma Abdulkadir Adan in Kenya, in a region where girls used to be forbidden to play football. Now it's changing their lives. As Fatuma herself said in a BBC documentary: 'People look at a football and they see this round, useless thing. For me it's the most powerful tool.'

Fatuma started running football tournaments in northern Kenya in 2008 with a goal of tackling many issues that hurt young girls. In that first tournament just twelve girls competed. 'Travelling with the girls we'd hear people cussing us and saying may you all break your legs. I was physically stoned and literally kicked out of the pitch.'

Moving forward a decade and more than 1,600 girls have competed. One of the girls in the 2018 tournament was fourteen-year-old Fatuma Gufu. Coming from a very humble background, everything would have been a barrier for her, explains Fatuma Abdulkadir Adan. But the young Fatuma says she wants to be the governor of Marsabit county in the future – a dream she would never have had without football.

Fatuma explains: 'Football changed me. I was so shy. My teams, we are with them for many years. We won matches. We even got a new jersey for the football team.

'I want to continue playing, but even if not, I will campaign for girls to continue. I want in the future to be a parent who is supporting football for girls.'

Doris Petra, Vice-President of the Football Kenya Federation, explains why initiatives like this are so important for young women like Fatuma: 'She comes from an area where women are not supposed to have a voice. They get married so early in life. They are not even taken to school.'

As well as bringing girls together to play football, in between games, HODI runs sessions tackling child marriage and breaking the silence around female genital mutilation. Three million girls a year across Africa are at risk of being victims of female genital mutilation.

This educational element is a critical component of the programme, and, along with the tournaments, HODI also runs a nine-month programme in schools.

Fatuma Abdulkadir Adan concludes: 'We are currently in a hundred and fifty-two villages. There are so many other villages that are out of our programme, but others hear the stories of these villages and they start asking "why don't we also start doing this? Why are we marrying off our girls?"

'We have broken the silence. Before it was a cool thing for a thirteen-year-old, a twelve-year-old girl to be married. Today if you marry off a thirteen-year-old the girls in those classes would complain. And not just the girls, the boys also.'

―――――

Moving the Goalposts, a sport for development charity in Kenya, is another pioneering organisation that uses football as a tool for gender equality, reaching out to young women who face huge challenges and complexities in life.

Sarah Forde, who founded the charity, believes that football can provide opportunities for girls, because seeing girls play football makes people wonder what more they can do. It makes people think about their prejudices against girls. 'I was convinced that sports could be used to address issues of girls dropping out of school, early marriages and pregnancies, as well as empowering young girls with life skills,' she says.

Moving the Goalposts strongly believe that by empowering girls and young women they can empower entire communities. Football is just one pillar of their programmes, which focus on providing fundamental economic and education opportunities through job and life skills and include education, livelihood, health, leadership and child protection.

The charity also recognises the patriarchal nature of African societies (also the case in many societies globally) with men and boys as the 'custodians of culture' and holding rigid views about gender roles and masculinity. This can be a big deterrent to women's and girls' empowerment.

'Without involving men and boys in gender equality and elimination of gender-based violence is like a doctor treating symptoms and ignoring the disease,' the charity says. They therefore also run a Young Men as Equal Partners programme which increases the number of 'gender transformative' men and boys who can be agents of social change and champion the rights of girls and young women.

Another hugely successful charity which intentionally uses sport as a tool of empowerment and education for women is Free to Run. Using adventure sports to develop female leaders in regions of conflict, the charity enables women and girls to safely, and boldly, engage in outdoor activity in conflict-affected regions including Afghanistan, Iraq and South Sudan.

Since 2014, the charity has worked to create positive change in the lives of over 1,100 women and girls living in regions of conflict, combining sports programmes, life-skills development and community outreach to help women reclaim public space and change views about the roles they can (and should) play in a society.

Participants run and hike with their team three to five times per week and also volunteer in their community, actively contributing to local projects. They are also taught life skills through sports, which include communication skills, conflict negotiation, leadership and service learning. Week-long leadership events then take participants outside their usual environments, and enable them to try new activities like camping, kayaking, cycling, ice skating and skiing. Groups come together from different cultures where they share their experiences and learn from each other.

Having enabled women and girls to pursue sporting challenges, the Free to Run programme then supports them to transfer these successes to their everyday lives so that they can be a force for positive change, shifting the attitudes of participants and their communities, and increasing the opportunities for women and girls to engage in public life. Participants who successfully complete a year or more of Free to Run programmes are encouraged to lead life-skills and sports sessions in their local schools, which creates a positive ripple effect for other women and girls in their own communities.

And it's not just more traditional sports having impact. I was fascinated to learn more about Free Movement Skateboarding, an organisation offering free, structured skateboarding workshops to young refugees, migrants and local people in Athens and its surrounding camps.

My daughter, Molly Horler, who has spent time investigating the impact of skateboarding for young women, highlighted something I hadn't before considered

In many communities where girls are typically prohibited from participating in sports, or don't due to societal norms, skateboarding can give them access to physical activity and its numerous benefits.

When Oliver Percovich [the founder of Skateistan, a charity empowering children through skateboarding and education] first took his skateboard to Afghanistan he was intrigued to find that girls' interest in skateboarding was equal to the boys, when they were so excluded from all other forms of sport in Afghanistan.

He realised this was because skateboarding presented somewhat of a 'loophole', it's unknownness to Afghan society, meaning there had been no opportunity for it to be socially prohibited for girls. The unknown nature of skateboarding often works to its advantage in communities where more traditional sport for development initiatives fail.

―――――――

The potential for sport to change the lives of women and girls was highlighted by UN Women in 2020:

In recent years, sport has demonstrated its enormous capacity to propel women and girls' empowerment. It mobilizes the global community and speaks to youth. It unites across national barriers and cultural differences. It is a powerful tool to convey important messages in a positive and celebratory environment – often to mass audiences. In addition, it teaches women and girls the values of teamwork, self-reliance and resilience; has a multiplier effect on their health, education and leadership development; contributes to self-esteem, builds social connections, and challenges harmful gender norms.

While it's fantastic to recognise the enormous impact of sport, it would be naïve to presume that sport programmes alone will change the lives of women and girls in the global south. These excellent initiatives need to be embedded in wider societal change.

As Maria Bobenrieth so articulately explains:

The joy of sport is transformative. The humanity of it. The love and the energy. If all we could do is bring joy for one hour a week for a few years, to some of these young women together, then their lives will be transformed. Joy transforms us more than anything else.

But there are many strategies. This is not a silver bullet. This strategy will only help you if you've got very good other strategies. We need schools. We need to make sure girls have access to good medical facilities. We need psychological support.

This is just one kind of really great booster in your toolkit.

———

In researching and writing this chapter I've been fascinated to learn about the impact the intentional use of sport can have on the lives of women and girls so far removed from what we see every day in the West.

Inspired by the work of remarkable women like Maria Bobenrieth, Radha Balani and Alexandra Chalat, it's an area I'm now keen to explore further.

CONCLUSION

Game On

Well-behaved women seldom make history.

Laurel Thatcher Ulrich

My goal for this book was to celebrate the vast progress we have seen for women in sport, while also highlighting the inequalities that still exist today. I wanted it to be a joyful book, acknowledging all that has been accomplished, as well as a rallying cry for future action.

In writing it I have learned much more about the history of women in sport. I was shocked and disappointed to discover that so many ridiculous medical and societal assumptions from over a hundred years ago still impact attitudes to women's participation in sport today.

But it is clear we are now witnessing positive change as never before.

There has been a huge increase in spectators, media coverage, sponsorship and professional contracts, with female athletes leading the way as powerful activists for social change. We've seen sportswomen celebrated as strong and powerful, with better gender balance on sports boards, female-focused sports science and research, and more women and girls participating in grassroots sport.

As I update this final chapter for the book's paperback edition, it's clear that the COVID-19 pandemic highlighted historical gender inequalities, with women's events, leagues and competitions curtailed more readily than men's throughout 2020. Many were concerned that this hiatus would have a long-term negative impact, undoing much of the progress we'd witnessed over the past decade. And yet, despite the delays and cancellations, the unstoppable rise of women's sport continued unabated throughout 2021 and into 2022.

Watershed moments included the FA's multi-million-pound deal with Sky Sports and the BBC to broadcast the Women's Super League for the next three seasons. Barclays also renewed its title sponsorship of the WSL and doubled its investment in women's football with a £30 million, three-year deal that includes title sponsorship of the Women's Championship. Meanwhile, in cricket, The Hundred drew spectacular crowds and high TV viewing figures, setting records for the women's game.

Hardly a week went by without news of another significant 'female first', whether that was Rachael Blackmore winning the Grand National, Sara Cox becoming the first female Premiership Rugby referee, Debbie Hewitt being appointed as the first female Chair of the FA or British cyclist Lizzie Deignan winning the first women's Paris–Roubaix race.

Sporting bodies, leagues and teams across the world, including FIFA, unbundled their women's rights, with global brands such as Google, Nike, Mastercard, Adidas, Deloitte, Budweiser, Heineken and Michelob flocking to sponsor women's sport.

New global events and formats emerged, including the Tour de France Femmes avec Zwift, the Arnold Clark Cup and World Rugby's WXV tournament.

Wales became the first country in the UK, and only the third in Europe, to drop 'women's' from the name of its female football league, and along with Ireland and Sweden it introduced equal pay for its men's and women's international football teams. Women's salaries in The Hundred doubled for 2022, a bold move that reflected the ECB's commitment to the women's game and their ultimate goal of gender parity in wages. UEFA doubled the prize money for the women's Euros in 2022, but sadly this is still less than 5 per cent of the men's Euros prize pot.

Social issues around women's sport were also addressed in 2021, with the MCC amending the Laws of Cricket to use gender-neutral terms 'batter' and 'batters', rather than 'batsman' or 'batsmen'; Cricket Australia committing to address the lack of statues of female cricketers; and the International Handball Federation finally responding to widespread accusations of sexism by changing its rules around women's uniforms to allow shorts and tank tops instead of bikinis.

Looking back at how much has been transformed for women's sport in the past decade, it's exciting to imagine what could be made possible in the future by this momentum.

As women's sport continues to evolve, let's not solely compare it to men's sport in order to judge its success, though. Women's sport differs on many levels and in many cases has more to offer – especially in the way it challenges society's gender stereotypes.

Things are changing, but not fast enough. It is down to all of us to keep pushing for more. We can all be influencers in this space.

★

Here are ten steps you can take to drive change:

1. **CALL OUT** the media when you see unequal coverage and praise them when they get it right.
2. **ASK** brands about the balance of their sponsorship. Support those that back women's sport.
3. **WATCH** more women's sport – live when you can, or on TV or digital platforms.
4. **STAND UP** for female athletes and broadcasters on social media – help close down those trolls.
5. **REFLECT** on and address your own conscious and unconscious biases towards women in sport.
6. **QUESTION** the diversity of those leading the sports you love.
7. **SUPPORT** campaigns and charities that progress the agenda for women's sport.
8. **SPEAK UP** when things are not fair – be more vocal with your support.
9. **TAKE PART** in sport and encourage the women and girls in your life to do the same.
10. **CELEBRATE** the success of female athletes and female leaders.

It's simply not acceptable that in 2021 women's sport should still be a poor relation to men's.

Women make up over half the population and, together with those forward-thinking men who appreciate the benefits of equality, our voices can be incredibly powerful.

Let's all be more proactive and unapologetically demand more for everyone.

Game on.

ACKNOWLEDGEMENTS

I could never have written this book without the kind support of many people.

The biggest thanks go to Matt for your love and patience, especially when I hid myself away upstairs, writing at weekends. Thank you for the exceptional room service in response to my random texts for tea and for taking care of life 'downstairs' as I wrote.

Thank you to my beautiful girls who have all played their part in the creation of this book. To Daisy for encouraging me to go for it in the first place, to Molly for opening my mind and for critically reviewing chapters and to Tess for being (fairly) willing to play cards with me when I needed a break from writing. I'm so proud of you all.

It hurts that my parents were not part of my book-writing journey. As avid readers I know they would have been very proud. Thanks, Mum, for raising me to believe I could do anything in life, and Dad for being such a sporting inspiration.

Thank you, Nick, Tim and Mark, for always supporting your little sister.

Huge thanks to Carmen Rendell for asking 'what's stopping you' when I mentioned I wanted to write a book in the summer of 2019. Such a powerful nudge. This was followed by much encouragement from Nicky Frobisher as I talked myself in and out of it in the following months. Nicky has been a cheerleader for many things in my life. Thank you for knowing I could do this – especially when I doubted myself.

To Kate Hannon, my fabulous friend, colleague and co-founder of the Women's Sport Collective, thank you for encouraging, questioning, challenging and supporting me throughout the entire process.

To the trailblazing women in sport who I spoke to for The Game Changers podcast and in researching the book – I am in awe of you all. What a privilege it was to sit down with Tanni Grey-Thompson, Chrissie Wellington, Sally Munday, Maggie Alphonsi, Kate Richardson-Walsh, Pamela Cookey, Jo Bostock, Katherine Grainger, Denise Lewis, Clare Connor, Anna Kessel, Jo Coates, Clare Balding, Karen Findlay, Liz Nicholl, Lauren Steadman, Eni Aluko, Kelly Smith, Jacqui Oatley, Sue Campbell, Jo Tongue, Maggie Murphy, Kelly Simmons, Casey Stoney, Hope Powell, Steph Houghton, Moya Dodd, Stacey Copeland, Ebru Koksal, Rose Reilly, Rimla Akhtar, Heather Rabbatts, Emma Hayes, Eleanor Oldroyd, Sarah Storey, Ali Oliver, Ebony Rainford-Brent, Katie Sadleir, Tracy Edwards, Judy Murray, Jessica Ennis-Hill, Gabby Logan, Rachel Yankey, Gail Newsham, Shelley Kerr, Mary Harvey, Sian Massey-Ellis, Jane Purdon, Jill Scott, Jessica Creighton, Dawn Scott, Julie Welch, Manisha Tailor, Jess Fishlock, Maria Bobenrieth, Amanda Vandervort and Lucy Bronze.

To the people behind *The Game Changers* podcast who enabled me to learn so much from these extraordinary women in sport – thank you Sam Walker, my brilliant executive producer, and thanks also to Tom Corbett at Barclays and Lisa O'Keefe and Kate Dale at Sport England for your support.

To Tammy Parlour and Jo Bostock, co-founders of the Women's Sport Trust, along with fellow trustees including Zarah Al-Kudsy, Claire Bennett, Sue Day, Liz Grant, Chris Hurst, Michael Inpong,

Suzanne King, Suzy Levy, Ben Smith, Laura Weston and Danielle Sellwood. I learn so much from you every time we meet and speak. This book would never have been possible without you.

I'm so grateful to the women who spoke to me for the book, kindly sharing your wisdom – Radha Balani, Carol Bates, Ali Bowes, Lex Chalat, Lynsey Douglas, Rebecca Myers, Emma Ross, Lisa Parfitt and Hannah Thompson. Thanks also to Anabel Sexton who so generously shared her research on the history of women's sport.

Other talented academics whose years of study inspired me as I researched the book include Nicole LaVoi and Mary Jo Kane from the Tucker Center, along with Toni Bruce and Susan K. Kahn.

I loved Anna Kessel's book *Eat Sweat Play* and having her personal support for this project meant so much to me. I'm also grateful to Richard Pike, Anna's agent, whose early guidance helped me shape the direction of *Game On*.

To my early readers for taking time to check chapters and provide suggestions – Ali, Laura, Kate, Julia, Rimla, Molly, Tammy, Jo, Chris, Anna and Julia Childs – thank you for your kind and useful feedback.

Game On is all about the power women's sport and I'd like to recognise and thank the incredible female coaches who have supported my own daughters on their sporting journeys. Brenda Pope, Clare Roe, Ali Hill, Clare van Spall, Julia Bird, Kate Hallett, Nolli Waterman and Giselle Mather – you are all extraordinary women.

Looking back now I'm grateful to my own wonderful teachers who normalised my love of sport, particularly Miss Turney (now Sue Strippel) at Norwood Green School and Miss Bamber at The Green School.

Then there is the incredible team at Unbound. From the very first day I spoke to Katy Guest – following an introduction from fellow Unbound author and rugby legend Catherine Spencer – her passion and enthusiasm for my book was evident. Katy was the most brilliant and kind supporter throughout the process of funding and writing.

Thank you to Anna Simpson for moving me through editing and production with such compassion and understanding. You made the whole thing so enjoyable.

I'm so grateful for all the behind-the-scenes support provided by Tamsin Shelton, Richard Collins, Catherine Best and David Atkinson in editing, proofreading and indexing the book, and also to Debbie Elliot for her fantastic guidance on publicity.

Thank you to everyone who pledged for this book. It's been a long time coming, but your belief in me meant so much. Very special thanks go my 'Total Game Changers' Mark and Vicky Anstiss and Nicky Lewis.

To Nick Read and Keith Kropman at Vitality it's been such a pleasure working with you – thank you for backing *Game On*. What you have done for women's sport in the UK is quite remarkable, and I know you're not finished yet.

Finally, in the words of the ultimate game changer, Billie Jean King, we stand of the shoulders of the women who went before us. So, here's to all those magnificent trailblazers who have ensured the unstoppable rise of women's sport.

INDEX

Index

Index

Index

Unbound is the world's first crowdfunding publisher, established in 2011.

We believe that wonderful things can happen when you clear a path for people who share a passion. That's why we've built a platform that brings together readers and authors to crowdfund books they believe in – and give fresh ideas that don't fit the traditional mould the chance they deserve.

This book is in your hands because readers made it possible. Everyone who pledged their support is listed below. Join them by visiting unbound.com and supporting a book today.

Game Changer
Mark and Vicky Anstiss
Nicky Lewis

Supporters
Eleanor Abrahams-Burrows
Lucy Adams
Sam Adams
Nicky Affleck
Ed Airey
Nicki Aitken
Kasey Allen
Nicole Allison
Nicola Alloway
Dave Alstead
Julie Amies
Rosie Anderson
Andy Anstey
Cooper Anstiss
Ed Anstiss
James Anstiss
Tim Anstiss
Craig Anthony
Elsa Arapi
Jane Ariztegieta Scott
Leanne Arnold

Keith Ashton

Amelia Ashton-Jones

David Atkinson

Shelley Austin

Jonas Baer-Hoffmann

Gurpri Bains

Catherine Baker

Karen Baker

Radha Balani

Emma Ballard

Heather Bamforth

Shakila Barabhuiya

Immy Barclay

Yentl Barremans

Beth Barrett-Wild

Jessica Barrows

Alison Bartoletti

Katie Bartoletti

Dave Barton

Liz Barton-Jones

Nicki Bass

Carol Bates

Justine Baynes

Sarah Beattie

Amelia Behrens

Georgia Bekyra

Lindsey Bell

Natascia Bernardi

Di Binley

Toni Birch

Matt Birkett

Melissa Birkhead

Cath Bishop

David Black

Belinda Blakeney

Amie Bletso

Alex Bliss

Elle Bloor

Sarah Blythe-Wood

Heather Boldon

Catherine Bond Muir

Gemma Bonnett-Kolakowska

Kate Bosomworth

Jo Bostock

Mel Bound

Jennie Bouron

Suuz Boven

Scott Bowers

Ali Bowes

John Boyd

Marianne Boyle

Ian Braid

Anna Braithwaite

Bev Bratton

Katie Brazier

Tricia Breach

Kristi Breisch

Ruth Brennan

Helen Bridgman

Penny Briscoe

Lisa Broomhead

Danielle Brown

Brian Browne

Jon Bruford

Katie Bryan

Rui Bu

Zara Buck
Chris Bullock
Patrick Burge
Mark Burgess
Louise Burke
Hannah Burt
Helen Bushell
Anica Bussell
Ellen Buttrick
Helena Byrne
Mike Caine
Natasha Callis
Rebecca Calvert
Mark Camp-Overy
Leandra Cardozo
Joshua Cardwell
Katy Cardwell
Michelle Carney
Matthew Carpenter
Cathy Carr
Patricia Carswell
Carter
Catherine Carty
Caroline Cater
Stephen Catton
Sue Catton
Chris Child
Julia Childs
Steve Chisholm
Carolina Chrispim
Kiki Christofi
Suzy Christopher
Catherine Clark

Emma Clarke
Lee Clarke
Carrera Clarke-Freitas
Amy Clayfield
Maeve Clements
Tony Clements
Jason Cobley
Emily Cockrill
Jilly Collins
Yvonne Comer
Pauline Connington
Clare Connor
Tamsin Connor
Sarah Cook
Jennie Cooper
Nick Cooper
Zoe Cooper Sutton
Stacey Copeland
Charlie Copsey
Liv Corbishley
Rebecca Corcoran
Laura Cordingley
Kate Costin
Biba & Esme Cottam
Alex Coulson
Avril Couper
Andy Cowe
Luke Cox
Ruby Cox
Suzie Cox
Tim & Julie Cozze-Young
Rosie Crampin
Helen Craven

Hannah Crawley
Tayler Cresswell
Ella Croft
Helen Crossley
Michelle Crotty
Helen Crowley
Danny Cullinane
Samantha Cullum
Jess Cully
Jamie Cunningham
Natalie Curtis
Yvette Curtis
Dominique Cutts
Kate Dale
Sally Dalton
Michelle Dand
Ian Daniell
Tracy Danks
Alex Danson-Bennett
Helen Dargue
Henry DaVega Wolfe
Anna-Victoria Davies
Conor Davies
Alice Davis
Sandra (SD) Dawson
Steven Day
Sue Day
Phil de Glanville
Emily Defroand
Cheryl Denise
Tanya Denning
Rebecca Derrick
Nathalie Deutsch

Liz Dexter
Fiona Dick
Ruth Dickinson
Sarah Dickson
Tara Dillon
Monique Collette Dingley
Steve Dinnie
Kellie Discipline
Michelle Dite
Karen Dobres
Samuel Dodson
Chris Donald
Anna Donegan
Michelle Dorgan
Margaret Doughty
Lynsey Douglas
Georgia Dowdeswell
Natalie Doyle
Jane Drapkin
Ben Dudley
Sally Dudley
Nasima Dunne
Nicola Dutton
Lynette Eaborn
Catherine Eastham
Laura Eddie
Sarah Edmonds
April Edwards
Charlotte Edwards
Tracy Edwards
Charlotte Ellis
David Ellis
Sophie Ellis

Siân Evans

Victoria Evans

Ruth Evered

Rebecca Fairlie-Clarke

Stuart Fenton

Julie Ferguson

Alicia Ferguson-Cook

Claire Fergusson

Maria Angelica Fernandes

Lucy Findlay

Fiona Finlayson

Kilian Fisher

Emelie Fitzgerald

Jasmine Flatters

Mark Fletcher

Amanda Foister

Cliona Foley

Amanda Fone

Ella Foote

Rachel Ford

Alison Leigh Forman

Tim Foster

Charlotte French

Lucy French

Karen Frend

Andrew Friedlander

Nick Frith

Nicky Frobisher

Sarah Gandon

Louise Garlick

Sharon Garner

Tom Garry

Claire Gatcum

Leigh Gell

Sally Gibbins

Imogen Gibbon

Natalie Gibson

Anya Gilbert

Dr Sarah Gilchrist

Ben Gittus

Tanya Godbeer

Alexandra Goldschmidt

Almudena Gomez

Michelle Goode

Lucy Goodman

Cat Goryn

Victoria Gosling

Steve Grainger

Liz Grant

Lj Gray

Imo Greatbatch

Rachel Gregg

Tallulah Gregory

Martin Gritton

Katy Guest

Jackie Gutierrez

Emily Jane Guy

Louise Hacking

Ben Hackney-Williams

Annie Hairsine

Calron Hall

Kate Hallett

Lizzy Halton

Jude Handley

Kate Hannon

Greg Harkins

Roxy Harpham

Tanya Harris

Graeme Harrison

Sophie Harrison

Yvonne Harrison

Amanda Hart

Rob Hartnett

Em Harvey

Maria Hasler

Mike Hawkes

Berni Hawkins

Leshia Hawkins

Georgie Heath

Kirsty Heath

Cassandra Heilbronn

Rebecca Hembrough

Patrick Henchoz

Alison Hill

Emily Hill

Jonathan Hill

Laura Hillier

Craig Hobbs

Paddy Hobbs

Emily Hodder

Hannah Holland

Katie Holmes

Lynsey Hooper

Sean Hooper

Marc Hope

James Hope-Gill

Daisy Horler

Matt Horler

Molly Horler

Tess Horler

Alison Howard

Elysa Hubbard

Elizabeth Hudson

Alex Hughes

Charlotte Hughes

David Hughes

Chris Hurst

Zara Hyde Peters

Gareth Ikin

Amanda Ing

Kim Ingleby

Carol Isherwood

Lenka Istvanova

Barry Jackson

Claire Jackson

Nat Jackson

Samia Jackson

Sarah Jackson

Amy Jacobs

Bill James

Russell James

Ben Jessup

Charles Jillings

Danny Johnson

Marieke Johnson

Samantha Johnson

Liesel Jolly

Sarah Jones

Nicola Joyce

Tom Judge

Natalie Justice-Dearn

Susan Keaney

Sarah Kelleher

Sarah Kendall

Nicola Kenton

Niamh Keoghan

Sally Kettle

Dan Kieran

Adele Kilby

Mary Killingworth

Sue Klesniks

Ebru Koksal

Jade Konkel

Barbara Kunkel

Lewis Laing

Dmitriy Lampert

Gabriella Lampert

Jenny Landreth

Douglas Langley

Elena Lapetra

Louise Latter

Angela Laventure

Jonathan Le Fondre

Becs Leach

Harriet Leach

Lorna Leach

Kirsty Leake

Sarah Leeves

Emma Legg

Eleanor Lestrange

Courtney Levinsohn

Emma Lewis

Madeleine Lewis

Nicky Lewis

Emily Liles

Lara Lill

Rhian Lilley

Craig Lister

Emma Liverseidge

Suzie Liverseidge

David Lixton

Karen Llewellyn

Rhona Lloyd

Samantha Lloyd

Lucy Lomax

Jon Long

Emma Longbottom

Joanne Love

Diccon Loy

Ciara Lucey

Terri Lynam

Gordon Maclelland

Beth Macleod

Steve Madincea

Catherine Makin

Amy Marks

Laura Marks

Ian Marron

Alexandra Marshall

Jo Martin

Emma Mason

Gemma Mason

Simon Massie-Taylor

Julie Masterson

Giselle Mather

Katie Matthews

Louise Matthews

Kate Maurici

John 'Max' Maxwell

Karen Maxwell

Eddie May

Rosie Mayes

Marg Mayne

Angela Mc Guire

Louise McCabe-Arnold

Tracey McCillen

Lisa McCormick

Claire McCosh

Milly McEvoy

Katie McGavigan

Ruth McGrath

Molly & Nancy McIntosh

Sinead McNulty

Emily McOrist

Steve McQuaid

Vicki Mcquaid

Laura McQueen

Sarah McQueen

Alina Menukhin

Mags Mernagh

Matt Merritt

Mark Middlemas

Alexis Middleton

Julie Middleton

Joshua Miethke

Carly Miles

Harriet Millard

Ben Miller

Eugene Minogue

Emma Mitchell

The Mitchell Girls

John Mitchinson

Jenny Mitton

Olivia Monkhouse

Amy Monkman

Jonathan Monks

Ugo Monye

Lucy Moore

David Morgan

Eliza Morgan

Lynne Morgan

Milly Morgan

Sally Morrell

Becki Morris

Darren Morris

Fionnuala Morris

Bianca Morriss

Shona Morriss

Caron Morton

Jo Moseley

Neil Mosley

Dani Mugridge

Sally Munday

Maggie Murphy

Bob Murray

Di Murray

Rebecca Myers

Liz Nagel

Paul Narraway

Carlo Navato

Jeremy Navrady

Jack Needham

Allie Nelkon

Dawn Newbery

Cathy Newnes-Smith

Gail Newsham

Jo Newson

Dan Newton

Scott Newton

Brett Nicholls

Katrina Northern

Lisa Norton

Tim O'Connor

Lisa O'Keefe

Jacqui Oatley

Nic Oldham

Graham Oliphant

Mark Ormerod

John Oxley

Mary Pacitti

Helen Pack

Clementine Painter

Adam Paker

Bethan Palmer

Jules Parke-Robinson

Steph Parker

Victoria Parker

Tammy Parlour

Claire Parnell

Eilidh Paterson

Katie Paterson

Jenny Patrickson

Pauline Edgar Library

Alun Peacock

Niamh Peacock

Alissa Pearce

Lisa Pearce

Sophie Penney

Simon Pennock

Lucy Pepper

Sarah-Jane Perry

Susan Petruccelli

Annamarie Phelps

Christina Philippou

Julia Philipson

Helen Phillips

Steve Philpott

Sarah Pickford

Dr Ian Pickup

Steve Plant

Ginelle Polini

Justin Pollard

Jill Poots

Brenda Pope

Amy Porter

Sarah Potts

Jane Powell

Jill Powell

Sophie Power

Alex Preece

Ashlea Prescott

Natalie Prescott

David Priddy

Laura Puddle

Julie Quinn

Ana Rabell

Mary Racz

Alice Radford

Olivia Rae

Nick Rance

Rebecca Randell

Matt Rapinet

Kathryn Ratnapala

Rhian Ravenscroft

David Reddin

Cassandra Rees

Chris Rees

Georgina Rettey

Sophie Reynolds

Yvonne Rhoden

Lily Rice

Ellie Richards

Naomi Riches

Caroline Richings

Ian Ridley

Katie Rigby-Brown

Vivien Rimmer

Jenni Rishworth

Caroline Roberts

Jane Roberts

Matt Roberts

Charli Robertson

Melissa Robertson

Sarah Robertson

Bryony Robins

Gemma Robinson

Nicholas Robinson

Clare Roe

J Simon Rofe

Matt Rogan

Lucy Roper

David Rose

Rebecca Rothwell

Helen Rowbotham

Sarah Rowell

@RugbySaracens

Victoria Rush

Wendy Russell

Karyn Sackey

Ruth Sacks

Becky Saffery

Richard Savage

Sarah Saxton

Steven Scales

Ash Scott

Emma Self

Danielle Sellwood

Fiona Semple

Anabel Sexton

Marios C Sfantos

Marios Christos Sfantos

Nadeem Shaikh

Jack Shakespeare

Angela Sharp

Claire Sharpington

Julie Shaw-Binns

Sarah Shephard

Preeti Sherry

Laura Siddall

Marianna Sikorowska

Kay Simnett

Lindsey Simpson

Georgina Slawinski

Jennifer Smith

Latoya Smith

Lydia Smith

Scarlett Smith

Tim Smith

Anne Smyth

Neel Sood

Ali Speechly

Catherine Spencer

Martin Spencer

The Sports and Play
    Construction Association

Anouk Spreckelsen-Brown

Atlanta St John

David Stalker

Beth Stallwood

Emily Starling

James Stebbing

Lizzie Steele

Alannah Stephenson

Sarah Stoney

Sue Storey

Sue Strachan

Caroline Street

Sue Strippel

Jieke Stroobant

Connie-Rose Sullens

Sara Sutcliffe

Austin Swain

Mimi Tarrant

Abby Taylor

Claire Taylor

Maria Taylor

Martha Taylor

Team Heroine

Alex Teasdale

Amy Tennant

Upneet Thandi

Lori Theisen

Sangy Theivendra

Carole Thelwall-Jones

Annie Thomas

Marina Thomas

Mark Rhys Thomas

Andy Thompson

Anna Thompson

Ashleigh-Jane Thompson

Tricia Thompson

Hannah Thompson-Radford

Charlotte Thomson

Laura Tiidla

Becca Todd

Pete Todd

Jack Tompkins

Torunn and Ellen

Ali Trauttmansdorff

Damian Treece

Maia Tua-Davidson

Henry Turner

Laura Turner-Alleyne

Jo Tyler

Eleanor Udall

Tim Underhill

Clare van Spall

Tulshi Varsani

Michele Verroken

Diane Vesey

Jenny Vincent

Samantha Vincent

Emma Vivo

Charlotte Wade

Leoni Waghorn

Lisa Wainwright

Tim Wainwright

Cary Wakefield

Nicola Walker

Sam Walker

Alex Wallace

Barbara Walsh

Jenny Walsh

Chloe Walton

Lisa Warburton

Bev Ward

Ella & Mia Ward

Laoise Ward

Natalie Ward

Steven Ward

Penny Wardale

Joelle Watkins

Cat Watson

Sarah Watts

Simon Webb

Vicci Wells

Anna Whowell

Greg Whyte

Margaret Wilby

Sue Wilkie

Tina Louise Wilkins

Florence Williams

Gail Williams

Morgan Williams

Sarah Williams

Rachel Williamson

Alexandra Willis

Justine Willmott

Amanda Wilmer

Heather Wilson

John Wilson

Lin Wilson

Marie Wilson

Stuart Wilson

Jo Wimble-Groves

Glynnis Wisbey

Women Sport Report 1

Jennifer Wong

Mark Wood

Poppy Wood

Jason Worthy

Adriana Wright

Dave Wright

Lisa Wright

Jill Wring

Stephanie Xavier

Tim Yarnall

Laura Yell

Caroline Youds

Rob Young

Laura Youngson

Bruna Zanin Juresic

Adam Zoltie

Alex Zurita